American Gothic Culture

Edinburgh Companions to the Gothic

Series Editors
Andrew Smith, University of Sheffield
William Hughes, Bath Spa University

This series provides a comprehensive overview of the Gothic from the eighteenth century to the present day. Each volume takes either a period, place, or theme and explores their diverse attributes, contexts and texts via completely original essays. The volumes provide an authoritative critical tool for both scholars and students of the Gothic.

Volumes in the series are edited by leading scholars in their field and make a cutting-edge contribution to the field of Gothic studies.

Each volume:
- Presents an innovative and critically challenging exploration of the historical, thematic and theoretical understandings of the Gothic from the eighteenth century to the present day
- Provides a critical forum in which ideas about Gothic history and established Gothic themes are challenged
- Supports the teaching of the Gothic at an advanced undergraduate level and at masters level
- Helps readers to rethink ideas concerning periodisation and to question the critical approaches which have been taken to the Gothic

Published Titles
The Victorian Gothic: An Edinburgh Companion,
    Andrew Smith and William Hughes
Romantic Gothic: An Edinburgh Companion,
    Angela Wright and Dale Townshend
American Gothic Culture: An Edinburgh Companion,
    Joel Faflak and Jason Haslam
Women and the Gothic: An Edinburgh Companion,
    Avril Horner and Sue Zlosnik

Forthcoming Titles
Scottish Gothic: An Edinburgh Companion,
    Carol Margaret Davison and Monica Germanà

Visit the Edinburgh Companions to the Gothic website at: www.euppublishing.com/series/edcg

American Gothic Culture

An Edinburgh Companion

Edited by
Joel Faflak and Jason Haslam

EDINBURGH
University Press

© editorial matter and organisation Joel Faflak and Jason Haslam, 2016
© the chapters their several authors, 2016

Edinburgh University Press Ltd
The Tun – Holyrood Road
12(2f) Jackson's Entry
Edinburgh EH8 8PJ

www.euppublishing.com

Typeset in 10.5/13 Sabon by
Servis Filmsetting Ltd, Stockport, Cheshire

A CIP record for this book is available from the British Library

ISBN 978 1 4744 0161 6 (hardback)
ISBN 978 1 4744 0162 3 (webready PDF)
ISBN 978 1 4744 1022 9 (epub)

The right of Joel Faflak and Jason Haslam to be
identified as the editors of this work has been asserted
in accordance with the Copyright, Designs and Patents
Act 1988, and the Copyright and Related Rights
Regulations 2003 (SI No. 2498).

Published with the support of the Edinburgh University
Scholarly Publishing Initiatives Fund.

Contents

Introduction   1
Joel Faflak and Jason Haslam

Part I: Gothic Histories, Gothic Identities

1. Gothic Monstrosity: Charles Brockden Brown's *Edgar Huntly* and the Trope of the Bestial Indian   25
   Christine Yao

2. Slavery and American Gothic: The Ghost of the Future   44
   Jason Haslam

3. Ethno-gothic: Repurposing Genre in Contemporary American Literature   60
   Arthur Redding

Part II: Gothic Genres, Gothic Sites

4. Southern Gothic   79
   Christopher Lloyd

5. The Devil in the Slum: American Urban Gothic   92
   Andrew Loman

6. Joyce Carol Oates Revisits the Schoolhouse Gothic   110
   Sherry R. Truffin

Part III: Gothic Media

7. American Gothic Television   129
   Julia M. Wright

8. American Gothic Art 145
   Christoph Grunenberg

9. Doppelgamers: Video Games and Gothic Choice 166
   Michael Hancock

Part IV: American Creatures

10. Screening the American Gothic: Celluloid Serial Killers in American Popular Culture 187
    Sorcha Ní Fhlainn

11. American Vampires 203
    Jeffrey Andrew Weinstock

12. Consumed out of the Good Land: The American Zombie, Geopolitics and the Post-War World 222
    Linnie Blake

Contributors 237
Index 241

Introduction
Joel Faflak and Jason Haslam

Three architectural sites are associated directly with Walt Disney: Disneyland, built under Disney's guidance and opened in 1955; EPCOT, or the Experimental Prototype Community of Tomorrow, a utopian city designed by Disney; and the house he purchased for his parents following the success, in 1938, of *Snow White*. Each of these sites can be said to stand in for a particular aspect of the American Dream: the promise of a continually innocent happiness and pleasure; the utopian social dreaming that is present in the political performatives of America from John Winthrop's 'city on a hill' sermon through to Obama's campaign for 'hope and change'; and the mundane happiness of the normative family, white picket fence and all. And yet, like these American fantasies, all three Disney sites are haunted, undermined by the realization of their hollowness, of violence, and of death. Shortly after moving into their new home, Disney's mother died of asphyxiation caused by a problem with the furnace (Mannheim 2002: 185). EPCOT's technological utopia 'was supposed to be a model for world cooperation' but 'instead became a giant ad for corporate futurism' (Waldrep 2013: n.p.); it was to be 'a precisely controlled city with carefully selected residents' – terrifying in itself – but became 'a teaching machine for corporate capitalism' (Fernandez 1995: 237). As our use of 'haunted' indicates, the disparity between the superficial perfection and happiness of these Disney sites and the partially hidden realities lying behind them are perhaps best represented through the cultural forms of the gothic.

As for Disneyland? Could it be that Disneyland is the most gothic site in the whole of the America? This enigmatic question requires much by way of explanation, from defining the gothic, to defining what is 'American' about the gothic, even to defining what, exactly, constitutes 'America' and where its borders may lie. To cite Jean Baudrillard's famous example of the uncanny force of simulation and simulacra, what he terms the 'hyperreal', 'Disneyland is presented as imaginary in order to make us believe that the rest is real' and provides the 'religious pleasure of the real America' (Baudrillard 1994: 12), precisely by helping us to forget the fantasies by which we live in the real world. We can thus also read the 'magic' of Disney as a gothicization of the real, a reminder of the pathological doubles of the 'real' or the 'normal', especially in a country constituted by its own zealous, religious and patriotic desire for originality and autonomy. As we discuss below, most overviews of the American gothic begin with one or more of these gestures, but are often framed within a particular disciplinary or media landscape. We begin this *Companion to American Gothic Culture* with our tale of a divided Disney to signal our own approach. Moving from analyses of eighteenth-century literature to twenty-first century video games, with chapters concerning visual art, film and television, alongside discussions of serial killers and monsters, of education and cityscapes, this *Companion* aims to demonstrate the centrality of the gothic to American culture writ large. We suggest that the definitions of America and those of gothic are so closely related as to be inseparable. In what follows in this Introduction, we articulate these definitions, as well as trace out the history of the cultural analysis of the American gothic. In the end, we return to Disneyland to answer the question we pose above, and introduce the structure and contents of the volume.

American Gothic

The gothic, gothic writing and gothic art emerged in Britain and Europe in the eighteenth century to express unseen, unknown and unacknowledged aspects of human existence left unexplained by religion or science. Generally read, gothic literature begins as an originary part of the Romantic denial of Enlightenment scientific assuredness. The fundamental humanism and objectivity of early Kantian metaphysics, Lockean political formulations, and Adam Smith's rational market are challenged by the gothic's focus on people's inability to fully control or understand themselves, let alone come to a full apprehension of the natural world. And this incapacity re-exposes science to the uncanny return of the mysticism of belief or the paranormality and superstition of a religion that science had apparently superseded. The supernatural forces of the gothic, combined with the madness and insensibility of its major characters, posits a much more chaotic world, one that belies reason as such. But, the gothic also points out that the chaos has lingered behind, and even supported, this rationalist gloss – witness Smith's reliance on an 'invisible hand' to govern his rational market (on Smith's invisible hand as gothic see Stefan Andriopoulos 1999). To cite the title of the most famous of Goya's engravings for *Los Caprichos* (1799), '*El sueño de la razón produce monstrous*' – 'The Sleep of Reason Breeds Monsters'. Or as Fred Botting argues in his account of the gothic, 'Darkness threatened the light of reason with what it did not know' (Botting 1996: 30), a sublime encounter that forces reason to recalibrate its overpowering 'experience of loss and negativity . . . through an imaginative and active process' (Botting 1996: 8) that attempts to re-inscribe codes and limits. Goya suggests that any system insisting upon its own rationality will breed its opposite, like the Reign of Terror that ensued from the first flush of French republicanism, or the Civil War that erupted from the elision of racialized political and social divisions that underwrote the enlightened birth of the American nation along a North/South but also East/West axis. Or we can see reason's perverse encounter with its own curiosity and desire, which is to mark in the Puritans' righteous insistence on their tenets of faith the pleasure of transgressing the 'normal' world they supposedly left behind.

That is to say, if the gothic emerged in the eighteenth century from a Western culture long haunted by its own history, as the Old World decamped to a new continent it viewed as blank slate rather than cultural palimpsest, as we shall see, it brought with it the uncanny return of historical forces and forms from which it otherwise thought to make a clean break. The American Dream was from its inception a haunted, gothic endeavour. Terry Castle reminds us that the gothic is powerfully aligned with the uncanny (Castle 1995). Put another way, the gothic reconstructs the façade of history in order to reveal its fractures, usually to remind us of hidden or repressed forces. In Freudian terms, familiar or *heimliche* aspects of our existence we try to forget often return in strange and unfamiliar or *unheimliche* form, such as seeing a man on the street whom one mistakes for one's father, except that one's father died ten years ago. Or, as we shall see in many of this Companion's chapters, staring into the face of racial 'others' (or, indeed, being in the latter position and staring back) and seeing (or rather, *not* seeing) the reflection of one's implication in the history of racial violence forgotten by a faith in America's pristine genesis. Or, as Christoph Grunenberg suggests in his account of American gothic art, staring into the faces in Grant Wood's iconic canvas and seeing the reflection of one's freakish 'normality'. One's disbelief is momentarily at once suspended and animated, creating a cognitive dissonance that opens a gap in our otherwise comfortable acceptance of reality. Like the sublime, the gothic generates polarizing sensations – fear and fascination, terror and awe, grief and elation – which in turn demand that we summon our inner resources to surmount the confusion, but also keep us off kilter. The gothic reminds us never to take for granted a certainty bought at the price of setting aside improbability, ambiguity, doubt – the kind of uncertainty that is the uncanny other of the European conquest of America's indigenous cultures, and later of its Manifest Destiny. The gothic thus summons and signifies this feeling or power of uncertainty as well as our desire to master it – the gothic as a both compelling and perilous mode. The gothic is also the way in which we respond to and register this struggle – the form of the gothic and the forms the gothic takes.

Between mode and form there is thus also an uncanny relationship, which is why gothic functions as both mode and genre, and why definitions of the gothic can be as varied as the gothic itself. Robert Miles's answer to the question 'What is "Gothic"?' is 'that the Gothic is a discursive site, a carnivalesque mode for representations of the fragmented subject' (Miles 1993: 4). Miles continues:

> Both the generic multiplicity of the Gothic, and what one might call its discursive primacy, effectively detach the Gothic from the tidy simplicity of thinking of it as so many predictable, fictional conventions. This may end up making 'Gothic' a more ambiguous, shifting term, but then the textual phenomena to which it points are shifting and ambiguous. (4)

Another word for the gothic here might be 'heterogeneous', reflecting a protean nature beyond one's capacity to contain or express its different realities, which difference further points to a failure or flaw in the human attempt itself, a viral, virulent fallibility embodied in the vampires, serial killers and zombies in Jeffrey Andrew Weinstock's, Sorcha Ní Fhlainn's and Linnie Blake's chapters respectively. Miles takes his cue from another key gothic theorizer, David Punter, who suggests that the gothic, by exhibiting otherwise '[c]ompulsive, repetitive, superficially meaningless behaviour somehow addresses a deeper "wound", a rift in the psyche . . . [which] Punter understands . . . as in some sense a collective psyche, one shaped by social and historical forces' (Miles 1993: 2). If one imagines the economic, industrial, military, political and scientific explorations and expansions of the seventeenth and eighteenth centuries as a radical confrontation with global diversity both natural and cultural, one can see how something like the gothic emerges to imagine this diversity in turn, more particularly to deal with the awe, shock and fear such encounters evoke.

The gothic's compulsive, repetitive form indicates a genre of stereotypical tropes (haunted houses, hidden chambers, freakish natural acts) and conventions (narratives of illegitimate, lost, or terrorized victims). Yet to paraphrase Deleuze, even repetition leaves the trace of a difference, the symptom of repetition's struggle to express the very reality it repeats. Put another way, the gothic's generic sameness evokes the same dull round of our habitual lives, but in order to reveal a terror masked by custom. The contrived reproduction of conditions induces a real response of fear in order to jolt us out of the complacency produced by the equally contrived nature of everyday life resulting from an industrialism, commercialism and technology essential to the American Dream well before 1776. The relationship between terror and custom is itself uncanny, however. In Horace Walpole's gothic urtext, *The Castle of Otranto* (1764), the author of the original 1764 Preface (Walpole, gothically displacing himself; in the second edition of 1765, he authors the Preface in his own name), stages his text as a stage management of the gothic itself: 'The characters are well drawn, and still better maintained. Terror, the author's principal engine, prevents the story from ever languishing; and it is so often contrasted by pity, that the mind is kept up in a constant vicissitude of interesting passions' (Walpole 1764: v–vi). 'Terror' is at once the text's fuel and 'engine', both force and the system it drives, which makes further ironic the tension between 'maintenance' and 'constant vicissitude'. Change is at once essential and inevitable; the text manufactures 'Terror' in order to show how one never knows where terror lies, which in turn calls upon the reader's desire and will at once to surrender to and surmount the fear, as in players' encounter with the hap of choice in Michael Hancock's essay on video games for this volume. This confrontation evokes Burke's or Kant's theories of the sublime, in which one's encounter with what one cannot align with one's capacity *to* know redraws boundaries between self and world. For Walpole, the gothic novel, like video games, simulates 'interesting passions' in order to stimulate a visceral response. In order to feel reality *as* real one must experience it as fake, must feel within our habitual world a reality it has forgotten. Something of this uncanny return of the real within the fake (the real that is only known through the fantasies by which is constructed, as Slavoj Žižek might say) informs Disney's perfecting of the animated feature as the signal expression of his utopian vision. One recalls that one of Disney's godfathers, the animation pioneer Winsor McCay, begins by 'animating' dinosaur fossils in his first animated short, *Gertie the Dinosaur* (1914).

Put another way, the gothic expresses paranoia that reason might be as volatile or anachronistic as the histories and customs it forced underground, which is why the gothic itself appears at once anachronistic and freakishly novel. This vertigo between change and stasis, the new and the old, pretence and authenticity, becomes particularly relevant to our understanding of American nationhood as a radical break with the past rather than the result of a gradual historical evolution, what the British poet William Blake, hoping that the sparks of revolution would carry across the Atlantic to reignite English republicanism from the ashes of its own stagnation, figures as apocalypse with millennium in his illuminated prophecy *America* (1793). But with this coinage comes the burden of origins, originating and originality – the hubris of doubtful authenticity. Upon declaring independence the Founding Fathers needed immediately to 'frame' a Constitution – to give concrete form to an inchoate desire commensurate, as Fitzgerald writes at the end of *The Great Gatsby*, with man's capacity for wonder, but the goal of which eludes his grasp in endless pursuit of a future that bears him 'ceaselessly into the past' (Fitzgerald 2004: 180). It was as if for the first time history and the nation were making themselves up out of thin air, an auto-fashioning that makes one anxious to find and repeat one's origins, and may explain the nation's perverse desire *not* to let go of the traumas by which it is otherwise formed.

Which is why 'American' and 'gothic' are at once real and hyper-real companions. Authenticity depends upon its ability to buy into the legitimacy of older forms, a combination of delayed satisfaction and evangelical promise that speaks to the logic of capitalism that helped to forge the American nation. Jerrold E. Hogle (1998) speaks of the gothic as the 'ghost of the counterfeit' that finds its form by repeating its own feigned nature and thus trading in its lack of currency and in the simulative nature of all signs. Gothic signs are legitimate *because* they are parodic, a series of commodities whose life and value depend on their circulation in a market-driven public sphere. The telling and re-telling of America's 'national narrative' (Savoy 1998: 14), as Eric Savoy notes, is essential to this process, but that narrative is always haunted by its dubious origins, by a doubt that it *has* origins. This story can never quite say what it means because it wants to repress its real origins, but also because it does not trust the ones it made up to simulate its genesis. In American gothic studies Savoy is key for expressing this haunting's psychoanalytical slant: 'the gothic "turn" toward compelling but unthematizable narrative might be conceptualized as the emergence of the Lacanian Real, which, according to Judith Butler, "is that which resists and compels symbolization"' (Savoy 1998: 8). And the trauma that at once 'resists and compels symbolization' is 'the specter of Otherness', particularly of slavery (14). The founding of America is predicated on the eradication rather than amalgamation of indigenous or racial others, of a topographical and cultural slate wiped clean, yet producing a dominant narrative that, like a palimpsest, is both constituted and sustained by the traces of the histories it has attempted to erase. Ironic and often tragic, then, is the fact that a nation denies an authentic reality staring it in the face in favour of a 'Real' authenticity the origins of which it never ultimately trusts – can never ultimately trust.

That the history of gothic artistic production in America is often defined as a significant redevelopment of British and European forms appears in nineteenth-century authors' own descriptions of the nation's literature, and even well in to twentieth-century formulations of American gothic literature. Donald A. Ringe, for one, writes in 1982 that 'American writers of fiction had . . . to walk the thin line between the two extremes, basing their works, as Simms puts it, on unstrained probability – the real, or the seemingly real – and using the marvelous only with great discretion' (Ringe 1982: 9). Many early American authors also bemoaned the new nation's supposed lack of history – more correctly characterized as a lack of Euro-American empathetic imagination, in which the history of the indigenous population is rendered moot and silent. As Christine Yao notes in her contribution to this volume, Charles Brockden Brown, America's first successful novelist, explained that the 'puerile superstition and exploded manners, Gothic castles and chimeras' were 'the materials usually employed' by European authors to bring 'forth the passions and engag[e] the sympathy of the reader', but these were unavailable to the American writer convinced of the need to represent the nation as such. Three decades later, James Fenimore Cooper adapts Brown's call to national arms as a lament: as Allan Lloyd Smith writes, 'Cooper complained in 1828 that there were no suitable materials for writers to be found in the new country, "no annals for the historian . . . no obscure fictions for the writer of romance"' (Smith 2012: 163). Analyses of the past were the purported purview of the writer, and especially of the gothic writer, and America – within its own mythology – is constantly invented anew, with a past that never accrues.

What Cooper missed that Brown does not, however, is the simple fact that America is not defined by an innocence constantly projected but by a violent history that constantly reasserts itself. The quotation from Brown, above, offered in his notice 'To the Public' at the beginning of *Edgar Huntly; or, Memoirs of a Sleep-Walker* (1799), continues by arguing that 'the incidents of Indian hostility, and the perils of the Western wilderness, are far more suitable' to an American writer, 'and for a native of America to overlook these would admit of no apology' (Brown 1799: 4). Brown's vision admittedly paints a Eurocentric approach to the 'new' land and its peoples, but he correctly situates American national identity and its gothic rendition within the violence of colonialism and expansion, or, looked at from another direction, within the utopian frameworks of American exceptionalism. And Disney rears his head again.

We will defer Disney's return briefly, however, in order to trace the traditional narrative of American gothic literary production, so as to situate it within our larger approach to American gothic culture. American gothic is no different from its European counterpart in this respect: American gothic presents us with a world uncontrolled and uncontainable by narrative, whether that is indicated by Huntly's uncontrolled, and unconscious, sleepwalking; the tortures of Edgar Allan Poe's pit; Henry James's governess and her narrative's incommensurable portrayal of ghosts (or the lack thereof); Flannery O'Connor's repressed and violently Freudian protagonists; or Stephen King's self-propelled car. But American gothic does have its own trajectories, just as it has its own history. As Brown writes, American writers had a plethora of specific material on which to draw. From the nineteenth century through to early and high modernism and into the postmodern explosion of gothic culture, American gothic has long lingered on the specifics of the nation.

A canonical history of American gothic, such as Fiedler's, would trace its roots from the beginnings of the long nineteenth century, with such writers as Brown and Cooper, as well as Washington Irving, who all struggle to define the new nation in relation both to its previous inhabitants and to its European heritage. From there, we would move to the Romantic tradition of Hawthorne and Poe, who begin the inward turn to psychology, both of the individual and of the larger collective. This turn would then lead to the modernism of James, who perfects the terror of an unknowable self. From there, American gothic is said to regionally fragment, with the Southern Gothic of Faulkner, Tennessee Williams, O'Connor and others becoming a dominant mode, transforming James's eruditions into the incestuous malingerings of American domesticity. This mode then leads to the contemporary moment, with writers ranging from Toni Morrison, Stephen King and Anne Rice exposing the horrors and traumas of an American history – of slavery, miscegenation, sexual violence – at once always present and always repressed. And accompanying this evolution towards the present, as most chapters in this volume attest, is the protean metamorphosis of the gothic from page or canvas to stage, film, TV and video games, which multi-modal networks at once sustain and are sustained by America's interminable fascination with the gothic.

American Gothic Criticism

But this canonical, formal history often lacks precisely the historical specificity Brown demanded and Fiedler gestures towards. While Brown ultimately denies the assertion that America has no past and so is unsuited to the gothic, still the mythology of American newness shaped approaches to its literary and larger cultural production well into the twentieth century. This fixation on America's shiny present finds its cultural zenith in the pulp science fiction of the 1920s and 30s, but is echoed in the same period by the New Critics, who would have shunned such mindless entertainment as the pulps, even as they shunned the gothic. Viewing the gothic as too plodding for serious study, still they turned to authors whose works are clearly gothic to discuss the unknowable, the aporia and paradox they saw at the centre of literature, be it Hawthorne, Melville, or even Dickinson with her focus on death as the site of ontological questioning but also as a gothically embodied figure, be it in the fly that buzzed as the speaker of one her poems dies, or the kindly gentleman who stops for another speaker as she 'could not stop' for him. In formalist and New Critical readings, Dickinson, Hawthorne, or James became less figures from a specific time with a specific history writing within a specific gothic mode, and more the experimental formalists, intent on language play.

Certainly such play is important to gothic writers, and later theorists of the gothic, including Savoy and Hogle, would see in such linguistic finesse both a precursor to postmodern and post-structuralist theory, and an analysis of the counterfeit nature of capitalism (Savoy 1998; Hogle 1998). But another of the reasons for that formal experimentation is precisely the desire to address the formative repressions of the American historical self. The materialist turn in American literary and cultural criticism, starting in the 1960s, saw the return of the gothic to its historical conditions, and this approach still largely dominates the field today. In some ways, Leslie Fiedler's foundational work proves the hinge between critical traditions, as Hogle has pointed out in an introduction to the theoretical history of the study of American gothic (Hogle 2014: 5). Introducing the formal elements that compose the European gothic, Fiedler goes on to note that 'of all the fictions of the West, our own is most deeply influenced by the gothic', noting that America's 'greatest works are gothic in theme and atmosphere alike'. Like Cooper, though, he questions how the gothic can apply to a country with 'neither a proper past nor a history' (Fiedler 1966: 142; 144). But Fiedler then writes, following Brown to a point, that 'certain special guilts awaited projection in gothic form', among which are 'the slaughter of Indians, who would not yield their lands to the carriers of utopia, and the abominations of the slave trade, in which the black man, rum, and money were inextricably entwined in a knot of guilt' (Fiedler 1966: 143). While Fiedler's turn to history and to a Marxist and materialist approach seems somewhat superficial compared to the materialist turn of the later decades of the twentieth century, still there is a profound recognition that the historical elements of European gothic are turned to specific elements of American history (though of course recent critics of British and other gothic literatures also note the effect the slave trade had on those literary products).

That said, the relation between the gothic and the history of both the Americas in general and the United States in particular is one that has been traced by several literary and cultural critics. These analyses generally focus on the disparity between the 'national narrative' of the American Dream and the historical realities of violence, subjugation and attempted genocide that materially support the construction of that narrative. From the landing of the Puritans to the Civil War, to Western expansion and Manifest Destiny, and to the American Century and the mythology of the 'post-racial' future, the history of America could be characterized as the murderous intent hidden by a welcoming smile. Smith, analysing nineteenth-century American gothic literature specifically, offers a useful model for reading the 'American' in American gothic more generally:

> Without a feudal past and those relics so convenient for the European Gothicist, castles and monasteries and legends, the American landscape seemed an unlikely place for such fictions. Yet four indigenous features were to prove decisive in producing a powerful and long-lasting American variation of the Gothic: the frontier, the Puritan legacy, race, and political utopianism. (Smith 2012: 163)

In each of these four categories, Smith argues, American gothic develops a particularly Manichean vision, be it within political, religious, or more generally ontological discussions.

Building on Smith's conclusions, we can see that from the encounter with the frontier American gothic engages a debate between the chaos of the 'wilderness' and the light of civilization, mirrored in the Romantics' and later the naturalists' gothic appropriation of the innocence of nature and the decadence of the city, arguments followed by Christine Yao, Andrew Loman and Christoph Grunenberg in this volume. This analysis could then also be used to explore the ways in which gothic discourse is employed both to further and analyse American imperial actions, be they cultural or material, a global perspective that Arthur Redding brings to his chapter. Recent revelations about the US use of torture, for example, have employed the rhetoric of terror (both in relation to terrorist acts against the US, as well as the state of terror engendered by the use of torture). Combined with the often explicit deployment of a 'civilized vs. savage' binary in the political sphere, this trope clearly elaborates on the frontier mythos Smith discusses.

The Puritan legacy picks up on such a depiction of the landscape to present a world populated and driven by either absolute good or absolute evil, tied to religious and sexual realms. In colonial America, Cotton Mather asserted that the Puritans were in a land populated by demons and devils, both supernatural and in their material agents, as the racist depictions of indigenous peoples would often portray them (see Madsen 1998: 33). Moving into the nineteenth century, as Brown outlines, the representation of indigenous peoples expanded on the frontier gothic Smith identifies, but the puritanical religious gothic lingered. Yet the Puritans themselves became the focus of gothic literature, especially in Hawthorne's oeuvre, where the sexual legacies of Puritan communities were shown to haunt America. In both *The Scarlet Letter* (1850) and *The Blithedale Romance* (1852), the conservative Hawthorne depicts the deadly effects of a sexual licentiousness, even as lingering in the shadows the suspicion remains that it is conservative dictates themselves that fuel the terror. These shadows then become the main focus of later gothic writers, as in Henry James's 'The Beast in the Jungle' (1903), where the haunting but never revealed beast is the always already hidden secret of sexual desire, be it heterosexual as in traditional readings of the story, or the closet of a queer desire, as in Eve Kosofsky Sedgwick's powerful – even undeniable – reading (Sedgwick 2008: 182–212). Later gothic writers would become more explicit in identifying the Puritan heritage of sex and its repression (or, following Foucault (1990), its 'repressive' dissemination) as the source and site of the gothic dissolution of the self-contained, self-reliant American identity. Southern Gothic writers from Faulkner, to O'Connor, to Morrison and beyond to such cultural products as Hitchcock's *Psycho* (1960) and Demme's 1991 *Silence of the Lambs* (both based on serial killer Ed Gein, as Sorcha Ní Fhlainn details in this volume), highlight the sexual terrors of American nostalgia and history, even as they show how those terrors are inextricably linked to race, class, region and other identifying markers.

The discussion of sexuality is, of course, part of a Gordian knot of identities that also include the other categories that Sedgwick refers to as the 'coarse axes' of identification (Sedgwick 2008: 22): class, gender and race. Smith's categories may not explicitly reference gender, but of course the frontier, the Puritan legacy, race and utopian political formations are impossible to discuss without turning to gender alongside all of these other identities. The gendered history of American and other democracies likewise proves a fertile field for gothic writers, as Hawthorne's Hester Prynne, or many of Shirley Jackson's characters, or Stephen King's Carrie would be at pains to remind us. Indeed, one cannot discuss the Puritan heritage nor its gothic refractions without examining the way in which they interact with the later formulations of domestic purity in the ideological structures of the 'Cult of True Womanhood' (see Welter 1966), nor to the later feminist invocations of the gothic, from Charlotte Perkins Gilman's 'The Yellow Wallpaper' (1892) through to Shirley Jackson's fugue-like story 'The Tooth' (1948), to more recent works by Joanna Russ, Poppy Z. Brite, Octavia Butler and others (see, for example, Weinstock 2008).

The third of Smith's American gothic categories, race, permeates these others in the history of American gothic culture. The legacies of colonialism and slavery, the Asian Exclusion Act and Japanese internment, among other historical and ongoing acts of racism, find their discursive echoes (and challenges) in American gothic, where the Manichean Puritan vision is replicated as 'us' and 'them'. Toni Morrison's meditations on whiteness, Teresa Goddu's discussions of slavery, and other analyses of gothic literature develop this thread. Here the link between the contemporary and the nineteenth century is perhaps strongest. From the use of gothic discourse by pro-slavery and abolitionist authors alike, to the lingering symptomatology of 'colour' in American gothic, one cannot escape the history of African American slavery, in particular, and its ongoing social and cultural effects. Poe's 'Black Cat' (1843), the fugitive slave narratives of Frederick Douglass (1845) and Harriet Jacobs (1861), and their exploitation in Harriet Beecher Stowe's *Uncle Tom's Cabin* (1852), among other works, show clearly that the gothic representation of slavery and race form the throughline of American gothic in the nineteenth century. But, as Morrison's *Beloved* (1987), Octavia Butler's *Kindred* (1979) and even Anne Rice's *Interview with the Vampire* (1976) show, the site of slavery is America's primal gothic scene, one that echoes even in works that, on their surface, have little to do with slavery (one can think here of the Wachowski Siblings' 1999 film, *The Matrix*, for one).

Slavery and the racism and subsequent racialized subjects it both relied on and engendered form the spine of American gothic and the critical analyses thereof. Smith's final inclusion of political utopianism is a useful move, however, and indicates how all of these categories are imbricated in American culture and the gothic forms by which it is frequently constituted. Smith writes:

> The utopian visions of freedom and prosperity that brought the early settlers to North America gained new vigor from Enlightenment arguments about the possibility of an ideal society and were enshrined in the founding constitutional principles of the United States. But along with the utopian inspiration came profoundly pessimistic insights into the dangers of trusting a society to the undisciplined rule of the majority, fear of faction in democratic government, the rule of the mob, and the danger of a collapse of the whole grand experiment. (Smith 2012: 165)

Smith presents here the seemingly incommensurable paradox of American self-definition, one that will not synthesize through the rational, self-fashioning dialectics that supposedly form the nation. Individual rights and mob rule; civil representation and government overreach; civilization and chaos; utopia and dystopia: the gothic represents these binaries as the fight between the forces of light and the forces of darkness, the rational and the irrational, the angelic and demonic, and so on. And obviously such binaries play out in the material oppositions that frame the nation and that make up Smith's other three categories: colonizer vs colonized; free vs enslaved; whiteness vs blackness; the ideologically asserted if mythical moral purity of the white nation vs the representation of the sexual licentiousness of racialized subjects; all contained within the 'self' of the hegemonic nation and its variously constructed 'others'.

Of course, by repeating these formulations the gothic also highlights and thus challenges them. If the racist cultural structures of American slavery and the white supremacy that grew from it paint moral purity in shades of white and 'perversions' primarily in browns, the gothic can gesture to the psychological and material mixtures that whiteness relies on. One can think here of the paint factory in Ralph Ellison's *Invisible Man* (1952), which generates its brightest white through the addition of drops of black substance. Toni Morrison analyses how the gothic explicitly employs the representation of race, and specifically blackness, to define (white) Americanness 'itself' in ways that echo all of the other categories heretofore discussed:

> As a disabling virus within literary discourse, Africanism has become, in the Eurocentric tradition that American education favors, both a way of talking about and a way of policing matters of class, sexual license, and repression, formations and exercises of power, and meditations on ethics and accountability. Through the simple expedient of demonizing and reifying the range of color on a palette, American Africanism makes it possible to say and not say, to inscribe and erase, to escape and engage, to act out and act on, to historicize and render timeless. It provides a way of contemplating chaos and civilization, desire and fear, and a mechanism for testing the problems and blessings of freedom. (Morrison 1992: 7)

Going on to analyse such authors as Poe and Melville, Morrison shows how these definitions of (white) Americanness begin to fall apart, or at least expose themselves as fetish objects for which no true nature exists. American gothic can thus be read as that which challenges and even denies the very signification of its first term.

Smith's four-part structure emphasizes the dominant materialist trend in contemporary gothic studies. That his piece discusses the nineteenth century makes this focus all the more understandable and proper. Materialist studies of the gothic, taking their cue from the turn to Marxist analyses and then to New Historicist approaches (as Hogle (2014) expertly details), remain a central focus of American gothic studies, and American Studies more generally, and many of our contributors add to our complex understanding of such approaches. American gothic studies, like critical approaches to the larger gothic field, have a long and continuing tradition of direct engagement with other methodologies, however. Adding these methodologies to materialist approaches helps to mitigate the risk of taking Fredric Jameson's dictum to 'always historicize' to its paradoxically mimetic extremes (Jameson 1981: 9), where American gothic becomes a reflection of a limited set of plots from the nation's repressed history. In addition to 'history', after all, the other key term in the previous sentence, which Morrison likewise uses, is 'repression', pointing to another major focus of American gothic and a central mode of the criticism thereof: psychology and psychoanalytic criticism. Not separated from the material realm, but instead focused on its personal and cultural mediation, the psychological realm of American gothic has become another of its defining features. Even as materialist discussions may dominate the current critical moment, their focus on race, gender, sexuality, empire and other politics are also available to psychoanalytic and even linguistic analyses.

Indeed, it is difficult not to see the gothic as an implicitly psychoanalytical mode and genre par excellence, for as Andrew Loman notes in his essay on the American urban gothic, citing two of our most powerful gothic theorizers, Freud is the 'true heir of Walpole and Radcliffe' (Williams 1995: 240) and 'psychoanalysis is a late gothic story' (Kilgour 1995: 221). The gothic's individual perversities and transgressions, hidden and terrorizing depths of knowledge, or ancestral miscegenations all speak to a broader national family romance in which personal ordeal is writ large as sociopolitical trauma. As Jason Haslam and Christopher Lloyd remind us in their chapters, very often the South is a primal scene of the nation's crimes and misdemeanours and the Southern Gothic a generic couch for remembering, repeating and working back through the past towards an ambivalent yet always hopeful future. But as Loman also reminds us, citing Toni Morrison's point about 'how dour, how troubled, how frightened and haunted our early and founding literature truly is' (Morrison 1992 35), it seems the entire American landscape is a psychic topography especially overdetermined by the American imagination's utopianism about the undeniability and unassailability of a progress the evangelical promise of which seems excessive, almost freakish in its zeal.

Reading this topography as an always manifestly positive form of a more disturbingly latent content thus also subtends a post-Freudian, Lacanian approach to the letter of the gothic as taken up by Hogle, Savoy and others. Such an attention to the text as symptom informs two seminal readings of James's fictions, for instance. In her account of *The Turn of the Screw* (1898) Shoshana Felman argues that we can only read the text's ambiguous content through its compulsively repetitive narrative form, an interminably delayed trajectory toward the truth that one might read as an allegory for the failure of Manifest Destiny itself (Felman 1977). A different failure informs Sedgwick's reading of James's 'The Beast in the Jungle', noted above, in which the ego-centred bachelor John Marcher, by preserving himself and others (specifically women) from an unnamed fate he knows might attack at any time, ends up writing homosexual panic as the id-like beast that both protects and devours the superego's heteronormative identities, like the letter that always finds its destination in Lacan's reading of Poe's 'The Purloined Letter' (1845). For if American identity is predicated on a utopia whose origins lay in a murky past, are unrealizable in the present, and thus remain always pitched, like Gatsby, toward an impossible future, we can read the story of America as somehow gothically stillborn – to re-cite Savoy, as an 'unthematizable narrative [that] might be conceptualized as the emergence of the Lacanian Real, which ... "resists and compels symbolization"'. In this way, the gothic tells the 'perfect' American tale, as Hogle might argue, through the displaced, simulated, alienated and overdetermined capitalist forms of its own manufactured, fractured identity. But in this way we must also remember, as Loman reminds us, that whenever we conjure the ghost of Freud, we must also welcome Marx to the seance.

America as Gothic

Importantly, while the critical and cultural history traced above focuses on the literary or otherwise textual gothic, the gothic has always been a multi-modal cultural discourse. There is a reason, after all, why the phrase 'American Gothic' is most readily identified with an iconic painting, and that one of Edison's first moving pictures was a 1910 version of *Frankenstein* or that McCay's first animated film literally (re)animated dead life forms. If, then, we view the gothic as a mode or discourse, rather than as a genre, the field of gothic studies opens from the literary to visual arts, film, video games and other media, to architecture, and beyond. It would be a mistake to see this trend as particularly American, of course: American gothic, like all cultural products and modes of discourse, has always been in a symbiotic relationship to a global cultural exchange. But if there is something particularly *American* about American gothic, it's the extent to which it forms the foundation of cultural practice across a range of media and cultural forms. While realism, and a concomitant pragmatism, has long been assumed to lie at the heart of American culture, it is equally true – as Julia M. Wright argues in her chapter on American gothic television – that the gothic has an equally long and multi-modal history. This gothic, as Wright argues, is the necessary self-analytic form of realism itself. American gothic consistently and simultaneously focuses on and immediately denies both national and generic dissolution. Hence while we can say that the gothic begins with Walpole's *Otranto* or Radcliffe's novels, we must also view the gothic – whether genre, mode, or discourse – as feeding upon a host of textual, aural, linguistic, spatial and visual resources in order to fuel its movement across and between media and cultural forms wherever required to speak to desires and anxieties that society cannot otherwise express by 'official' means, as we shall see in the individual chapter descriptions at the end of this Introduction. And yet 'official' is rather ironic, here, for the gothic has gone from a maladapted, bastardized, or otherwise cheap, innocuous and superficial aesthetic force to a viral cultural load that now burdens the mainstream as a necessary reminder of what has, can, or could go wrong.

This fact is one of the reasons we opened this Introduction with Walt Disney. If American utopianism and American gothic have gone hand-in-hand socially, politically and culturally, since Winthrop's 'city on the hill' became Mather's terrorized landscape (a transformation outlined by Deborah Madsen (1998), though not in terms of the gothic per se), then one would expect Disney's purposefully utopian cultural constructs to be as terrible as they are entertaining. And, indeed, they are. Disneyland does not just stand in for America within the nation's self-image, constructing a hollow simulacrum of national identity, as Baudrillard discusses (Baudrillard 1994: 12–14); it also becomes the haunting ghost of America's self-recognition as a gothically abject, rather than democratically utopian, nation. Nowhere is this shown so clearly as in the 1973 Michael Crichton film, *Westworld*. An amusement park that nostalgically trades on a frontier life that never was, 'Westworld' shows what happens when the nation's own self-congratulatory utopian discourse of freedom turns on itself, when the hollow, purposeless ideologies of American self-reliance generate violent robots whose only purpose is to kill all humans (or at least, in a projection of self-loathing, kill all Americans). In Crichton's incisive vision, Disneyland – and by extension, America – becomes what it truly is: not 'the happiest place on Earth', but 'the most gothic place on Earth'. And it is from this encompassing vision of America *as* the gothic that this *Companion* takes its structure. Moving both across history and through multiple media and forms of analysis, the *Companion* sees the gothic as a primary discourse through which American culture discusses itself and the material nation from which it arises.

Our first section, 'Gothic Histories, Gothic Identities', begins to map the historical, sociopolitical and aesthetic terrain upon which the American gothic propagates. Our first three essays remind us that the American nation, hardly springing Athena-like from the minds of its Founding Fathers, instead unfolds as a long analytical encounter with a past it would rather forget: the stories it tells itself in order to forge a new identity always haunted by its struggle to work through the ghosts of past struggles. Christine Yao explores Brown's depiction of Native Americans as cannibalizing beasts in *Edgar Huntly*, a gothic fantasy with brute material effects. Turning Native Americans into chimeric presences, like figments of the American imagination, the novel's overdetermined structure ensures their uncanny return within a national narrative that would cannibalize the past without remainder – beginning with Plymouth Colony, haunted by Columbus's earlier confrontations with the 'New World', and mobilized violently westward. Jason Haslam reads this troubled narrative back to the future of its 'originary trauma' in slavery, which American gothic names as both metaphor and institutional reality. Yet in doing so, does the gothic compulsively repeat or analyse this trauma? In Haslam's survey from slave narratives (Jacobs, Douglass) to Poe to Toni Morrison or Octavia Butler, American gothic must continually re-ingest the poison of slavery, 'that which *must* be renarrativized if the past is not to overwrite the future'. Or as Haslam asks, 'Could the walking dead actually be the talking cure?' Arthur Redding's account of 'ethno-gothic' then reminds us that colour is less black and white than fifty shades of anxiety about miscegenation, which finds powerful expression in the gothic's bastardized, aborted, hybrid, protean forms, especially for a national audience otherwise trained in the hegemonic stories of a hybrid white identity both constituted and haunted by the strains of its differences. Contemporary fiction, rather than rejecting a gothic un-scripting of racial others, re-inhabits the genre's national home built by slavery in order to re-purpose its still haunting stereotypes toward a more hopeful occupation – what Redding calls a 'globalized counter-gothic' that, by accepting that racism never seems to die, can (and must) tarry differently with its spectres.

Our next section, 'Gothic Genres, Gothic Sites', writes American gothic through three contested topographies: the South, the school, the city. Here space and place function *as* genre, as sites written and overwritten by traumas of the past. For Christopher Lloyd, the South has also possessed a 'fertile' gothic imagination: American gothic is figuratively but also literally rooted in the South, suggesting Teresa Goddu's point that the gothic emerges rather than escapes from the reality it expresses. Slavery and the Civil War plant this *Ungrund*, but Lloyd's three contemporary examples from cinema and TV suggest that the South, always an 'aberrant space' haunted by traumas of sex, violence, race and gender, also offers the opportunity to queer the past toward a reparative future. In Andrew Loman's examination of American urban gothic, the terrors of social disintegration and alienation attending the rapid urbanization and modernization of the late antebellum (1840–60) produced an equal explosion of gothic mysteries mired in the city distinct from the country. This urban subgenre expresses less a coherent if vexed national identity than a broad discursive field of competing local, regional, national, and international racial and classed differences constituting the city as an equally paradoxical hybrid of progress and failure. Finally, Sherry R. Truffin's exploration of 'Schoolhouse Gothic' writes Goya's primal scene of Enlightenment as a horrifying national classroom epitomized by two bastions of educational privilege, Harvard (in Faulkner's *The Sound and the Fury* (1929)) and Princeton (in Joyce Carol Oates's *The Accursed* (2013)). Here the problem is not 'human reason itself' but 'reason enmeshed in capitalist exploitation, bent on domination, and unchecked by the equally human capacity for respect or empathy'.

The three essays in our next section, 'Gothic Media', address TV, art, and video games respectively as key gothic mediations of American identity. Julia M. Wright addresses how the unfolding history of television series evokes a trend toward greater realism, yet which later realism is, ironically, often borrowed from earlier gothic depictions of reality. In this way TV 'reality' deploys the gothic as thought experiment, a carefully constructed cultural artefact (hearkening back to Walpole's manipulation of reality) that plays out reality as a gothic artificiality in which we then suspend our disbelief. Or as Wright argues, 'Gothic television is not only uninterested in representational accuracy or verisimilitude, but also continues to question the very possibility of such representation'. For Christoph Grunenberg the gothic in American art 'functions as a kind of moral valve, releasing repressed memories and revealing the traumas that haunt American society throughout its history and presence', 'more a state of mind than a distinct style, defined by a plurality of expressive modes and presentational strategies'. From late eighteenth- and early nineteenth-century American landscape painting, to Grant Wood's iconic 'American Gothic', to Edward Hopper's night scenes, to Kara Walker's grotesque tableaux of the Southern Gothic we thus witness in American art early gothic symptoms that increasingly survive unabated as a full-blown cultural syndrome, an infallible visual barometer and diagnosis of, and thus witness to, the nation's moods. And on the subject of video games as art-gothic, Michael Hancock makes the visual uncannily viral by exploring how the avatars of humanity exist on both sides of the gaming screen. Doubling and repetition, as if to materialize Beckett's point of trying again, failing again, and failing better, face players with the ghosts of future attempts and past failures, turning human motion and emotion into an aesthetic, mechanized gothic existence that the overt gothicization of video games is meant to de-familiarize. Yet the ultimate ghost in the machine of their Enlightenment *Bildungsroman* is choice, a self-determination through which the 'video game exposes the gothic self' always 'beyond one's rational control'.

Our final section, 'American Creatures', welcomes home three monsters of the American gothic. For Sorcha Ní Fhlainn celluloid and TV serial killers embody the 'counter-narrative American Dream: the consumerist and consumption-driven American nightmare', turning the American gothic inwards to expose a festering sociopathy that turns assembly-line killing into a mechanical, generically durable reproduction of America's 'destructive individualism'. Increasingly, then, the serial killer is less monster than uncanny moral specimen, as in the TV series, *Dexter* (2006–13), which tarries with rather than rejects outright the main character's morality because it externalizes the Law's perverse pleasure as the fine line between justice and vigilantism, proving that the superego has an id of its own. The vampire undergoes a similar cultural rehabilitation in Jeffrey Andrew Weinstock's chapter. Early nineteenth-century controlling women or the bloodthirsty cannibals of Yao's essay, stereotyping dark fantasies about sexual or racial otherness, were prototypes for the vampire's post-*Dracula* reincarnated peril to the lifeblood of the 'pure' if overdetermined American body politic. Yet in more recent times the 'outsiderdom of the vampire, its queer sexuality, its refusal to respect authority all become causes of celebration rather than castigation'. Vampires' monstrous and miscegenating survival, metamorphosing across and between media and cultural forms, makes them the undead metaphor par excellence for the nation's shifting yet never-stilled desires and anxieties.

The same gothic survival informs the zombie apocalypse now of our final essay by Linnie Blake. Here the terror that Walpole re-manufactured in England becomes in the country that left its mother behind a land of real terrors feeding upon the offspring of its auto-ontogeny – a 'particularly potent metaphor' for 'our age of infrastructural collapse, societal degeneration, mismanaged pandemic scenarios and governmental indifference and corruption'. Such gothic disaster takes us full circle as well to Cotton Mather's fears of a civil body corrupted by infection and dehumanization. But it also takes us back to the future of a ghost haunting the American psyche all along, one that called for, and apparently ensures the undead survival of, the nation's 'originary trauma'. The religiously zealous, morally upright, pristinely utopian future imagined by Mather's heirs has for Blake produced that most frightening of enslavements: the triumph of a global neo-liberalism that, in the name of democratic individualism, sustains itself all over again by a frightening reliance on the racial othering and marginalization of the very individual cultures to which it offers to give rein in the free marketplace. The Main Street of Disney's middle-class, middle America dream of a better future writ large as the global networks of an Experimental Prototype Community of Tomorrow whose futuristic template, more dominatingly present and more terrifyingly tied to Eisenhower's military-industrial complex than even Disney might have imagined, will keep the undead cultural machinery of American gothic working for some time to come. We thus end the volume with the gothic reminder that the unfettered vicissitudes of free market, coupled with overdetermined dreams of democratic individualism, might just be the most terrifying monster of all. Winthrop's 'city on the hill' has now become a gated global community in which the power of money is the magical wall separating the 1 per cent from the other – and othered – 99 per cent by which such unthinkable affluence and privilege constitutes and sustains itself. And yet we can thank the gothic for reminding us – over and over again – of what the terrors of such an outcome look and feel like, hopefully always scaring us back to some sense and semblance of reality.

References

Andriopoulos, Stefan (1999), 'The Invisible Hand: Supernatural Agency in Political Economy and the Gothic Novel', *English Literary History* 66.3: 739–58.
Baudrillard, Jean (1994), *Simulation and Simulacra*, trans. Sheila Faria Glaser, Ann Arbor: University of Michigan Press.
Botting, Fred (1996), *Gothic*, New York: Routledge.
Brown, Charles Brockden (1799), *Edgar Huntly; or, Memoirs of a Sleep-Walker*, Philadelphia: H. Maxwell.
Castle, Terry (1995), *The Female Thermometer: Eighteenth-Century Culture and the Invention of the Uncanny*, New York: Oxford University Press.
Ellison, Ralph (1995), *Invisible Man* [1952], New York: Vintage.
Felman, Shoshana (1977), 'Turning the Screw of Interpretation', *Yale French Studies*, 55/56, 94–207.
Fernandez, Ramona (1995), 'Pachuco Mickey', *From Mouse to Mermaid: The Politics of Film, Gender and Culture*, ed. Elizabeth Bell, Lynda Haas, and Laura Sells, Bloomington: Indiana University Press, 236–54.
Fiedler, Leslie (1966), *Love and Death in the American Novel*, 2nd edn, London: Jonathan Cape.
Fitzgerald, F. Scott (2004), *The Great Gatsby* [1925], New York: Scribner.
Foucault, Michel (1990), *History of Sexuality. Vol. 1: An Introduction*, trans. Robert Hurley, New York: Vintage.
Hogle, Jerrold E. (1998), 'Frankenstein as Neo-Gothic: From the Ghost of the Counterfeit to the Monster of Abjection', *Romanticism, History, and the Possibilities of Genre*, ed. Tilottama Rajan and Julia M. Wright, Cambridge: Cambridge University Press, 176–210.
Hogle, Jerrold E. (2014), 'The Progress of Theory and the Study of the American Gothic', *A Companion to American Gothic*, ed. Charles L. Crow, Oxford: Wiley Blackwell, 3–15.
Jameson, Fredric (1981), *The Political Unconscious: Narrative as a Socially Symbolic Act*, Ithaca, NY: Cornell University Press.
Kilgour, Maggie (1995), *The Rise of the Gothic Novel*, New York: Routledge.
Madsen, Deborah (1998), *American Exceptionalism*, Edinburgh: Edinburgh University Press.
Miles, Robert (1993), *Gothic Writing 1750–1820: A Genealogy*, New York: Routledge.
Mannheim, Steve (2002), *Walt Disney and the Quest for Community*, Burlington, VT: Ashgate.
Morrison, Toni (1992), *Playing in the Dark: Whiteness and the American Literary Imagination*, Cambridge, MA: Harvard University Press.
Ringe, Donald A. (1982), *American Gothic: Imagination and Reason in Nineteenth-Century Fiction*, Lexington: University Press of Kentucky.
Savoy, Eric (1998), 'The Face of the Tenant: A Theory of American Gothic', *American Gothic: New Interventions in a National Narrative*, Iowa City: University of Iowa Press, 3–19.
Sedgwick, Eve Kosofsky (2008), *Epistemology of the Closet*, updated with a new preface, Berkeley: University of California Press.

Smith, Allan Lloyd (2012), 'Nineteenth-Century American Gothic', *A New Companion to the Gothic*, ed. David Punter, London: Wiley-Blackwell, 163–75.

Waldrep, Shelton (2013), *The Dissolution of Place: Architecture, Identity, and the Body*, Burlington, VT: Ashgate, e-book.

Walpole, Horace (1764), *The Castle of Otranto, A Story. Translated by William Marshall, Gent.*, Dublin. Printed for Tho. Lownds, London.

Weinstock, Jeffrey Andrew (2008), *Scare Tactics: Supernatural Fiction by American Women*, New York: Fordham University Press.

Welter, Barbara (1966), 'The Cult of True Womanhood: 1820–1860', *American Quarterly* 18.2: 151–74.

Williams, Anne (1995), *Art of Darkness: A Poetics of Gothic*, Chicago: Chicago University Press.

Part I

Gothic Histories, Gothic Identities

Chapter 1

Gothic Monstrosity: Charles Brockden Brown's *Edgar Huntly* and the Trope of the Bestial Indian

Christine Yao

In gothic fiction, monstrous acts committed by monstrous creatures mark spatial and symbolic frontiers: horror is generated not only when deviant acts such as cannibalism are carried out by bestial monsters on the fringes of society, but also these savage acts can collapse the conventional categories of the human and the monster. Within the framework of the American gothic, these integral tropes of cannibalism and bestial savagery – visible in works as diverse as Edgar Allan Poe's *The Narrative of Arthur Gordon Pym* (1838) and *The Texas Chainsaw Massacre* (1974) – can be traced back to the colonial legacy representing American Indians as animalistic and cannibalistic.[1] The monsters that haunt the American gothic signal the return of the traumas of national history and the speaking of suppressed voices from the ongoing violence of America's colonial past. Jeffrey Jerome Cohen claims the figure of the monster is 'an embodiment of a certain cultural moment – of a time, a feeling, and a place', demanding analysis 'within the intricate matrix of relations (social, cultural, and literary-historical) that generate them' (Cohen 1996: 4, 5). In what follows, I focus on the development and sedimentation of the savage image of American Indians in early American history through the monstrous tropes of the American gothic, concluding this genealogy with Charles Brockden Brown's 1799 novel, *Edgar Huntly*. In his introduction to *Edgar Huntly*, Brown discusses the inspirational devices available to the American writer: 'Gothic castles and chimeras, are the materials usually employed for this end. The incidents of Indian hostility, and the perils of the western wilderness, are far more suitable; and, for a native to America to overlook these, would admit of no apology' (Brown 1988: 3). If for Brown, acclaimed as the pioneer of American gothic, the American setting equivalent to 'Gothic castles' are the 'perils of the western wilderness', Native Americans are the monstrous equivalent of the mythical chimera. With both the chimera and the Indian posited as inhuman and antagonistic Others,

Brown positions the Indian as a quintessential element of the American gothic genre, and as both integral and liminal. *Edgar Huntly* participates in what Colleen E. Boyd and Coll Thrush call the 'Indian uncanny': a racialized formulation of Sigmund Freud's concept of the uncanny, which reveals the discomforting connections between the unfamiliar uncanny, '*das Unheimliche*, or 'the unhomely', and the familiar '*das Heimliche*, the homely' (Boyd and Thrush 2011: ix; Freud 2003: 134). The Indian uncanny exposes the disturbing tensions within familiar North American histories: it expresses 'the moral anxieties and uncertainties provoked by the dispossession of a place's Indigenous inhabitants', appropriates and misinterprets indigenous beliefs, and finally 'disrupt[s] dominant and official historical narratives as expressions of liminality', drawing attention to conflicts of production and power behind forms of knowledge (Boyd and Thrush 2011: ix).

The Indian uncanny in *Edgar Huntly* is not the ghostly presence of the deceased, but is the vital force of living individuals. Cohen notes that monsters do not just signal cultural limits, but also are 'a form suspended between forms that threatens to smash distinctions' (Cohen 1996: 6). In Brown's novel the colonialist figurations of bestiality and cannibalism become unmoored from their associations with Native Americans: the titular white protagonist descends into savagery not only through his violent acts against the Lenni-Lenape Indians, but also through the ironic reversal of these tropes, transforming Edgar into one of the monsters he fights against. My reading of *Edgar Huntly* brings together colonial histories, animal studies and indigenous philosophies in order to interrogate how the binary between the civilized and the savage is not a static either/or state: the twin monstrous tropes of difference indicate the paradoxical fear of underlying sameness and interdependence that would collapse fundamental boundaries between categories viewed as ontologically opposed. To Edgar Huntly, the interdependence of kinship – as that is viewed through an indigenous perspective – is a chimerical monstrosity, a perspective representative of the mindset of American settler colonialism. These kinships are chimerical in that they mix categories seen as different, and, like the mythical chimeras, are seen only as monstrous by a Western paradigm that denies shared associations between the colonizer and the colonized.

Monstrous Histories, Monstrous Subjects

The monsters that populate the American gothic owe their inhuman characteristics to a history of subjugation and dehumanization that goes back to Christopher Columbus's voyages. Two dominant tropes about indigenous savagery emerge from this ur-moment of colonialism in the New World, both predicated upon the threat they pose to the Western conceptions of civilization: the human as animal; and the human as cannibal. On Christopher Columbus's second voyage, Dr Diego Alvarez Chanca wrote a letter to the city of Seville, containing this observation of an indigenous village in the aftermath of a violent clash between the Spanish and Indians: 'These people are so like animals that they have not the intelligence to find a proper place to live' (Columbus 1969: 147). Dr Chanca meets this scene of violence with representational violence: denigrating Indians through a comparison to savage animals even as he imposes Western criteria for civilization. Although the idea of anthropophagy existed prior to Columbus's voyages, the term 'cannibal' was coined as result of his explorations: 'cannibal' is a corruption of 'Carib', part of Columbus's dubious distinction between the 'good' Arawak Indians and the 'bad' Caribs (Hulme 1986: 68). On his third voyage, Columbus details an exchange with some inhabitants who describe:

> a land bordering on theirs, to the west, which was very high and not far away. But they all told me not to go there because the inhabitants ate men. I presumed from this that these inhabitants were Caribs like the other cannibals I had met. But I have thought since that they may have meant not cannibals but wild animals. (Columbus 1969: 215)

Here we can see not only the accusation of cannibalism as a shifting signifier of difference, but Columbus's self-serving confusion between the animal and the cannibal, demonstrating the twin nature of these dehumanizing tropes in the colonial project. Cannibalism and the bestial are similar insofar as both must be read as monstrous difference. Much as the savage person becomes the same as an animal, the alleged cannibal's diet also presumes this similarity, taking the human as meat indistinguishable from the animal. By his fourth voyage, Columbus has become such an expert on eaters of flesh that he is able to objectify indigenous peoples based on appearance alone: 'I found other tribes who ate human flesh, as their brutal appearance showed' (Columbus 1969: 298). The founding moment of colonization in the Americas both constructed and naturalized the twin monstrous tropes used to represent indigenous peoples, thereby legitimizing the moral authority to conquer and colonize.

Turning from the first moment of Spanish colonialism in America to the first moments of colonialism in seventeenth-century New England, these monstrous tropes still haunt the American wilderness in the writings of William Bradford, governor of Plymouth Colony, and John Winthrop, governor of Massachusetts Bay Colony.[2] Upon arriving in America via Cape Cod on 6 September 1620, Bradford comments on the predicament of the colonists: there are 'these savage barbarians [who were] readier to fill their sides full of arrows than otherwise', and the landscape was 'a hideous and desolate wilderness, fall [sic] of wild beasts and wild men' (Bradford 1952: 62). Similarly, in Winthrop's entry for 5 October 1642, he muses on unrest in the colony:

> For such as come together into a wilderness, where are nothing but wild beasts and beastlike men, and there confederate together in civil and church estate, whereby they do, implicitly at least, bind themselves to support each other, and all of them that society, whether civil or sacred, whereof they are members. (Winthrop 1996: 416)

Both Bradford and Winthrop equate Native Americans with wild animals through parallelisms, thereby justifying violence against these monstrous Indians and the establishment of the Puritan colonies as bastions of civilization and order in the paradoxically populated yet empty wilderness.

As in Columbus's diaries, cannibalism appears in early American documents in order to characterize Native Americans as bestial savages, thereby justifying colonization and the dispossession of Indian land. *Mourt's Relation*, believed to be written primarily by Edward Winslow with some contributions from William Bradford, depicts the events following the landing of the Mayflower and the establishment of Plymouth Colony. Published in 1622, in contrast to Bradford's manuscript *Of Plymouth Plantation* which was only published in 1856, *Mourt's Relation* was meant to act as 'a promotional effort' in order to encourage new settlers to come to the colony (*Mourt's* 1963: xv). The association between the Indians and cannibalism, therefore, serves as a crucial example of how allegations of cannibalism worked as propaganda within the colonialist context.[3] In November 1620, the settlers went on an expedition and discovered burial grounds: despite deciding to leave the first graves in peace 'because we thought it would be odious unto them to ransack their sepulchres', upon finding the second burial grounds, the colonists decide to go against their earlier attitude of respect and exhume the contents (*Mourt's* 1963: 21). Engaging in proto-anthropological work, they speculate about the contents of the grave and its corpse, observing that the skull had 'some of the flesh unconsumed' (*Mourt's* 1963: 27). The implication becomes that the Indians were cannibals, giving the settlers a moral authority to colonize and civilize the land. Even the more liberal Roger Williams, who was an advocate for more equable interactions with Indians, records hearsay about cannibals throughout *A Key Into the Language of America*. According to Williams, *mohowaúgsuck* is Narragansett for 'The Canibals, or, Men-eaters, up into the west, two, three or foure hundred miles from us' and *cummóhucquock* translates as 'They will eat you' (Williams 1997: 16). The idea of savage Indians endures, haunting the popular early American genre of the captivity narrative and justifying the violence of the Indian wars. 'Cannibal' still acts as the horizon of civilized humanity, a marker of difference that transforms Indians into the originary monsters of American gothic fiction.

The conflict between colonists and Native Americans plays out on the ideological front, demonstrating the incommensurability of settler and indigenous paradigms when it comes to the place of humans among other living beings. Gregory Cajete emphasizes that Native American thought does not make the same distinctions between the human and the animal as Western epistemologies do, due to the mutual and fluid interrelation of the worlds of the human, the spiritual, and the animal: not only are animals seen as having souls, but the distinct category of 'animal' does not exist in most Native languages (Cajete 2000: 152). While specific names exist for specific animal species, the general category of 'animal' cannot be abstracted for, as Cajete stresses, the Native view of animals cannot be divorced from the animals' roles in their respective environmental, useful and symbolic contexts (150). In contrast, Western thought is dependent upon the animal/human binary that comes out of the opposition between nature and culture which, as Eric Cheyfitz points out, is 'a model the West has exported imperially with increasing force since 1492' (Cheyfitz 2009: 143). According to Colleen Boggs, animality is used to create 'a position of nonsubjectivity and of socially sanctioned abjection', which she traces through American history from the Puritan bestiality trials to Abu Ghraib (Boggs 2010: 99). The Native American relationship with animals clashes with the Western abjection of animals; indeed, early American history is the site of the further reification of the Western animal/human binary, with the colonizers violently treating Native Americans like abjected animals, unable to comprehend the Native perspective that would allow for more complex relationships between living beings.

Derrida's work on animality further explains the logic on which the animal/human boundary is dependent, positioning it as part of the creation and maintenance of social power. In order to think through the Western paradigm, Derrida analyses the figures of the beast and the sovereign: the first, not exactly the animal but rather the bestial; the second 'a sovereignty that is most often represented as human or divine, in truth anthropo-theological' (Derrida 2009: 14). If the dualism of the beast and the sovereign are seen in a relation of opposition, then the beast acts as the subordinated state in the obverse of the power of the sovereign. Both are what Derrida calls 'situated by definition at a distance from or above the laws, in nonrespect for the absolute law, the absolute law that they make or that they are but they do not have to respect' (Derrida 2009: 17). Within this scheme they are diametrically opposed, because animality is 'the place where the law does not appear, or is not respected or gets violated', while the sovereign subject is 'the form of the Law itself, of the origins of laws, the guarantor of laws' (Derrida 2009: 17). Thus, the animal, the place of abjection and violation, is a constitutive part of the fundamental structure required for the production of the power of sovereignty and the law.[4] In other words, 'civilization' can only exist in relation to its opposite, the 'frontier'. By deploying the trope of bestial non-human identity, the colonizers of the New World add a weapon to the arsenal of colonialist tactics that abjects the Indians outside of the law into the bestial state even as the colonizers authenticate their sovereign power as the makers of law. This strategy is the power of naming: as Derrida says, '*Animal* is a word that men have given themselves the right to give' (Derrida 2008: 32). The dehumanization of such groups as Native Americans through animalistic representations persists because of, and to further relationships to, institutions of power. The creation of monsters that bridge the categories of animal and human is an ideological necessity.

American gothic fiction draws upon these tropes in order to exploit their horror and explore the tensions around these 'monsters' and the power relationships they represent and reinforce. The terror in American gothic fiction often comes from questioning exactly who the monsters truly are, reflecting the complexity of historical ambiguities that in turn complicate the attempts to maintain the strict divisions required by ideology. Even as the Puritans imagined on their physical and symbolic frontiers the threat of animalistic and cannibalistic Indians, the decoupling of 'cannibal' from a definitive racial category meant the horrifying realization that the settlers, too, could be cannibals. For the New England colonists, the Starving Time tragedy in Jamestown earlier in the seventeenth century provided evidence for cannibalism emerging amongst the settlers themselves. The Starving Time occurred as a result of the Powhatan Confederacy's attempt to force the colonists from Virginia by isolating them from food supplies; combined with a poor growing season, only sixty people were left alive (Edmund S. Morgan, cited in Herrmann 2011: 47). The disturbing implication for colonists was that the Indians, those seen as bestial and possibly cannibalistic, could create conditions for Americans to become cannibals themselves, completely reversing the use of cannibalism in discourses of Othering.

Maggie Kilgour posits that 'cannibalism involves both the establishing of absolute difference, the opposite of eater and eaten, the dissolution of that difference, through the act of incorporation which identifies them, and makes the two one' (Kilgour 1998: 240). Thus, the myth of cannibalism is 'now explicitly revealed to be a story about *ourselves*, not others, as the cannibal has moved from the fringes of our world to its very centre' (247). Both eater and eaten are recognized as meat, collapsing the distinction between animal and human. In his essay 'Of Cannibals', influential early modern writer Montaigne declares: 'I think there is nothing barbarous and savage in this nation [America], from what I have been told, except that each man calls barbarism whatever is not his own practice' (Montaigne 1943: 77). Idealizing Indian society as pure and primitive, Montaigne paints the act of cannibalism as one of community and unity: prisoners are treated 'with all the hospitality they can think of' and once killed, 'they roast him and eat him in common and send some pieces to their absent friends' (Montaigne 1943: 84). While Montaigne does judge this act as 'barbarous horror', he reverses the expectations of savage and civilized, calling Western tortures and executions barbarous and decries them as worse than cannibalism: 'I am heartily sorry that, judging their faults rightly, we should be so blind to our own' (85). Eric Cheyfitz comments that Montaigne's depiction of cannibalism demonstrates 'the basis of most Native American civilization: kinship. Cannibalism expresses, or figures forth, a radical idea of kinship that cuts across frontiers of hostile groups' (Cheyfitz 1991: 149); the act signifies the composite constitution of the self and Other as well as the kinship economy which is composed of interconnectivity between all things on a foundation of 'the essentially equivocal' (Cheyfitz 1991: 149).[5] Returning to genre, Eric Savoy proposes a theory for the American gothic: because the past cannot be forgotten or repressed, the genre attempts to resurrect the 'specter of Otherness that haunts the house of national narrative', but cannot entirely explain or speak to these traumas (Savoy 1998: 14). For the genre of the American gothic, Jamestown's status as a foundational story for colonialism in America opens one of many possibilities for the collapse of whiteness into the tropes of savagery tied to Native Americans positioned at the heart of the national project.

Edgar Huntly's Colonial Haunting

Ever since Jared Gardner's foundational discussion of the representation of race in *Edgar Huntly*, scholars have understood the novel's portrayal of Native Americans as political, not merely psychological. Building on this conclusion, it can be argued that the tropes that characterize the monstrosities of the American gothic draw upon the power of the sedimented history of the representations of Native Americans; the horror of these monstrosities resonates with the fundamental divide between the civilized and the savage in the Western paradigm. But often the true horror of these gothic tales – from Edgar Allan Poe to Stephen King – arises when the fragility of this problematic binary collapses, exposing the true monsters among the so-called civilized and opening the possibility of monsters that lurk in the hearts of all. Given American gothic's obsession with the past, I look to the genre's own past by reading the monsters of Charles Brockden Brown's *Edgar Huntly*, the first American gothic novel, in light of the genealogy of colonialist tropes about Native Americans outlined above.

Set in 1787, *Edgar Huntly*'s protagonist goes on a quest for justice after the sudden murder of his friend Waldegrave, but finds himself entangled in both the uncertain inheritances of his friend's other dealings and the alleged crimes of the servant, Clithero Edny. Edgar finds himself fascinated by Clithero's past and soon he inexplicably adopts Clithero's habit of sleepwalking, sharing his friend's predilection for morose wanderings in the apparently empty wilderness, which serves as a sympathetic background. The second half of the narrative abruptly transitions with Edgar awakening in a dark cave with a panther as his companion, and as an eventual meal, before he discovers that the wilderness is not so empty after all: he engages in the brutal slaughter of Lenni-Lenape Indians as he attempts to make his way back to civilization in the midst of an apparent war over the unlawful seizure of Indian land. The strange resolution of one of these disparate narrative threads reveals that Waldegrave's murderer was one of the Indians, an epiphany sometimes questioned by critics.

The dangerous instability of race and identity in *Edgar Huntly* has been a topic of scholarly discussion from Gardner's argument about the influence of debates around the Alien and Sedition Acts to Katy Chiles's exploration of Brown's engagement with the mutability of race in eighteenth-century natural history. Amidst these important investigations into historical context, I call for attention to the symbolic valences of Brown's rhetorical figuration of Native Americans in his manifesto about the American gothic. To return to Brown's introduction, hostile Indians populate the perilous western wilderness as the equivalent of chimeras in gothic castles. By identifying Indians with the chimera, Brown does not merely cast Native Americans as monstrous; he specifically describes them as *chimerical*. The fantastical chimera, as an amalgamation of different beasts, undermines naturalized and essentialized identity.[6] Colonial tropes of Native American monstrosity share with the chimera the characteristics of both collapsing differences and fundamental sameness; both the figures of the animalistic and the cannibalistic Indians suggest the chimerical, insofar as they describe organic links between categories seen as mutually exclusive within the normative Western paradigm. The Indian as chimera becomes a threat to cohesive white American identity: the chimera suggests the constitutive interrelationship not only between Native Americans and white Americans, but also between human and animal, an organic kinship that we have seen the binary Euro-American paradigm fundamentally denies. From the normative American perspective, to be chimerical is to be monstrous, and vice versa.

The use of the word 'chimerical' in *Edgar Huntly* gestures toward this dilemma. Appearing only during Clithero's narration of his complicated past, 'chimerical' is associated not just with confusion, but also with such feelings as love and sympathy: the villainous Arthur Wiatte views love and friendship as 'chimerical' delusions that can 'in people of sense, be rectified by experience' (Brown 1988: 44); Clithero must act on his love or else remain in what he calls a 'chimerical project' of lovesickness (Brown 1988: 49); love beyond a certain age is called 'chimerical and marriage folly' (Brown 1988: 58); and Clithero justifies his attempt to murder his benefactress Mrs Lorimer because he accidentally killed her twin, Arthur, reasoning that 'the force of sympathy might be chimerical', and so he may as well save her from emotional devastation by performing a mercy killing (Brown 1988: 74). Love and sympathy are labelled as chimerical feelings: they are viewed by these characters as foolish, or even worse, dangerous. Seen as feelings that should be overcome, Arthur's and Clithero's actions to suppress these chimeras paradoxically lead to behaviours and actions that cause the men to be viewed as monstrous.

Significantly, Clithero's narration, which dominates the first half of the novel, takes place in Ireland – the site of the castles and chimeras that Brown identifies as the main tropes of the European gothic tradition. When the narrative returns to Edgar in Norwalk, Pennsylvania, the American gothic equivalent of the chimerical monsters are revealed. In the second half of Brown's novel, Edgar sleepwalks himself into a dark cave where his confrontation with the panther is closely followed by his clash with the local Lenni-Lenape Indians; he faces his chimeras, discovering that he, too, is monstrous. To Edgar, the panther possesses a 'grim and terrific visage' when it is hunting him; later, Edgar describes the 'tawny and terrific visage' of one of the Lenni-Lenape Indians just before he shoots him (Brown 1988: 120, 183). Here, he continues the tradition, outlined earlier, of dehumanizing Indians by equating them to savage animals. What is provocative, however, is that he does not just make the Indians into beast-like men, but makes the panther into a man-like beast: before this sleepwalking incident and during his search for Clithero, he is struck by a panther's cry's 'resemblance to the human voice' – that is, its similarity to the category of human in general, not just the Indian 'savages' (Brown 1988: 118). The panther falls into a dark pit, giving Edgar a temporary reprieve. But his victory is short: this blurring of categories sets up Edgar's complete collapse into chimerical confusion when he awakens from his sleepwalking in possibly the same dark pit with what is possibly the panther, having literally descended to the feline's level. Edgar unwittingly enacts what Aimé Césaire calls the dehumanizing paradox of colonization: 'the colonizer, who in order to ease his conscience gets into the habit of seeing the other man as an animal, accustoms himself to treating him like *an animal*, and tends objectively to transform *himself* into an animal' (Césaire 1972: 31).

Much has been made of the fact that Edgar's brutal and unprovoked massacre of five Indians makes him the same savage monster as those Indians who had massacred his family in the past: Richard Slotkin declares that Edgar 'has become the thing he hunts'; Robert D. Newman claims 'the underlying irony of the novel is the revelation of the savage potential of the white man'; and many critics note that Edgar uses a tomahawk and resorts to the kind of trickery that was represented as stereotypical of Native Americans (Slotkin 1973: 389; Newman 1988: 68; Christophersen 1993: 135). Yet what I want to analyse with greater precision is the fact that Edgar's fall into savagery with the panther is signalled by the same chimerical signifiers he associates with the Indians. In the pit, the ravenous Edgar admits he 'felt a strong propensity to bite the flesh from my arm. My heart overflowed with cruelty, and I pondered on the delight I should experience in rending some living animal to pieces, and drinking its blood and grinding its quivering fibres between my teeth' (Brown 1988: 157). The image of his potential self-cannibalization not only links him to the racist heritage of the native-as-cannibal, but also allegorizes his self-destructiveness and the dissolution of difference. Indeed, shortly after this admission he kills and consumes the panther: 'I review this scene with loathing and horror', he claims, both admitting to the monstrous aspect of his actions while attempting to rationalize them, 'If this appetite has sometimes subdued the sentiments of nature and compelled the mother to feed upon the flesh of her offspring, it will not excite amazement that I did not turn from the yet warm blood and reeking fibres of a brute' (Brown 1988: 160). The ambiguity of 'brute', given Edgar's obsessive use of 'savage' to describe both animals and Indians, blurs human and animal differences.

In his analysis of this much-read passage, John Carlos Rowe comments that numerous critics have discussed how 'the term "savage" effectively links the other terms in some sort of metonymic chain: Indian, panther, Clithero, are all predicates of the inchoate "savagery"' (Rowe 2000: 46). This chain, I suggest, acts as a reminder of the erasure of differences akin to the autophagic cycle: Edgar's eating of the panther, after the slippages among animal, Indian and his subjectivity as a white American, is tantamount to cannibalism. During the sequence in which he hunts and kills the party of Indians, his chimerical confusion extends to his ability to discern differences between these categories. Cautiously looking for enemies, he first sees 'movements which appeared like those of a beast' akin to 'a wolf, or panther, or bear' but realizes it is 'an human adversary' (Brown 1988: 191). For Edgar, the behavioural codes necessary for recognizing animal and savage Indian overlap, as he observes that the man 'moved upon all fours, and presently came near enough to be distinguished. His disfigured limbs, pendants from his ears and nose, and his shorn locks, were indubitable indications of a savage' (Brown 1988: 191). After this stream of shifting observational uncertainty, he retroactively claims that he was 'at no loss to interpret these appearances' in order to rationalize his ambush and slaughter of the lone surviving Indian (Brown 1988: 191).

When Edgar begins to return to civilization, he calls upon his reserves of strength and stamina, declaring:

> I disdained to be out-done in perspicacity by the lynx, in his sure-footed instinct by the roe, or in patience under hardship, and contention with fatigue, by the Mohawk. I have ever aspired to transcend the rest of animals in all that is common to the rational and brute, as well as in all by which they are distinguished from each other. (Brown 1988: 203)

Thus, the contradiction within his efforts to transcend the overlapping categories of the animal and the Indian is revealed: he must adopt the traits he assigns to these degraded entities. Edgar has reached the point of being able to decouple racial signifiers from their supposed essences: later, he even accidentally attacks a force of villagers from Solebury looking for him, mistaking the white Americans for the Lenni-Lenape Indians. With the same unquestioning certainty as in his previous interpretations, he reads the villagers as Indians since they were walking in a straight line 'peculiar to the Indians' (Brown 1988: 211). Edgar's chimerical perspective allows him to see the kinship between living beings; however, he cannot fully embrace this radical divergence from the Western paradigm and therefore must see the chimerical as monstrous. As a consequence, he repeatedly seeks to destroy that which was the monstrous other now uncannily like his own self.

Narrative Monstrosity and American Gothic

But what of the savage monstrosity of American gothic writ large? I want to suggest that Brown uses *Edgar Huntly* not only to establish the essential monstrous tropes of the American gothic and their connection to Native Americans, but also to present the importance of remembering this linkage between narrative trope and ongoing historical reality. In his 1803 pamphlet *An Address to the Government of the United States on the Cession of Louisiana*, Brown ventriloquizes the voice of a fictive French councillor in order to steer public and government opinion toward seizing Louisiana; through this device, Brown also levies critiques against the hypocritical foundations of America: 'Devoted to the worst miseries is that nation which harbours in its bosom a foreign race, brought, by fraud and rapine, from their native lands who are bereaved of all the blessings of humanity' (Brown 1803: 73). This French persona views the horrors of slavery as intertwined with the colonial history of Native American conflicts:

> The only aliens and enemies within [America's] borders, are not the blacks. They are indeed the most inveterate in their enmity; but the Indians are, in many respects, more dangerous inmates. Their savage ignorance, their undisciplined passions, their restless and war-like habits, their notions of ancient right, make them the fittest tools imaginable for disturbing the states. (Brown 1803: 74)

Even as Brown ostensibly writes this pamphlet with an eye to the future of America, he acknowledges that the past cannot be suppressed, creating fault lines that weaken the nation.

The accuracy and complexity of Brown's portrayal of this Native American past has been questioned and sometimes seen as indicative of flaws in the design of the narrative. Sydney J. Krause draws attention to treaties and land frauds in Pennsylvania that resulted in seemingly deserted areas such as the novel's Norwalk, going back to William Penn's agreement with the Lenni-Lenape or Delaware Indians and the subsequent abuse of the Walking Purchase Treaty. Norwalk as a setting is a place 'where the past hangs heavy, where its energies, its angers, its terrors from "about thirty years ago" still haunt', claims Kafer (Kafer 2004: 176). Some of the various ways *Edgar Huntly's* Indians have been read include Indians as 'phantoms of the mind', 'phantoms of the culture', 'and as Lenni-Lenapes living in late-eighteenth-century Pennsylvania' (Christophersen 1993: 156). According to Christophersen, even with the novel's awareness of Indian victimization, their narrative status as 'boogeymen of the wilderness' means that 'even the Indian's identity as an exploited population interests Brown only as it illuminates white America' (Christophersen 1993: 156). Criticisms about Brown's use of Native Americans pair with dissatisfactions over the novel's structure: Fiedler dismisses the Native American component of the conclusion as 'irrelevant to what has become the real theme of the book', calling the novel 'a charmingly, a maddeningly disorganized book', an accusation which has plagued the novel ever since (Fiedler 1960: 144). At the beginning of the novel Edgar admits to his fiancée Mary Waldegrave the difficulty he has in putting together a wholly coherent narrative: 'That the incidents I am going to relate can be recalled and arranged without indistinctness and confusion? That emotions will not be re-awakened by my narrative, incompatible with order and coherence?' (Brown 1988: 5). By pairing *Edgar Huntly*'s representation of Native Americans with the strange and sometimes frustrating unveiling of the narrative, I argue that we can see how the novel is structured on the belated unveiling of both Indian presences and history.

The first half of the narrative is bereft of Indian presences – indeed, Clithero and Edgar wander the wilderness of Norwalk as if it were an abandoned gothic castle. Clithero is drawn to Norwalk during his guilt-ridden sleepwalking, which acts as the site of Clithero's confession to Edgar; the caves and crags of Norwalk are the backdrop of pathetic fallacy to the emotional confusion and psychological drama of the characters. Throughout the first part of the novel, Edgar relates his intimate knowledge of Norwalk's flora and fauna as well as the limestone composition of its geography that makes the region prone to caves: 'Perhaps no one was more acquainted with this wilderness than I' (Brown 1988: 92). But his knowledge and enjoyment of Norwalk as a place is predicated upon the wilderness as empty. He declares, 'I love to immerse myself in shades and dells, and hold converse with the solemnities and secrecies of nature in the rude retreats of Norwalk' and presumes that Clithero is likewise drawn to its 'charms of solitude, of a lonely abode in the midst of mountainous and rugged nature' (Brown 1988: 90, 91). As he explores the wilderness, Edgar muses that:

> It was probably that human feet had never before gained this recess, that human eyes had never been fixed upon these gushing waters. The aboriginal inhabitants had no motives to lead them into caves like these ... Since

the birth of this continent, I was probably the first who had deviated thus remotely from the customary paths of men. (Brown 1988: 99)

Edgar echoes William Bradford's and John Winthrop's assumptions about the land as *terra nullius*, invoking the history of American colonialism.

Edgar only remembers that his beloved Norwalk is populated by the Lenni-Lenape Indians in the latter half of the novel. When he stumbles across the Indian camp he suddenly recalls the Indian wars as they pertained to that part of Pennsylvania. Disoriented upon seeing the sleeping figures and concluding that they are Indians, he wonders, 'Had some mysterious power snatched me from the earth, and cast me, in a moment into the heart of the wilderness? Was I still in the vicinity of my paternal habitation or was I thousands of miles distant?' (Brown 1988: 164). Although Edgar somehow considers the presence of Indians mutually exclusive from the area he knows, he quickly realizes he is still in Norwalk and claims, 'I need not tell thee that Norwalk is the termination of a sterile and narrow tract, which begins in Indian country' (Brown 1988: 165). Despite his earlier ignorance, he recounts the history of the Indian wars from 'a long course of injuries and encouragements [that] had exasperated the Indian tribes; that an implacable and exterminating war was generally expected' to 'a band of them [who] had once penetrated into Norwalk, and lingered long enough to pillage and murder some of the neighbouring inhabitants' (Brown 1988: 166). This incident is burned into his memory, claims Edgar, because his parents and a baby sibling were murdered: 'You will not be surprized that the fate of my parents, and the sight of the body of one of this savage band, who, in pursuit that was made after them, was overtaken and killed, should produce lasting and terrific images in my fancy' (Brown 1988: 166). He rationalizes his slaughter of these Indians through this epiphany about the massacre of his parents, which he claims has so traumatized and formed him – a decidedly unsatisfying revelation given there was no indication of this apparently haunting personal past in the previous half of the novel.

The conclusion of *Edgar Huntly* continues belatedly to reveal the hitherto invisible centrality of the Lenni-Lenape Indians to both Norwalk and to Edgar's own narrative. Critics such as Matthew Sivils and Janie Hinds agree that the novel hinges on the under-examined figure of a Lenni-Lenape woman known as Old Deb. As Edgar makes his way back to Solebury, she is introduced when he goes to her hut; in a parallel to the seemingly abandoned wilderness of Norwalk, Old Deb is absent from her hut when Edgar seeks shelter there. During his home invasion Edgar gives an extensive account of her personal history and a surprisingly sympathetic history of the dispossession of Indian land. A matriarch of the Lenni-Lenape Indians, she alone remained on the land as a gesture of sovereignty when the rest of her tribe emigrated due to colonist expansion. In her eyes, the 'English were aliens and sojourners, who occupied the land merely by her connivance and permission, and whom she allowed to remain on no terms but those of supplying her wants' (Brown 1988: 199). Old Deb reigns with her three wolf-like dogs; tellingly in the context of Indians as beasts, we are told 'These animals differed in nothing from their kinsmen of the forest, but in their attachment and obedience to their mistress' (Brown 1988: 198). With Indians as 'their kinsmen of the forest', the dogs and the Lenni-Lenape are presented in the context of indigenous kinship. Hinds attends to the anthropomorphic language used to describe Deb's dogs, arguing that 'Deb is, in short, multiply hybrid: she is part of her tribe and she is related to the story's animals inasmuch as Edgar entangles the entire tribe's sensory attributes with those of predatory creatures' (Hinds 2004: 337). Given Edgar's earlier investment in the image of the savage and bestial Indian, it is a revelation to discover that Edgar and Old Deb have a pre-existing friendship of sorts: visiting one another on a frequent basis, 'she seemed to contract an affection for [him]' and he took 'some pains to study her jargon, and could make out to discourse with her' (Brown 1988: 200). Sivils reads these interactions as part of her battle for tribal sovereignty, retaining her presence on the land as well as the survival of her culture with Edgar 'unwittingly help[ing] preserve the culture whites are destroying' (Sivils 2001: 302). Edgar's life is intertwined with the previously maligned and disavowed Indians through his relationship to Old Deb, the chimerical Indian who introduces Edgar to indigenous ways long before his violent turn with the panther.

The wilderness of Norwalk has come to the town of Solebury: upon his return Edgar finds himself in the middle of a conflict between the Lenni-Lenape Indians and the townspeople. Deb herself emerges near the novel's end as a defiant member of this quickly suppressed uprising: 'She was not to be awed or intimidated by the treatment she received, but readily confessed and glorified in the mischief she had done; and accounted for it by enumerating the injuries which she had received from her neighbours' (Brown 1988: 270). It is Deb who has the knowledge and authority to give a straightforward chronology of the novel's events and actions from the Indian perspective, including the solution to the mystery of Waldegrave's death: during the preparations for the invasion, one of the Lenni-Lenape had entered Solebury with the intent to murder and had found the hapless Waldegrave as his victim (Brown

1988: 271). Fiedler, among others, voices the complaint that this revelation about Waldegrave 'when it comes seems utterly anticlimactic', and the general dissatisfaction with the integration of the Indians into the novel (Fiedler 1960: 144). But what we see with Old Deb is the fundamental role of Native American resistance to the novel's underlying narrative; indeed, *Edgar Huntly*'s gothic plot cannot be understood without its American chimeras.

In Brown's *Edgar Huntly* the tropes of gothic monstrosity and their monstrous effects are felt and shown before the Indians themselves appear. While Indians are cast as the American chimeras, the interlinking kinship that constitutes the chimerical extends to all living beings, despite its disavowal by the Western paradigm. History cannot be completely repressed: the tropes of colonization of the New World used to justify violence against Native Americans come back to haunt Edgar with a vengeance in order to try to make him face his own chimerical nature, which he cannot help but reject as monstrous. According to Savoy, in the genre of the American gothic, prosopopoeia is the primary device of the allegorical turn, allowing for the traumatic return of the bloody history of America and for the ghosts of the past to speak (Savoy 1998: 14). In Brown's novel, however, Old Deb is able to speak on behalf of herself and her people; the Indian uncanny reminds us that the history of American Indians is not dead and long past, for despite their seeming absence, they are shown to be very much present and alive. Through the narrative deferral of the appearance of Indians, the structure of Brown's novel allegorizes the relationship between the American gothic's monstrous tropes and the history and ongoing presence of Native Americans. *Edgar Huntly* suggests that when it comes to monstrous tropes in the American gothic, Native Americans may seem to be absent but their presences and history will eventually be revealed, demonstrating their continual survival and resistance.

Notes

Thanks to Eric Cheyfitz, Shirley Samuels and my peers at the English Department Roundtable for their thoughtful comments and feedback on this essay as it developed. An earlier version of this essay was presented at The Society of Early Americanists Eighth Biennial Conference.

1. In his landmark *Love and Death in the American Novel*, critic Leslie Fiedler articulates the origins of the American gothic genre in the 'certain special guilts' resulting from the 'dream of innocence [that] had sent Europeans across the ocean to build a new society immune to the compounded evil from the past from which no one in Europe could ever feel himself free', but which led to 'the slaughter of the Indians, who would not yield their lands to the

carriers of utopia' (Fiedler 1960: 127). Fiedler highlights Charles Brockden Brown as the progenitor of the genre.
2. In his foundational work on the American myth of regeneration through violence, frontier clashes between colonists and Native Americans are the source of what Richard Slotkin calls 'the structuring metaphor of the American experience' (Slotkin 1973: 5).
3. Indeed, in *The Man-Eating Myth*, William Arens questions the existence of cannibalism among indigenous peoples due to the specious and biased nature of historical records and implicates his anthropological discipline in the perpetuation of the myth. He lists some of the ways in which the accusation of cannibalism can be deployed: attributed to other groups in order to delineate between civilization and barbarism; used as a temporal marker 'in the progress of [one's] own cultural development' that relies on notions of primitivism; and wielded against current members within one's own group 'to explain the existence of constant evil and misfortune' (Arens 1979: 159).
4. One might want to compare Derrida's ideas about the beast and the sovereign to Giorgio Agamben's concepts about bare life and sovereign power in *Homo Sacer*.
5. While cannibalism in this sense is a distortion of the Native concept of kinship, Jeff Berglund explores how contemporary Native American authors such as Leslie Marmon Silko and Sherman Alexie reappropriate the discourse of cannibalism in their work (Bergland 2006).
6. In Donna Haraway's iconic essay 'A Cyborg Manifesto' she fleetingly uses the term 'chimera' almost as a synonym for her concept of the 'cyborg': 'By the late twentieth century, our time, a mythic time, we are all chimeras, theorized and fabricated hybrids of machine and organism; in short, we are cyborgs' (Haraway 1991: 150). Unlike the cyborg, the chimera (while also a hybrid) is an organic assemblage of different elements and, one might say, a less voluntaristic model of interconnectedness; also, 'chimera' is a term more temporally relevant to an early America bereft of the particularly modern technologies identified by Haraway.

References

Arens, William (1979), *The Man-Eating Myth*, New York: Oxford University Press.
Berglund, Jeff (2006), *Cannibal Fictions: American Explorations of Colonialism, Race, Gender, and Sexuality*, Madison: University of Wisconsin Press.
Boggs, Colleen Glenney (2010), 'American Bestiality: Sex, Animals, and the Construction of Subjectivity', *Cultural Critique*, 76, 99–125.
Boyd, Colleen E. and Coll Thrush (2011), 'Bringing Ghosts to Ground', *Phantom Past, Indigenous Presence*, ed. Colleen E. Boyd and Coll Thrush, Lincoln: University of Nebraska Press, vii–xl.
Bradford, William [1856] (1952), *Of Plymouth Plantation 1620–1647*, ed. Samuel Eliot Morison, New York: Knopf.
Brown, Charles Brockden (1803), *An Address to the Government of the United States on the Cession of Louisiana to the French and on the Late Breach of Treaty by the Spaniards*, Philadelphia: John Conrad & Co.

Brown, Charles Brockden [1799] (1988), *Edgar Huntly; or Memoirs of a Sleep-Walker*, ed. Norman S. Grabo, New York: Penguin Books.

Cajete, Gregory (2000), *Native Science: Natural Laws of Interdependence*, Santa Fe: Clear Light Publishers.

Césaire, Aimé (1972), *Discourse on Colonialism*, trans. Joan Pinkham, New York: Monthly Review Press.

Cheyfitz, Eric (1991), *The Poetics of Imperialism*, New York: Oxford University Press.

Cheyfitz, Eric (2009), 'Balancing the Earth: Native American Philosophies and the Environmental Crisis', *Arizona Quarterly*, 65.3: 139–62.

Chiles, Katy L. (2014), *Transformable Race: Surprising Metamorphoses in the Literature of Early America*, Oxford: Oxford University Press.

Christophersen, Bill (1993), *The Apparition in the Glass: Charles Brockden Brown's American Gothic*, Athens, GA: University of Georgia Press.

Cohen, Jeffrey Jerome (1996), 'Monster Culture (Seven Theses)', *Monster Theory*, ed. Jeffrey Jerome Cohen, Minneapolis: University of Minnesota Press, 3–25.

Columbus, Christopher (1969), *The Four Voyages*, trans. J. M. Cohen, New York: Penguin Books.

Derrida, Jacques (2008), *The Animal That Therefore I Am*, trans. David Willis, ed. Marie-Louise Mallet, New York: Fordham University Press.

Derrida, Jacques (2009), *The Beast and the Sovereign*, trans. Geoffrey Bennington, ed. Michel Lisse, Marie-Luise Mallet and Ginette Michaud, Chicago: University of Chicago Press.

Fiedler, Leslie (1960), *Love and Death in the American Novel*, New York: Criterion Books.

Freud, Sigmund (2003), *The Uncanny*, trans. David Mclintock, London: Penguin Books.

Gardner, Jared (1994), 'Alien Nation: Edgar Huntly's Savage Awakening', American Literature, 66.3: 429–61.

Haraway, Donna Jeanne (1991), *Simians, Cyborgs, and Women*, New York: Routledge.

Herrmann, Rachel B (2011), 'The "tragicall historie": Cannibalism and Abundance in Colonial Jamestown', *William and Mary Quarterly*, 68.1: 47–74.

Hinds, Janie (2004), 'Deb's Dogs: Animals, Indians, and Postcolonial Desire in Charles Brockden Brown's *Edgar Huntly*', *Early American Literature*, 39.2: 323–54.

Hulme, Peter (1986), *Colonial Encounters*, London: Methuen.

Kafer, Peter (2004), *Charles Brockden Brown's Revolution and the Birth of American Gothic*, Philadelphia: University of Pennsylvania Press.

Kilgour, Maggie (1998), 'The Function of Cannibalism at the Present Time', in *Cannibalism and the Colonial World*, ed. Francis Barker, Peter Hulme and Margaret Iversen, New York: Cambridge University Press, 238–59.

Krause, Sydney J. (1994), 'Penn's Elm and *Edgar Huntly*: Dark "Instruction to the Heart"', *American Literature*, 66.3: 463–84.

Montaigne, Michel de (1943), *Selected Essays*, trans. Donald M. Frame, New York: Walter J Black.

Mourt's Relation: A Journal of the Pilgrims at Plymouth (1963), ed. Dwight B. Heath, Bedford, MA: Applewood Books.

Newman, Robert D. (1988), 'Indians and Indian-Hating in *Edgar Huntly* and *The Confidence Man*', *MELUS*, 15.3: 65–74.

Rowe, John Carlos (2000), *Literary Culture and U.S. Imperialism*, Oxford: Oxford University Press.

Savoy, Eric (1998). 'The Face of the Tenant: A Theory of American Gothic', *American Gothic New Interventions in a National Narrative*, ed. Robert K Martin and Eric Savoy, Iowa City: University of Iowa Press, 3–19.

Sivils, Matthew Wynn (2001), 'Native American Sovereignty and Old Deb in Charles Brockden Brown's *Edgar Huntly*', *American Transcendental Quarterly*, 15.4: 293–304.

Slotkin, Richard (1973), *Regeneration Through Violence*, Middletown, CT: Wesleyan University Press.

Williams, Roger (1997), *A Key Into the Language of America*, Bedford, MA: Applewood Books.

Winthrop, John (1996). *The Journal of John Winthrop, 1630–1649*, ed. Richard S. Dunn, James Savage and Laetitia Yeandle, Cambridge, MA: Harvard University Press.

Chapter 2

Slavery and American Gothic: The Ghost of the Future
Jason Haslam

> [W]hat is commonly assumed to be past history is actually as much a part of the living present as William Faulkner insisted. Furtive, implacable and tricky, it inspirits both the observer and the scene observed, artefacts, manners and atmosphere and it speaks even when no one wills to listen.
>
> Ralph Ellison (1995: vxi)

It has become a critical truism to say that the gothic as a literary form is inextricable from the institution of slavery, especially, but not solely, in the United States.[1] Violence (physical, spiritual, sexual, cultural); the grotesque; otherness; incarceration; living death; and the arbitrary exercise of power: these are both literary devices of the gothic and the material practices of various forms of social oppression, from the transatlantic and American slave trade, to current practices of mass imprisonment, to the patriarchy, to heteronormativity, to capitalism and its wider divisions of populations. Slavery in the US, however, does stand apart, because it was the debate over slavery that nearly kept the nation from forming as such, and which later sundered the US into two warring nations. The historical congruence of the rise of classic nineteenth-century American gothic and the institution of slavery, when read next to the relation of generic conventions to material practices of slavery, may indicate a causal relationship (in which slavery is the base of the American gothic superstructure). But, more generally, when combined with the long-standing connections between the gothic mode and American literature, film and other cultural forms, it appears not only that American culture is gothic throughout, as Fiedler hinted (Fiedler 1966: 29), but also that large swathes of it are defined by the mutual mediations of the gothic and slavery. In this reading, the gothic relies on metaphors and depictions of slavery just as abolitionist and pro-slavery cultural forms rely on gothic aesthetics and devices: 'slavery's Gothic history and the Atlantic world's Gothic fictions', as Teresa A. Goddu writes, are 'mutually constituted' (Goddu 2013: 72). First providing a structural analysis of these relations and of the approaches to the topic, in order to sketch the current state of American gothic criticism in relation to slavery, this essay will then move to an understudied figure: the uncanny spectre of freedom that not only haunts representations of slavery, but which also reframes the gothic portrayal of slavery as an agential, generative and forward-looking device of healing that responds to the endless repetition of America's primal scene of slavery.

The Traumatic Structures of Slavery and the Gothic

It is safe to say that, at the most basic, there are two primary relations between slavery and gothic literature and culture. First, slavery as a concept can be used as a gothic device: employed as a metaphor for a character's powerlessness in the face of larger, insurmountable forces (be they psychological or social), or as a metonym or comparison for other oppressions (gendered, national, classed and so on), slavery lends itself to being used as one of any number of gothic devices to set a larger tone and address larger gothic themes. Second, gothic discourse, to use Robert Miles' term (Miles 2002), can be used to address the material oppressions of the actual practice of slavery. In other words, in one form, slavery is the metaphorical vehicle of the gothic, in the other it is the target of the gothic's literary devices.[2]

It should go without saying, of course, that many texts engage some or all of these functions to varying degrees. Harriet Jacobs's slave narrative, *Incidents in the Life of a Slave Girl* (1861), obviously uses gothic-inflected discourse to describe the brutal realities of life as a slave, even as she employs slavery itself as a gothic parallel for sexual and gendered violence, while the latter is represented as a material effect of the horrors of slave laws and institutions, in a spiral of gothic slavery. Samuel R. Delany's late twentieth-century sword-and-sorcery *Flight from Nevèrÿon* (1985), conversely, can present slavery as both materialist practice and metaphor, in a meditation on sexuality and power through a depiction of BDSM, even as he inverts the racial dynamics of American slavery in order to comment on and undermine the racist and heteronormative logics of contemporary US social structures. Generally speaking, however, there remains a distinction between the (metaphorical) use of slavery to further a text's gothic elements, and a text's use of the gothic to address slavery as an institution.

If the split described above can be labelled a divide between the aesthetic and the sociopolitical gothic depiction of slavery, the critical approach to the topic, dating at least back to Fiedler, is less divided in this sense, focusing primarily on the sociopolitical aspects, in which the practices of slavery are represented through the literary devices of the gothic. Such is not to say, however, that the criticism on slavery and American gothic is completely unified. Instead, one can draw a rough divide between those critics who focus on the use of gothic discourse within descriptions of slavery, and those who examine traditionally conceived gothic works for their (allegorical or other) representations of slavery. In this way, the above divide is maintained, but subsumed under the sociopolitical approach.

Within this approach, the allegorical or symptomatic reading, on the one hand, analyses gothic texts that, while not dealing explicitly with the material history and practices of slavery, can still be said to invoke that history, often gesturally or even unconsciously. Pioneered in some ways by H. L. Malchow's readings (1996) of British gothic this form of analysis finds itself naturally suited to the allegorical nature of the nineteenth-century gothic romance in America. One can point to critical analyses of Edgar Allan Poe and Nathaniel Hawthorne, among other canonical authors (some of whom rarely dealt with slavery directly). Often tied to discussions of race and racism, these analyses argue, following the general critical vein opened by Toni Morrison in *Playing in the Dark* (1990), that the material practices of slavery were so pervasive as to leave deposits and resonances even within texts that purportedly have nothing to do with it. As Goddu, citing Robert Hemenway, argues in her foundational text, 'the gothic's oppositional symbolism', often including 'black/white' binaries, 'carries "a sociological burden even when there is no conscious intention of racial statement"' (Goddu 1997: 74). Morrison likewise writes that such symbolic echoes of race and slavery occur more often than not in nineteenth-century American literature: 'It would have been an *isolato* indeed', she writes, 'who was unaware of the most explosive issue in the nation. How could one speak of ... almost anything a country concerns itself with ... without having as a referent, at the heart of the discourse, at the heart of the definition, the presence of Africans and their descendants? It was not possible. And it did not happen' (Morrison 1990: 50). Slavery, or the concomitant representation of race and racism, remains as a trace in these texts, a lingering excess that often finds its expression in the haunting aspects of gothic literature.

Poe is an often-used example for such allegorical-symptomatic readings. Both Goddu and Morrison read Poe's works as complex meditations on whiteness and how it is constructed in relation to blackness.

Poe's fixation on containment, trials and punishment has also been recently reread in relation to legal and other constraining social institutions of his time (see Dayan 1999; Haslam 2008). Lesley Ginsberg, in a foundational essay on the topic, combines these two forms of analysis, arguing that

> the gothic machinery of Poe's 'The Black Cat' – with its graphic and 'damnable atrocities', its 'PERVERSENESS', its murdered corpse, 'clotted with gore' – are resounding echoes of antebellum slavery discourses, allusions which allow the story to be read not only as an examination of the narrator's purported 'peculiarity of character' but also as an investigation into the peculiar psychopolitics of the master/slave relationship, a bond whose sentimentalized image was at the heart of the South's proslavery rhetoric. (Ginsberg 1998: 99)

If the gothic elements of Poe's tale are read as the 'trace' of slavery and other white supremacist social structures, then Poe's tales both articulate and reinforce the rhetoric of slavery, while – even if unintentionally – offering the reader an entry point into their critique. The 'gothic machinery' as symbolic referent to material conditions proves to be, at best, a slippery form of signification.

On the other hand, an increasing number of critics are examining texts about slavery – often non-fictional works, including slave narratives – for their use of gothic discourse. In this critical approach, which could be called a discursive one, the gothic becomes one register within a larger set of textual strategies used to represent slavery. In these analyses, certain elements of gothic discourse – horror, the grotesque, extreme violence, and so on – are said to paint the scene of slavery in a particular way, to generate specific effects for the reader. Whether used in non-fictional works (such as slave narratives, pamphlets, political speeches, and so on) or fictional works (ranging from *Uncle Tom's Cabin* (1852) to *Beloved* (1987) and beyond) such texts use the gothic to explore the degradations and violence committed in the name of slavery and often do so for explicit political purposes (abolition in late eighteenth- and early nineteenth-century works; to address the social consequences of slavery and racism in later works). Within this type of analysis, one can also include pro-slavery and racist works, which use the gothic to opposite ends: to present the chaos of a post-abolition world, for example, or to paint African Americans as the demonic other who needs to be defeated – in this category one could list material ranging from responses to Nat Turner's rebellion to D. W. Griffith's *Birth of a Nation* (the infamous 1915 film adaptation of Thomas Dixon's 1905 novel, *The Clansman*). For abolitionists, anti-abolitionists, and their later incarnations alike, the gothic was used to spur political action, as a way of presenting a terror that must be fought. Gothic discourse thus both stood apart from and in some cases was put in service to the equally common and powerful sentimental tradition.

Following the influential work of Goddu, fugitive slave narratives have become a regular source for this discussion of the use of gothic discourse. The scene in *Narrative of the Life of Frederick Douglass* (1845) in which Douglass describes the gruesome whipping of his aunt, or the chapter 'Sketches of Neighboring Slaveholders' in Jacobs's *Incidents in the Life of a Slave Girl* (both discussed by Goddu) are instances in which 'actual events produce gothic narratives' (Goddu 1997: 145). And yet, as Goddu says, the fugitive slave or former slave author must be at pains to indicate that slavery is not a gothic *fiction* but a reality, one that 'exceeds ... representation' (146). Goddu's account of *Incidents* is worth rehearsing for both its allegorical-symptomatic and discursive readings of Jacobs's text. She writes that there are

> two strategies by which the gothic represents the unspeakable event of slavery. First, by signifying the event of slavery through narrative effects, the gothic both registers actual events and turns them into fiction. Its conventions can both rematerialize and dematerialize history: some gothic narratives insist upon the actuality of slavery by refusing to collapse the referent of the narrative with its effects; others displace the event of slaver into fictional form in order to contain its horrors. However, ... even in the act of displacement, traces of the material remain to be read by those invested in remembering the horrors of history. (132)

Goddu's analysis of texts prefigures my division of criticism, insofar as one set of texts fictionalizes slavery, while the other uses gothic discourse to 'insist upon [its] actuality'.

Clearly both of these traditions arise from the materialist turn of American cultural studies, especially as this turn develops out of New Historicism. My division, in fact, directly echoes Louis Montrose's analysis of New Historical praxis, which

> may be characterized chiastically as a reciprocal concern with the historicity of texts and the textuality of history. By the *historicity of texts*, I mean to suggest the cultural specificity, the social embedment, of all modes of writing – not only the texts that critics study, but also the texts in which we study them. By the *textuality of history*, I mean to suggest, firstly, that we can have no access to a full and authentic past ... unmediated by the surviving textual traces of the society in question ... and, secondly, that those textual traces are themselves subject to subsequent textual mediations. (Montrose 1989: 20)

This chiasmus can also be mapped onto the relationship between American gothic and slavery. The allegorical-symptomatic approach deals with the historicity of the traditionally conceived gothic text: written within the particular national context of America, with the ever-present history within that of its 'peculiar institution', such texts become part and parcel of the 'social embedment' of slavery itself. The discursive approach, meanwhile, focuses on the 'textuality of history', in the gothic framing of slavery itself: mediated by its surrounding cultural context, slavery becomes necessarily filtered by the gothic, and literary authors, autobiographers, journalists, historians, filmmakers and others will use the traditions of the gothic in their representation of its historical reality, both for particular effect (as in the case of Jacobs or Stowe, for example) or because the form lends itself to the comparison. In America, the historicity of the gothic and the gothic nature of history are linked together by the chains of slavery.

The gothic thus becomes a primary method through which to present the reality and lingering effects of American slavery, whether in terms of the directly terrifying nature of slavery itself, or its lingering, often disguised ideological effects on American society and psyches. And, again, it is necessary to recognize that the division between these two critical practices are not hard and fast, since critics often address how a single text can deploy its gothic devices in both ways. Morrison's *Beloved* is a case in point. Discussing the ways in which the traumas inflicted by the practices of slavery can physically, mentally and spiritually haunt recently freed men and women, even as the community strives to prevent slavery's repetition, *Beloved* explores the difficulties of telling a story that is not one to 'pass on' (Morrison 2006: 315), meaning that the story will not die, but that its material reality and physical and emotional trauma also should not be repeated into the future. Slavery and its individual and social effects become an always already present yet repressed, haunting gothic figure, at once spoken and unspoken, to echo Goddu's language.[3]

These critical maps thus point to a shared, and clearly necessary, foundational assumption by critics: slavery serves as an originary trauma of American gothic (and, indeed, of the national narrative itself). Both allegorical-symptomatic and discursive critics read slavery as the gothic past that haunts America: in certain readings, slavery becomes the primal scene with which gothic authors replace the foundational traumas of class violence and aristocratic abuses in the European traditions of the gothic (although several interventions have also placed the slave trade back in the centre of British gothic, especially, where it also clearly belongs).[4] In other readings, the gothic becomes the only discursive tradition capable of rendering the material horrors of slavery. But in both, the gothic becomes the 'natural' fit for representing slavery, because of the gothic's ability, to use an oft-repeated phrase, to 'speak the unspeakable', or, in other words, to deal with trauma. Both approaches are in a materialist frame, of course, but that frame is ultimately a psychoanalytic one.

Certainly the notion of slavery as trauma is indisputable, and its social and cultural effects as trauma have been much discussed.[5] Likewise, the literary use of the gothic to attempt to understand or come to terms with that trauma is well known. A useful case study can be found in Octavia Butler's gothically inflected science fiction novel, *Kindred* (1979). On its surface, the novel presents the now typical argument about the gothic and slavery: the African American narrator, Dana, and her white husband, Kevin, are transported into the past through an unexplained mechanism related to her genetic connection to her slave-owner ancestor, Rufus. Dana and Kevin experience the true horrors of slavery, with scenes of physical and sexual abuse presented in ways that echo their gothic renditions in the slave narratives of Frederick Douglass and Harriet Jacobs. While the cultural memory of slavery has been repressed or otherwise mitigated in their own time, this time travel allows them to understand the effects of slavery that still exist in the present of the late twentieth century.

These traumas are then duplicated on the body of the twentieth-century narrator: finally killing her slave-owning ancestor, she is transported back to the future, but loses her arm in the process. Where the slaver's 'fingers had grasped', her arm becomes trapped in a wall, and when she pulls away, she loses it in an 'avalanche of pain, red impossible agony!' (Butler 1988: 261). A physical reminder of the trauma slavery enacted on slaves' bodies and on the body politic of the nation (as well as a subtle critique of continuing racial oppression in America, under the guise of Adam Smith's 'invisible hand' of capitalism), the narrator's missing arm is an (in)visible reminder of the fact of slavery, one that has been otherwise erased (the plantation where she was enslaved having burned down, with records and even graves of the individuals all but lost). When her husband says, at the end, that 'now that the boy is dead, we have some chance of staying [sane]', the statement can be read as either the healing nature of dealing with the trauma of the past, or simple wish fulfilment. But, in either case, their lives will never be the same, as the narrator continues to 'look[ ] back at the brick building of the Historical Society', glancing back to a history that will *always* haunt – indeed, the Historical Society is earlier described as one of their 'haunts' (Butler 1988: 264; 263).[6]

Trauma is thus a temporal event that nonetheless flattens history: everything before the traumatic event is rendered, if not moot, then impossible to access in its pre-traumatic form, and everything after that moment constantly and continually reverts to the scene of trauma: trauma becomes the lens through which everything is read, darkly. To quote from Geoffrey H. Hartman's classic summation, 'there is a limit to recovery, or a limit to the effort at visualization. Every time we are tempted to say 'I see' when 'I understand' is meant, we do not see, or else do not understand' (Hartman 1995: 540). Or, as Eric Savoy writes, 'Paradoxically, the various kinds of trauma represented by the gothic – the proximity of Otherness which occasions allegorical approximation – constitute both a return and a loss, and the gothic might be broadly conceptualized as a cultural ritual of inscribing the loss of coherent ego formation, the negation of national imaginary' (Savoy 1998: 11). The trauma of slavery both constitutes and denies the very notion of an American self, even as the event of slavery is both repressed and continually invoked. The hauntings, doublings and suspense of the gothic can thus be read as the symptomatic effects of that originary social trauma.

Gothic Reconstruction and Haunting Forward

But what of the *recovered* subject? The promise of psychoanalysis is not the recovery of pre-traumatic innocence, but instead the re-narrativization of trauma such that the subject can move forward. And what is the gothic representation of slavery – in either of the modes discussed above – but precisely a re-narrativization of the originary trauma that lies at the origin of American identities? Can we reread certain (though by no means all) gothic representations of slavery not as symptoms or traumatic repetitions of that endlessly present past, but instead as attempts to re-narrate the American subject into a self-reflexive future? Is the gothic not a compulsive repetition of trauma, but instead the analysis of that trauma? In other words, could the walking dead actually be the talking cure?

Speaking of 'postmodern slave narratives' in general, and Butler's work in particular, A. Timothy Spaulding gestures towards an answer to these questions, writing that such works 'intrude upon history as a means to re-form it' (Spaulding 2005: 4). Likewise, Goddu's concept of 'haunting back', in which gothic horror is redirected onto slavers themselves, is part of such a process. As she writes, 'While the gothic threatens to resurrect a history that can never be exorcised, it also offers a way to signify against that history', allowing gothic to 'serve […] as a mode of resistance' (Goddu 1997: 155). If the 'traces' of slavery remain hidden, trauma's effects remain, but if they are discussed, mitigation and healing can occur. The gothic, Goddu writes in the concluding line to her major study, 'is a route toward that articulation' (159). But both authors still look to history as the defining feature, the traumatic source of such texts. Moreover, as the 'threatening' clause above indicates, for Goddu even this use of the gothic becomes, to a point, a 'problem': 'The problem of how literary narration could displace historical reality was especially troubling', she writes, 'for the author of the slave narrative' (136). When 'textuality' overwrites 'historicity', she suggests, material fact and politics are lost. 'Literariness', 'textuality' or the gothic itself here becomes the first connotative step toward Barthesian myth, where the details of material life are replaced by stories, and the possibility for political change is emptied out by the hollow nature of fictional representation (Barthes 1973: 143). This ontological problem – one that dates back at least to Kant[7] – is especially a problem for the authors of slave narratives, Goddu suggests, whose writing and self-presentation are directed toward gaining material freedom both for the authors themselves and for their larger communities. The gothic is particularly dangerous here because of its unrealistic, ephemeral nature.

To characterize slavery as both material condition (which should not be fictionalized) and as trauma is to cause other problems, however, because trauma is that which *must* be re-narrativized if the past is not to overwrite the future. To live beyond the repetition of the trauma, a subject's trauma must not be repeated, but retold, as Goddu makes clear above. Savoy frames this simultaneous denial of and demand for a narrative account of self in both psychoanalytic and linguistic terms. He writes that traditional narrative accounts of a nation, the 'seamless authenticity of national narrative', can be disrupted when 'another history' (or the history of the other) enters. He writes:

> the national narrative of American freedom is disrupted by the history of slavery. This disruption creates a 'chasm' within the coherent structures of self and past. This chasm is opened by the strategies of gothic signification, for it is not simply the case that a horrific 'alternate' history emerges as a cohesive or fully explanatory corrective that is superimposed upon nostalgic history. Rather, it irrupts by fits and starts in a semiotic that is fragmentary, one that is more suggestive than conclusive. As such, the gothic 'turn' toward compelling but unthematizable narrative might be conceptualized as the emergence of the Lacanian Real, which, according to Judith Butler, 'is that which resists and compels symbolization'. (Savoy 1998: 7–8)

Thus, the trauma of slavery leads to a gothic irruption in the national narrative, one that sunders the coherency of that narrative into a semiotic chaos. But, this is not simply an irruption of meaninglessness. Taking Judith Butler's statement to its full extent, the gothic irruption both 'resists and compels' meaning, and in this sense the gothic rendering of slavery can resist the hegemonic definitions of nation, community, self and race, and out of the chaos thus created, new symbols can emerge: this gothic irruption in fact 'compels' such new signification. And what is the Real in terms of the gothic irruption from within slavery (if we permit ourselves to allow the Real to signify in this comparison, if only under erasure)? Could it be that it is the always already denied freedom of enslaved subjects, presented as a 'ghost of a counterfeit' (Hogle 2012), haunting from their own future? Is the gothic only used to re-present the past, or can it offer something altogether new?

If it can do the latter, then the gothic may not risk displacing the historicity of slavery's actual practices, but instead allow for a reconstruction – not of slavery per se, but of the ways in which the national narrative frames those practices and their effects on individuals, communities and the nation. To revisit an example that Fiedler uses, when Huck Finn says 'All right, then, I'll *go* to hell', he is invoking the ultimate target and vehicle of gothic metaphor not to replay the traumas of slavery, but to try, at least, to move beyond them – 'a forbidding description of freedom itself', Fiedler writes (Fiedler 1966: 143): a gothic of the future is presented here. And when placed back into the material context of slavery (which *Huckleberry Finn* insists upon, of course), the gothic is not solely representative of trauma, or a revisiting of the trauma in this reading. The gothic here is a generative, not a limiting or repetitive, framework through which to re-articulate the originary trauma of slavery; not repeating the risk of future enslavements, such re-articulations attempt to ensure that it not happen again, and indeed look to a brighter day. Like the spirituals that W. E. B. DuBois analyses in *Souls of Black Folk* (1903), these generative gothics can articulate the horrors of slavery while still looking toward hope, but just as the gothic materializes the terror of the Burkean sublime, it also presents a hope in this case more material than spiritual.[8]

I recognize that this may read as too utopian a vision, especially within a gothic framework, and that such a utopian vision can slide into a wilful ignorance toward the injustices gothic authors strive to articulate. Certainly not all gothic renditions of slavery lend themselves to being read as transformative in this way. And, just as importantly, some of the texts that do focus on repetition serve as a form of warning narrative to the future, tempering the hope for a better future that I am reading here with a cultural form of planning for the worst. One can definitely read Morrison's 'story not to pass on' in this light. But, even when functioning as such warnings, the implicit structuring principle is the possibility of a future free of the material repetition of the traumatic scene or its compulsive, symptomatic repetition. It is important to recognize that at least some – though, again, by no means all – gothic representations of slavery in American culture are not solely about the horrors of the past, but are also about hope for the future. Cathy Caruth's foundational statement on trauma, history and narrative, *Unclaimed Experience* (1996), gestures toward this possibility. Even as she argues that trauma oscillates 'between the story of the unbearable nature of an event and the story of the unbearable nature of its survival' (Caruth 1996: 7), at the end of her study she gestures, in a Lacanian turn that in its phrasing echoes Morrison's novel, to hope for a more bearable future: 'the passing on of the child's words' (both words of a dream and words of death) transmits 'not simply . . . a reality that can be grasped in these words' representation, but the ethical imperative of an awakening that has yet to occur' (112). What if the gothic is that ethical imperative, and the gothic representation of slavery a demand to awaken to the reality of freedom? Several wide-ranging and artistically variable examples spring to mind: from slave narratives to (perhaps problematically) Quentin Tarantino's *Django Unchained* (2012). To focus my conclusion, however, I will briefly examine two particular deployments of this generative gothic: Harriet Jacobs's graveyard scene and Octavia Butler's *Kindred*. The gothic figure in these works is not simply slavery nor its traumas, but the complicated and always fraught relationship between freedom and slavery: freedom is the gothic creature that resists and revolts against the constraints of a reality bound by the all-too-mundane horror of the practices and after-effects of American slavery.

As Goddu has shown, Jacobs's *Incidents in the Life of a Slave Girl* engages the gothic throughout, often to present the horrors of slavery, as well as to 'haunt back', in Goddu's terms, against the horrors of the slaveholders' actions. 'Piling narrative upon narrative, Jacobs marshals a multitude of cases as evidence of slavery's real terrors', all the while 'refus[ing] to spoof the gothic or undermine the reality behind its effects', Goddu writes (Goddu 1997: 146; 149). Jacobs's seven years in the garret is the most obvious example, but her time in Snaky Swamp is another:

> As the light increased, I saw snake after snake crawling round us. I had been accustomed to the sight of snakes all my life, but these were larger than any I had ever seen. To this day I shudder when I remember that morning. As evening approached, the number of snakes increased so much that we were continually obliged to thrash them with sticks to keep them from crawling over us. The bamboos were so high and so thick that it was impossible to see beyond a very short distance. . . . I passed a wretched night; for the heat of the swamp, the mosquitos, and the constant terror of snakes, had brought on a

burning fever. I had just dropped asleep, when they came and told me it was time to go back to that horrid swamp. I could scarcely summon courage to rise. But even those large, venomous snakes were less dreadful to my imagination than the white men in that community called civilized. (Jacobs 1987: 112–13)

John J. Kucich points out that this scene 'counters Stowe's romanticized image of Dred's maroon hideaway in the Great Dismal Swamp', in part by invoking 'African spiritualist' imagery (Kucich 2004: 33). But, it also clearly points to a demonic Eden after the fall, overrun by serpents whose phallic nature echo the sexual violence she faces in slavery, as Marilyn C. Wesley notes (Wesley 1997: 68), something Jacobs makes clear in the final sentence quoted. This passage reinforces Goddu's argument, that Jacobs uses the gothic to figure, but not cover over, the actual violence and traumas of slavery.

But the earlier graveyard scene is different. Jacobs's autobiographical narrator, Linda Brent, contemplates her parents' graves:

The graveyard was in the woods, and twilight was coming on. Nothing broke the death-like stillness except the occasional twitter of a bird. My spirit was overawed by the solemnity of the scene. For more than ten years I had frequented this spot but never had it seemed to me so sacred as now. A black stump, at the head of my mother's grave, was all that remained of a tree my father had planted. His grave was marked by a small wooden board, bearing his name, the letters of which were nearly obliterated. I knelt down and kissed them, and poured forth a prayer to God for guidance and support in the perilous step I was about to take. As I passed the wreck of the old meeting house, where, before Nat Turner's time, the slaves had been allowed to meet for worship, I seemed to hear my father's voice come from it, bidding me not to tarry till I reached freedom or the grave. I rushed on with renovated hopes. My trust in God had been strengthened by that prayer among the graves. (Jacobs 1987: 90–1)

I have written elsewhere that in spite of the deaths of Jacobs's parents and of Nat Turner, as well as the destruction of the meeting hall by whites (described earlier in her text), still this passage highlights that the African American community, slave and free, signified by these images, continues in Brent and her living family (Haslam 2005a: 60). But this sublime moment, and Jacobs's ability to move forward, is enabled by the gothic: her father's voice, speaking from beyond the grave, is not 'speaking the unspeakable' of trauma and its repetition, but is imbued with the power to allow her to escape. It is precisely the 'gothic irruption' of a community, found in both death and freedom (symbolized by her father and by Nat Turner's armed insurrection), that allows Jacobs to rewrite her personal, and the national, narrative of slavery into one of resistance: 'freedom or the grave' are necessarily imbricated here, as the gothic is an indication of a space of reinterpretation, creating a warning about the past repeating itself while also, ultimately, leading her not to get stuck in the swamp of past traumas, but towards 'renovated hopes' for the future.

My epigraph from Ellison's introduction to *Invisible Man* speaks to the difficulties with this reading, however. The gothic, in many readings, is constituted by the blurring of temporality itself: the (dead) past invades the (living) present and disrupts the status quo. What I am suggesting is not a counter-reading of that structure, but a change in emphasis: if the gothic does disrupt the status quo, then perhaps it does not resurrect the traumatic past, but instead challenges the inevitable conformity that hegemonic forces attempt to imprint on the future. The blurring of the modes of science fiction and the gothic in Butler's novel, as in Ellison's (and throughout the history of both forms from at least *Frankenstein* forward), points to this generative possibility. I do not want to suggest that this is a positivist or Romantic reading, in which the gothic can generate an always positive future, or in which I mistake the transcendent for the haunting. Necessary to remember here is that hope is fleeting. But the gothic does allow for the possibilities inherent in semantic confusion; what matters is the perspective taken on and from that confusion.

Perhaps the best example again comes from Butler's *Kindred*. On one of Dana's early trips back, she speaks to a young Rufus, attempting to explain why she suddenly appears in his life. He asks:

'But . . . what's it like? What did Mama see that she won't tell me about?'
  'Probably the same thing my husband saw. He said when I came to you, I vanished. Just disappeared. And then reappeared later'.
  He thought about that. 'Disappeared? You mean like smoke?' Fear crept into his expression. 'Like a ghost?'
  'Like smoke, maybe. But don't go getting the idea that I'm a ghost. There are no ghosts'.
  'That's what Daddy says'.
  'He's right'.
  'But Mama said she saw one once'.
  I managed to hold back my opinion of that. His mother, after all . . . Besides, I was probably her ghost. (Butler 1988: 24)

The gothic here does something quite different than merely repeating the trauma of the past. The ghost is not from the past, but from the future.[9] If the novel is read as Dana's story about her haunting of Rufus, then what haunts him is the knowledge that black people can be, should be, and will be free, able to come and go as they please, and that as self-empowered agents they know this themselves. This freedom is rendered ghostly because the material structures of slavery and racism make it, in Jerrold Hogle's terms, a counterfeit. But the reality of freedom and of its dreams haunts those who would try to deny it.

Notes

1. On the gothic and slavery both within and outside of the US see, to take a very brief selection, Castronovo 2004; Ginsberg 1998; Goddu 1997; 2007; 2013; Greeson 2001; Haslam 2005b; Henry 2004; Marshall 2011, esp. 123–49; Smith-Rosenberg 2010: 413–64; Soltysik Monnet 2010; Wardrop 2002; and Winter 1992.
2. I am here echoing, in part, Monika Fludernik's analysis of the use of prison as metaphor, in which prison is either the target or source domain – as in 'PRISON IS X' and 'X IS (a) PRISON' (Fludernik 2005).
3. For Goddu's own reading of *Beloved*, see Goddu 1997: 154–5.
4. See Winter's study, especially.
5. For an extended discussion of slavery, trauma and African American identity, see Eyerman 2001.
6. Another version of this form of time travel narrative is presented in Haile Gerima's film *Sankofa*, which similarly deals with coming to terms with the largely forgotten history of slavery.
7. On Kant, the sublime and the gothic, see Mishra 1994.
8. One could think here of the song DuBois quotes, offered referred to as 'I'll Hear the Trumpet Sound': 'You may bury me in the East, / You may bury me in the West, / But I'll hear the trumpet sound in that morning' (DuBois 1986: 539).
9. Vallas also notes that Dana 'becomes a kind of ghost from the future' (Vallas 2000: 103) but still paints the past as what haunts.

References

Barthes, Roland (1973), *Mythologies*, sel. and trans. Annette Lavers, London: Jonathan Cape.
Butler, Octavia [1979] (1988), *Kindred*, Boston, MA: Beacon.
Caruth, Cathy (1996), *Unclaimed Experience: Trauma, Narrative, and History*, Baltimore: Johns Hopkins University Press.
Castronovo, Russ (2004), 'The Art of Ghost Writing: Memory, Materiality, and Aesthetics', in *In Search of Hannah Crafts: Critical Essays on* The Bondwoman's Narrative, ed. Henry Louis Gates, Jr, and Hollis Robbins, New York: Basic Books, 195–212.
Dayan, Colin (Joan) (1999), 'Poe, Persons, and Property', *American Literary History* 11:3, 405–25.
Delany, Samuel R. (1985), *Flight from Nevèrÿon*, Hanover, NH: Wesleyan University Press.
Douglass, Frederick [1845] (1996), *Narrative of the Life of Frederick Douglass, an American Slave, Written by Himself*, ed. William L. Andrews and William S. McFeely, New York: Norton.

DuBois, W. E. B. [1903] (1986), *The Souls of Black Folk*, in *Writings*, ed. Nathan Huggins, New York: Library of America, 357–547.
Ellison, Ralph [1948] (1995), *Invisible Man*, New York: Vintage International.
Fiedler, Leslie A. (1966), *Love and Death in the American Novel*, London: Jonathan Cape.
Eyerman, Ron (2001), *Cultural Trauma: Slavery and the Formation of African American Identity*, Cambridge: Cambridge University Press.
Fludernik, Monika (2005), 'Metaphorical (Im)Prison(ment) and the Constitution of A Carceral Imaginary', in *Anglia: Zeitschrift für Englishe Philologie* 123:1, 1–25.
Ginsberg, Lesley (1998), 'Slavery and the Gothic Horror of Poe's "The Black Cat"', in *American Gothic: New Interventions in a National Narrative*, ed. Robert K. Martin and Eric Savoy, Iowa City: University of Iowa Press, 99–142.
Goddu, Teresa A. (1997), *Gothic America: Narrative, History, and Nation*, New York: Columbia University Press.
Goddu, Teresa A. (2007), 'American Gothic', in *Routledge Companion to Gothic*, ed. Catherine Spooner and Emma McEvoy, New York: Routledge, 63–72.
Goddu, Teresa A. (2013): 'The African American Slave Narrative and the Gothic', in *A Companion to American Gothic*, ed. Charles L. Crow, Oxford: Wiley Blackwell, 71–83.
Greeson, Jennifer Rae (2001), 'The "Mysteries and Miseries" of North Carolina: New York City, Urban Gothic Fiction, and *Incidents in the Life of a Slave Girl*', *American Literature* 73:2, 277–309.
Hartman, Geoffrey H. (1995), 'On Traumatic Knowledge and Literary Studies', *New Literary History* 26:3, 537–63.
Haslam, Jason (2005a), *Fitting Sentences: Identity in Nineteenth- and Twentieth-Century Prison Narratives*, Toronto: University of Toronto Press.
Haslam, Jason (2005b), '"The strange ideas of right and justice": Prison, Slavery and Other Horrors in *The Bondwoman's Narrative*', *Gothic Studies* 7:1, 29–40.
Haslam, Jason (2008), 'Pits, Pendulums, and Penitentiaries: Reframing the Detained Subject', *Texas Studies in Literature and Language* 50:3, 268–84.
Henry, Katherine (2004). 'Slavery and Civic Recovery: Gothic Interventions in Whitman and Weld', in *The Gothic Other: Racial and Social Constructions in the Literary Imagination*, ed. Ruth Bienstock Anolik and Douglas L. Howard, Jefferson, NC: McFarland, 32–53.
Hogle, Jerrold E. (2012), 'The Gothic Ghost of the Counterfeit and the Progress of Abjection', in *A New Companion to the Gothic*, ed. David Punter, Oxford: Blackwell, 496–509.
Jacobs, Harriet [1861] (1987), *Incidents in the Life of a Slave Girl Written by Herself*, ed. Jean Fagan Yellin, Cambridge, MA: Harvard University Press.
Kucich, John J. (2004), *Ghostly Communion: Cross-Cultural Spiritualism in Nineteenth-Century American Literature*, Lebanon, NH: Dartmouth College Press.
Malchow, H. L. (1996), *Gothic Images of Race in Nineteenth-Century England*, Stanford: Stanford University Press.

Marshall, Bridget M. (2011), *The Transatlantic Gothic Novel and the Law, 1790–1860*, Farnham: Ashgate.
Miles, Robert (2002), *Gothic Writing, 1750–1820: A Genealogy*, 2nd edn, Manchester: Manchester University Press.
Mishra, Vijay (1994), *The Gothic Sublime*, Albany: State University of New York Press.
Montrose, Louis (1989), 'Professing the Renaissance: The Poetics and Politics of Culture', in *The New Historicism*, ed. H. Aram Vessey, New York: Routledge, 15–36.
Morrison, Toni (1990), *Playing in the Dark: Whiteness and the Literary Imagination*, New York: Vintage.
Morrison, Toni [1987] (2006), *Beloved*, New York: Knopf.
Sankofa (1993), written and directed by Haile Gerima, Mypheduh Films.
Savoy, Eric (1998), 'The Face of the Tenant: A Theory of American Gothic', in *American Gothic: New Interventions in a National Narrative*, ed. Robert K. Martin and Eric Savoy, Iowa City: University of Iowa Press, 3–19.
Smith-Rosenberg, Carroll (2010), *This Violent Empire: The Birth of an American National Identity*, Chapel Hill: University of North Carolina Press.
Soltysik Monnet, Agnieszka (2010), *The Poetics and Politics of the American Gothic Gender and Slavery in Nineteenth-Century American Literature*, Farnham: Ashgate.
Spaulding, A. Timothy (2005), *Re-Forming the Past: History, The Fantastic, and the Postmodern Slave Narrative*, Columbus: The Ohio State University Press.
Stowe, Harriet Beecher [1852] (2010), *Uncle Tom's Cabin*, ed. Elizabeth Ammons, New York: Norton.
Vallas, Stacey (2000), 'The Ghosts of Slavery', in *Gendered Memories*, ed. John Neubauer et al., Amsterdam: Rodopi, 101–11.
Wardrop, Daneen (2002), '"What Tangled Skeins Are the Genealogies of Slavery!": Gothic Families in Harriet Jacobs' *Incidents in the Life of a Slave Girl*', *The Literary Griot*, 14:1–2, 23–43.
Wesley, Marilyn C. (1997), 'A Woman's Place: The Politics of Space in Harriet Jacobs's *Incidents in the Life of a Slave Girl*', *Women's Studies* 26:1, 59–72.
Winter, Kari J. (1992), *Subjects of Slavery, Agents of Change: Women and Power in Gothic Novels and Slave Narratives, 1790–1865*, Athens, GA: University of Georgia Press.

Chapter 3

Ethno-gothic: Repurposing Genre in Contemporary American Literature
Arthur Redding

> A white man decomposing is a ghastly sight.
> D. H. Lawrence, *Studies in Classic American Literature*

American Gothic and Racial Dread

Along with D. H. Lawrence, who everywhere underlined the anger, fear and destructiveness of the American imagination, critics as diverse as Leslie Fiedler, Toni Morrison, Teresa Goddu, and Eric Savoy all agree that traditional American gothic literature has been in large part motivated by racial dread and anxieties about the purportedly destabilizing effects of miscegenation. 'From the moment at which our serious literature began', notes Fiedler, 'there were established in the American psyche images of the savage and the colored man as threats to stable and organized life' (Fiedler 1966: 148). Morrison notes that early American gothic and romance were strikingly 'frightened and haunted' (Morrison 1992: 35) by the Africanist presence in the US. And for Goddu, gothic 'registers its culture's contradictions, presenting a distorted, not a disengaged, version of reality' which is deeply and often alertly entwined with 'historical horror – revolution, Indian massacre, the transformation of the marketplace . . . slavery' (Goddu 1997: 3). Savoy in turn asserts that it is 'the specter of Otherness that haunts the house of national narrative' (Savoy 1998: 14). It comes as small wonder, then, that in his important study of Native American fiction, Louis Owens asserts that contemporary 'American Indian novelists . . . are in their fiction rejecting the American gothic, with its haunted, guilt-burdened wilderness and doomed Native and emphatically making the Indian the hero of other destinies, other plots' (Owens 1992: 18). Insofar as Native Americans, Blacks and other swarthy-skinned characters have served – and continue to serve – as synecdochal figures of menace and terror in dominant cultural narratives, contemporary ethnic writers strive to undo prevailing racist and racially inflected stereotypes.

Curiously, however, and paradoxically, a number of contemporary writers self-consciously deploy and rework gothic tropes and idioms. That is, instead of simply 'rejecting' gothic, as Owens advises, contemporary writers are everywhere refashioning the genre. This repurposing takes on two general aims. The first is critique and exposure, as writers capitalize on the inherent anxieties of American gothic in order to make explicit the racialism embedded in the hegemonic cultural narratives of opportunity and upward mobility available via the assimilationist ideology of an ethnic 'melting pot'. Second, such gothic redeployments permit contemporary ethno-gothic fictions imaginatively to disinter the voices of those legions who have died and disappeared, unmourned. Leslie Marmon Silko's *Gardens in the Dunes* (1999), for example, pays explicit if ironic homage to such Victorian masters of the genre as Wilkie Collins; part of the action, which spans the globe, takes place in the gardens of an 'old stone cloister that once sheltered Norman nuns' (Silko 1999: 236) near Bath, England, 'the land of stones that dance and walk after midnight' (237), as Aunt Bronwyn, proprietress of the estate, explains. In Silko's novel, Indigo, an orphaned child of the Sand Lizard people, is fostered by the progressive, sensitive and intelligent Hattie, who, with her husband Edward, hopes to raise Indigo as a properly civilized lady. It is Hattie's 'civilized' world that unravels and decomposes, however, as she increasingly perceives and confronts the hypocrisies and brutalities of the Western, imperial, Anglo-Saxon and Christian order, in whose ultimate benevolence she had so long been invested. At a crucial juncture, in Aunt Bronwyn's garden, Hattie encounters an eminently Victorian ghost, a 'loud knock' accompanied by 'a strange glow emanating from within' (247) the garden gates. Such is Hattie's intuition as she unlearns her Western ways, and such is Silko's parody of the genre, that Hattie's feelings of 'apprehension and dread' at this apparition resolve into 'such joy she wept' (248).

While few other writers are as explicit in their intertextual references to gothic scenarios as Silko, other well-known examples of works published in the past thirty or forty years that cite, undo and rework gothic conventions over the past four or five decades abound: Rudolfo Anaya's, *Bless Me, Ultima* (1972); Maxine Hong Kingston's ghost-filled *The Woman Warrior* (1976); Gerald Vizenor's *Bearheart* (1978; 1990), and other works. As Michelle Burnham notes, Native American interventions into gothic also include Anna Lee Walters's *Ghost Singer* (1988); Louis Owens's *Sharpest Sight* (1995); Sherman Alexie's *Indian Killer* (1996) and Joseph Bruchac's *Whisper in the Dark* (2005) – a list to which I would add A. A. Carr's *Eye-Killers* (1995), as well as works by First Nations writers from Canada, notably Tomson Highway's *Kiss of the Fur Queen* (1998) and Eden Robinson's *Monkey Beach* (2000). To mention a few more, by other writers of colour: Toni Cade Bambara's *The Salt Eaters* (1980); Cristina García's *Dreaming in Cuban* (1992); Randall Kenan's *Let the Dead Bury their Dead* (1992); and Ana Castillo's *So Far from God* (1993). The list goes on, and should rightfully include films as well; while gothic and horror cinema are ubiquitous in Hollywood, a few notable films participate in re-calibrating and subverting the standard tropes of racial, class or ethnic terror. We can single out Guillermo del Toro's *Pan's Labyrinth* (2006) or *The Devil's Backbone* (*El espinazo del diablo*, 2001) – all of his films, really. With its haunted house on 124 Bluestone Road; its unflinching interrogation of unrelieved racial violence; its giving of imaginative voice to representative victims of the 'Sixty Million and more' whose lives, deaths and even names have never been discerned or acknowledged; and its theorization of the collective persistence of 'rememory 'out there, in the world' (Morrison 1987: 43), Morrison's own *Beloved* (1987) is perhaps the single best known instance of the repurposed gothic that characterizes much of the writing by ethnic and minority writers in the US after 1968. 'It's still there, waiting, that must mean that nothing ever dies' inquires Denver of her mother, Sethe, in *Beloved*, after Sethe has explained to her the resolutely public nature of ghosts. 'Sethe looked right in Denver's face. "Nothing ever does", she said' (44).

While the influence of Latin American magical realism on such works of fiction cannot be overstated, and while fictions assessing the dilemmas of 'hyphenated' and hybrid identities tend self-consciously to re-invigorate and valorize the folktales, legends, rituals and oral traditions of indigenous and immigrant cultures that have been too long disparaged, muted and denigrated by an American Anglo-Saxon hegemony and an American emphasis on assimilation, many novels also blend these textual strategies with the traditional trappings and machinery and landscapes of European and American gothic. In a post-1960s writing, inflected, at times, by nationalist projects of cultural revival, figures of haunting, in particular, have been deployed by writers to demonstrate how nothing ever dies, to depict the ghostly persistence of histories and traditions of cultural knowing that are palpably present and yet irretrievably absent, inaccessible, mute, dishonoured or unrecognized. Such fictions ventriloquize histories marked by trauma, violence, slavery and genocide, histories that have been sacrificed, histories whose subjects are buried in mass graves, whose ways of knowing and being in the world are missing from available annals.

The project of historical gothic is today being supplemented by a globalized counter-gothic, works that diagram and contest long festering American national anxieties about the country's 'porous borders'. Such fears have been well stoked within Nativist discourse post 9/11, obviously, and accentuated during the years of the Obama administration, a president viewed by many conservatives as foreign, subversive and, well, downright spooky. If the buried, disallowed and disparaged revenants of indigenous pasts and the serial brutalities attending the European conquest of the New World haunt the contemporary historical imagination of American literature, then we can also discern the gothic dimensions of writing that assesses contemporary movements of displaced individuals and diasporic communities across the globe and interrogates the challenges facing political and economic refugees today. That is to say, gothic modes, figurations, conceits and trappings – often injected with the overt political ironies that the traditional genre scants – form a powerful strain within the contemporary World Literature of diaspora and displacement. Such well-known writers as Salman Rushdie or the Nigerian fantasist Ben Okri have typically deployed gothic and magical realist techniques in their celebrated works, and, more recently, works by several putatively 'American' writers of global diasporas such as the Nigerian/American Teju Cole or the Jordanian-American Diana Abu-Jaber are blending (often very muted) gothic elements with other literary forms in their fiction.

Clearly the repurposing of gothic through inhabiting its modes in order to resist them is a pan-American, even global phenomenon. We might consider, for example, *The Hungry Ghosts* (2013), by the Canadian/Sri Lankan writer, Shyam Selvadurai, which is by no means a gothic or even a magical realist work – indeed in its elegant weaving of personal and familial melodrama into epic horrors of war it might best be characterized as Tolstoyan. Nonetheless, the book proffers in the 'hungry ghost' an image of haunted desire as a figure for unappeasable loss, cultural dislocation and the persistence of the past:

> In Sri Lankan myth, a person is reborn a peréthaya because, during his human life, he desired too much – hence the large stomach that can never be filled through the tiny mouth. The peréthayas that appear to us are always our ancestors, and it is our duty to free them from their suffering by feeding Buddhist monks and transferring the merit of that deed to our dead relatives. (Selvadurai 2013: 24–5)

Shivan, the son of a Tamil father and Sinhalese mother, protagonist of Selvadurai's comic and melancholic coming-of-age novel, is doubly divided, doubly caught between opposing cultural systems (Sinhalese/

Tamil, Sri Lankan/Canadian), traverses a complex and mobile set of cultural borders. All of these borders and conflicts are, in a metaphorical or real sense, haunted. The pitched conflicts of war, civil and imperialist, traumatize survivors; its legacies are often gothic too, as, for example, in Robert Olen Butler's tales of Vietnamese, *A Good Scent from a Strange Mountain* (1992). Deserts, gardens, haunted houses, borderlands, war zones, jungles, metropolitan urban centres – all the gothic geographies of the contemporary world are traversed. Ghosts everywhere mark and police limits and thresholds, exchanges, miscommunications and difference. The 'rejection' of gothic, it seems, involves in large part a working through and repurposing of gothic traditions to new ends.

In *Cultural Haunting*, her important 1998 theorization of these gothic refashionings, critic Kathleen Brogan has posited that what can be characterized, rather sweepingly, as contemporary 'ethno-gothic' fiction, 'signal[s] an attempt to recover and make social use of a poorly documented, partially erased, cultural history' (Brogan 1998: 2). Citing works as diverse as William Kennedy's *Ironweed* (1983), Paule Marshall's *Praisesong for the Widow* (1983), T. Coraghessan Boyle's *World's End* (1987), Louise Erdrich's *Tracks* (1988), Cynthia Ozick's short fiction collection, *The Shawl* (1989), Sandra Cisneros's *Woman Hollering Creek* (1991), and Askold Melnyczuk's *What Is Told* (1994), Brogan's study convincingly asserts that contemporary gothic works are a 'pan-ethnic phenomenon, registering a widespread concern with questions of ethnic identity and cultural transmission' (Brogan 1998: 4), which, taken together, mark the emergence of a new, hybrid, contemporary genre. Drawing on ethnography, trauma theory and Freudian psychoanalysis, Brogan understands haunting as a return of the repressed, a formulation she shares with such other psychoanalytically inclined theorists of American gothic as Goddu or Savoy. In turn, then, contemporary ghost stories exorcise their ghosts through narrating 'second burials', rituals that bring mourning to a successful and productive, if provisional, completion:

> For heir-ethnographers, those who stand both inside and outside traditions, ethnicity should be construed not just in terms of memory but more specifically as a function of mourning, the form of memory that most directly confronts loss. . . . In tale after tale of cultural haunting, mourning is an essentially integrative process through which the living struggle to integrate the dead in the new reality (and the new identities) they construct. These stories work to reconnect experience to memory by redefining the legacy bequeathed by earlier generations. Once dangerously possessed by a denied, forgotten, or otherwise sheared-off past, the protagonists of haunted texts come newly into possession of their reimagined history. (Brogan 1998: 171)

Another influential theoretical approach to the problem takes the workings of historiography into account. In his essay 'Between Memory and History' Pierre Nora argues that, in the contemporary world, 'the quest for memory is the search for one's history' (Nora 1994: 289). That is, the project of memory today requires 'every social group to redefine its identity through the revitalization of its own history. . . . Those who have long been marginalized in traditional history are not the only ones haunted by the need to recover their buried pasts' (291). The task of memory has three features, according to Nora: 'archive-memory', 'duty-memory' and 'distance-memory'. Memory is archival, because it is no longer 'experienced from the inside' but increasingly 'exists only through its scaffolding and outward signs' (290); it becomes a duty as the free-floating individual finds herself increasingly unmoored from the traditional communal and affective props undergirding identity formation: 'The atomization of a general memory into a private one has given the obligation to remember a power of internal coercion' (292). Finally, given this task of reconstituting 'our fractured past' what we perceive is 'no longer a retrospective continuity but the illumination of a discontinuity' (293). What this implies is that two of the most dominant forms of contemporary literature – historiographical meta-fiction and memoir – are sharing in the same broader but elusive cultural project of reconstituting a provisional model of selfhood. The overlapping borders between the memoirist's attempt to wrestle the wayward routes of self-formation into narrative structure and the historical novelist's endeavour to sniff out the germs of the contemporary within a historical regime of trauma, rupture and discontinuity, constitute a working definition of contemporary gothic. Nora himself slips into a gothic idiom to describe the insistently literary nature of this enterprise: 'memory has never known more than two forms of legitimacy: historical and literary. These have run parallel to each other but until now always separately. At present the boundary between the two is blurring' (300). Accordingly, as Brogan explains, 'ghosts . . . figure prominently whenever people must reconceive a fragmented, partially obliterated history, looking to a newly imagined past to redefine themselves for the future' (Brogan 1998: 19).

Plotting Haunting

One question we will want to examine as we dig more deeply into a few select examples is how, precisely, these tasks of mourning, re-imagination, and intergenerational cultural transmission and renewal are dramatically plotted. The structural patterns underlying a number of quasi-gothic *Bildungsromans* – more commonly, *Künstlerromans* – chart the pressures facing a young person wrestling with the anxieties of adolescence and the social demands of resolving cultural conflict. Many of the works mentioned above deploy a gothic idiom to portray these dilemmas. In folklore and urban legends, episodes of poltergeists, hauntings and demonic possession are often linked to adolescents undergoing transition to sexual maturity. Significantly, too, so many of these narratives are coming-of-age stories, featuring young or adolescent protagonists growing up between cultures and striving for self-formation and self-articulation. A young person of 'mixed blood' grows up in a family that is at once internally divided and, as part of a minority group, threatened by a more powerful, external and dominant culture. He or she is at once compelled to resolve intra-cultural differences and to hash out a relative peace with the dominant culture that symptomatically excludes him or her, often on account of religious, ethnic, national or racial differences, from its powers and privileges. For ghosts are not only figures of the past, but mark and police the abyss between cultures. In Kingston's *The Woman Warrior*, for example, most of the ghosts are in the stories about China that Maxine is told by her mother, Brave Orchid: Wall Ghost, Frog Spirit, Sitting Ghost. Yet, even in America, on Gold Mountain, the children refer to non-Chinese as ghosts:

> America has been full of machines and ghosts – Taxi Ghosts, Bus Ghosts, Police Ghosts, Fire Ghosts, Meter Reader Ghosts, Tree Trimming Ghosts, Five-and-Dime Ghosts. Once upon a time, the world was so thick with ghosts, I could hardly breathe; I could hardly walk, limping my way around the White Ghosts and their cars. There were Black ghosts too, but they were open eyed and full of laughter, more distinct than White Ghosts.
> What frightened me most was the Newsboy Ghost. (Kingston 1977: 96–7)

En route to overcoming these barriers, the young protagonist will develop a sometimes antagonistic relationship with a (typically female) mentor figure one generation removed from his parents – a grandmother, often, or a great aunt.

As Louis Owens has noted, most of American Indian fiction is mixed-blood, or hybrid, in its sympathies and outlook: this tends to be as true of immigrant and bicultural works as of those by indigenous writers. Protagonists must resolve intertribal antagonisms as well as contest anti-Indian biases from outsiders. The template for such stories was no doubt established as far back as D'Arcy McNickle's classic *The Surrounded* (1936), in which the protagonist, Archilde León, is the estranged son of a Spanish father and Salish mother, yet the same narrative infrastructure can be discerned in many Native American works of the so-called American Indian Renaissance, such as James Welch's comic surrealist *Winter in the Blood* (1974) or Leslie Marmon Silko's *Ceremony* (1977). In *Ceremony*, the hazel-eyed Tayo returns to Laguna reservation following his service in the Asian Pacific. Spurned as a half-breed by family members and his tribe, suffering from what would be diagnosed in later years as 'post-traumatic stress disorder', Tayo is, at the novel's opening, 'white smoke', something of a ghost himself. Through the intercession of the medicine man, Old Betonie, who cautions him that it has become 'necessary to create new ceremonies' (Silko 1977: 126), Tayo's challenge is to heal himself, his tribe, his land, which is suffering from drought, and, ultimately, all of human and cosmic history. He will 'complete' the ceremony by confronting and at least provisionally staving off the murderous 'bad witchery' that has conjured up human evils ranging from everyday racism to atomic warfare. At the uranium mines of the Cebolleta land grant in New Mexico, Tayo arrives 'at the point of convergence where the fate of all living things, and even the earth had been laid', where 'the lines of cultures and worlds were drawn in flat dark lines on fine white sand, converging in the middle of witchery's final ceremonial sand painting' (246).

The same narrative pattern can be discerned in other works as well. The fate of six-year- old Antonio Marez y Luna, protagonist of Rudolfo Anaya's *Bless Me, Ultima*, is pinioned by the antipathies between the family of his mother, a Luna, who are farmers and priests, tillers of the earth, and that of his father, a Marez, wild and wayward *vaqueros*, llaneros, riders of the wind, who live by the motto that 'man was not to be tied to the earth, but free upon it' (Anaya 1994: 6). Tony's intrafamilial conflict is accentuated by the pressures he faces as a Chicano in an Anglo school, and he is torn, too, between paganism and his mother's Catholicism, which he will come to reject as hypocritical and judgmental. Apprenticed to the *curandera*, Ultima, an ancient woman who arrives to stay with his family, Tony assumes a role as witness and confessor at the violent deaths of outcasts and innocents in his community, and participates in a series of ceremonial exorcisms. In an ultimately redemptive tale, Tony is able to glean the beginnings of a 'new religion' (247) by accepting and reconciling the differences inside himself and those between himself and the larger world, learning from Ultima that 'the tragic consequences of life can be overcome by the magical strength that resides in the human heart' (249).

This moral hardly serves as a 'gothic' lesson, to be sure; the novel, linguistically and generically hybrid, like so many of the works I have been discussing, is more a child's fantasy of wonder than a horror story. Yet the gothic elements can be traced in precisely those factors that remain stubbornly outside the symbolic universe of the work, forbidden entry into Tony's new religion of inclusive sympathy. In his role as priestly confessor, Tony has forgiven the three sacrificial victims on their deathbeds: the murderer Lupito, whom the war has made crazy, and who is killed by a posse of men from the town of Guadalupe; the town drunk, Narciso, shot dead by the evil Tenorio as he hurries to warn Ultima of a plot against her life; and Tony's classmate, the atheist rebel Florence, drowned a short while after Tony refuses to condemn him in a mock confessional orchestrated by the other schoolchildren. Yet if these outcasts can be integrated into the spiritual community of difference, others cannot. Towards the end of the book, the rancher Téllez finds his family and home cursed, and summons Ultima for assistance. Undertaking the exorcism, Ultima understands the situation to have arisen from the long history of conquest and occupation:

> 'A long time ago,' she began, 'the llano of the Agua Negra was the land of the Comanche Indians. Then the comancheros came, then the Mexican with his flocks – many years ago three Comanche Indians raided the flocks of one man, and this man was the grandfather of Téllez. Téllez gathered the other Mexicans around him and they hanged the three Indians. They left the bodies strung on a tree; they did not bury them according to their custom. Consequently, the three souls were left to wander on that ranch. The brujas who laid the curse knew this, so instead of placing the curse on a member of the family and taking the chance of getting caught, they simply awakened the ghosts of the three Indians and forced them to do the wrong. The three tortured spirits are not to blame, they are manipulated by brujas.' (Anaya 1994: 227)

At the borderlands, as Lois Parkinson Zamora has noted, 'novelists write out of a sense of cultural displacement – displacement of traditional communities, indigenous and rural, and the resulting ruin of the land' (Zamora 1995: 541). In this passage Ultima outlines the heritage of dispossession and racialized violence that, for all its devotion to *mestizaje*, the coming-of-age story has largely scanted, a history that *brujas* manipulate to their own purpose. Though Ultima, with the assistance of Tony and his father, arranges for a second burial for the unhappy *bultos* and successfully rids the family of their haunting, she confesses to Tony (the fourth deathbed absolution he administers) that she may have erred in her life's mission by trying to interfere with – rather than facilitate – human destiny. Ultima dies at peace, promising her young protégé that 'harmony will be reconstituted' (Anaya 1994: 260). Yet it is the displacement of an historical 'evil' onto the maleficence of witches that amounts to an ideological sleight of hand. Long-suffering ghosts may be pacified and laid peacefully to rest only if a scapegoat can be designated to assume the burden of communal sin and punished. Ghosts are exonerated, on the condition that *brujas* bear the brunt of the blame: the two Trementino girls, daughters of Tenorio, denied burial on hallowed ground by the parish priest, and denied, too, their voice within Anaya's fable. These two nameless women are the unassimilable exiles who haunt the borders of this fable of inclusive harmony. As Tony's father tells him, 'most of the things we call evil are not evil at all; it is just that we don't understand those things and so we call them evil' (248) – well, some need to be labelled evil nonetheless, and so cast out. Tony's new religion, in its own way, needs fully as much to judge and condemn as has the Christian God Tony has rejected. The ethical logic of judgment and blame stands in stark contrast to Silko's narrative, where it is precisely the hero's *refusal* to exact revenge against witches that redeems Tayo, and which, temporarily at least, frees the world from animosity.

Which is not to say that *Ceremony* does not have its exiles as well. In a well-known gloss of Silko's novel, which attempts to make the feminist case for the work, Paula Gunn Allen has catalogued two distinct types of women in the novel. The first, largely benevolent, are those who 'belong to the earth spirit and live in harmony with her, even though this attunement may lead to tragedy. Those in the second are not of the earth but of human mechanism; they live to destroy that spirit, to enclose and enwrap it in their machinations, condemning all to a living death' (Allen 1992: 118). Curiously absent from Allen's seemingly exhaustive list of characters, however, is one of the most singular women in *Ceremony*: Helen Jean, a young drifter picked up by Tayo and his friends, whose history replicates, in part, that of Tayo's wayward mother. Allen overlooks Helen Jean despite her central place in the novel, despite her capacity to speak on her own behalf: a full six pages of the book are told from Helen Jean's point of view, one of the very few characters apart from Tayo who serve autonomously as focalizer – whose point of view, that is, is presented directly to the reader, without intermediary quotation marks. Neither an accomplice nor an antagonist, simply a scorned young woman desperate to make do, Helen Jean is in some sense the unredeemed 'ghost' that haunts *Ceremony*, the exile who cannot be fully integrated into the new symbolic order.

The sacrificial logic at work in these novels is clear enough: in an attempt to purify and cleanse the village, the ghosts who sin and who suffer are appeased and reburied; in some sense, as Brogan has argued, the work of mourning is thereby completed, and the social community renewed. What so often happens in gothic works, however, is the short-circuiting of full integration, the failure successfully to exorcise the unruly ghosts, who even when buried, even when buried again, linger. Note, for example, that at the conclusion to Morrison's *Beloved* the ghost is not wholly absent, and the ostensible 'healing' of the protagonist, Sethe, is left an open question: 'Me?' Sethe wonders aloud at the novel's end. 'Me?' (Morrison 1987: 322). It is the capacity to recognize and indulge those figures who are nonetheless condemned to remain what we might term 'exiles from the representational fold' that most insistently characterizes the contemporary gothic.

Unspeakable Subjects and the Ghosts of Empire

These ghosts, then, remain, to use one of Morrison's recurrent terms, ultimately 'unspeakable'. Endowed with language, they are everywhere refused full entry into the symbolic order, even as they continue to haunt, even as they refuse to be appeased. The problem, in a word, is legibility; the problem is how a ghost may be welcomed into symbolic or representational language without reducing her or his or its 'speech' to anything we can safely understand or interpret. In Cristina García's ghost-filled *Dreaming in Cuban* (1992) it is the aspiring artist, Pilar Puente, who is challenged with the task of reconciling an estranged family whose Cuban loyalties have been split by the revolution. The family matriarch, Celia del Pino, has dedicated herself to Castro; Celia's ill-fated daughter Felicia, who remains in Cuba, is an adept of Santeria; her other daughter, Lourdes, is raped by revolutionary soldiers and moves with her husband and daughter to the US, settling eventually in New York City, where she establishes the Yankee Doodle Bakery, a haven for exiled Cubans plotting Castro's overthrow. As Brogan provides an exemplary reading of García, I will merely mention the consistency of the plot structure: again, we witness internal division (between revolution and religion); an external divide between minority and majority cultures (Cuba and America); the need for mentoring and connection from the grandmother; the 'mixed-blood' adolescent struggling for self-articulation amid these intergenerational divides; and, as all of these borders are traversed, and guarded, by ghosts, the hybridized gothic as the genre in which best to recount the family epic. To complete her mission, Pilar must travel to Cuba to meet her grandmother, Celia del Pino, with whom she shares a mystic, telepathic bond. In New York City, Pilar undergoes her own initiation into the rites of Santería, as she is recognized by the proprietor of a *botánica* as a 'daughter of Chango' (García 1992: 200), who directs her that 'You must finish what you began' (200). Like her mother, Lourdes, Pilar will be sexually assaulted upon leaving the shop; after nine days of ritual cleansing, she returns, Lourdes in tow, to Cuba. '"We have no loyalties to our origins", Abuela tells me wearily. "Families used to stay in one village reliving the same disillusionments. They buried their dead side by side"' (240).

As an artist, both painter and musician, and as historian and storyteller, Pilar wrestles with the formal concerns of legibility and representation: her task is to find a language adequate to the complexities of her family heritage. Illegibility and the difficulties of discerning, translating, recording and transmitting messages form a recurrent motif in the novel. When Celia confronts the giant ghost of her dead husband, he 'moves his mouth carefully, but she cannot read his immense lips' (García 1992: 5). Pilar dreams of people 'chanting in a language I don't understand' (34). She tells her school psychiatrist that 'painting is its own language ... Translations just confuse it, dilute it' (59). When Lourdes is raped, 'the soldier lifted the knife and began to scratch at Lourdes's belly with great concentration. A primeval scraping. Crimson hieroglyphics'. She tries 'to read what he had carved. But it was illegible' (72). As Celia dreams, 'voices call to her in ragged words stitched together from many languages, like dissonant scraps of quilt' (95). And, while 'Pilar records everything' (7), she would 'like to record other things' (28); she learns that 'capturing images' is 'an act of cruelty' (48). And while at one pole the novel is devoted to the transformative power of the imagination, the motto that 'imagination, like memory, can transform lies to truths' (88), at another the novel runs up against the inadequacy of finding or forging a language capacious enough to record mute, illegible and ghostly histories. At the climax, Pilar admits: 'Nothing can record this, I think. Not words, not paintings, not photographs' (241).

Of yet another resonant ethno-gothic text, Fae Myenne Ng's *Bone* (1993), Andrew Hock Soon Ng has proposed that 'the loss and emptiness that characterizes the lives' of the people depicted 'point to their ghostly existence. They are always on the brink of vanishing from the symbolic order but, like spectres, will never truly disappear because they are not even worthy of exorcism' (Ng 2014: 259). Two considerations follow: first, in his assessment of the prevailing gothic sensibilities that inform so much of Asian-American literature, too, Ng makes the important point that contemporary writing is involved in a reciprocal relation with the strictures of genre: our experience of gothic is recalibrated. To recognize the instabilities of genre categories is not merely to acknowledge that contemporary ethno-gothic writing is generically hybrid – unsurprisingly, as the theme and social problem of so much of this writing is cultural displacement and social hybridity – but more troublingly, as Allan Lloyd Smith has demonstrated, 'Gothic foregrounds issues of ontology in reader and text, while subduing or subverting the explanatory structures that might, in a realist or modernist text, control, explain or direct affectivity' (Smith 1996: 10). Second, if contemporary gothic writing is characterized by the persistent shaping presence of a past that is unknown, dismissed or traumatic, then it follows too that the present must also be acknowledged as unstable, vaporous, unreal, shivering and spectral. The solid, familiar world is 'haunted'; the contemporary world, therefore, for all its materiality and depth, is also wraithlike. This is the 'trick' of such films as M. Night Shyamalan's *The Sixth Sense* (1999) or Alejandro Amenábar's *The Others* (2001): the slow or dramatic reveal that 'we the living' are the ghosts.

Gothic works to dissolve the solidity of our lived lives; this is a more or less Derridean point about the spectrality of the everyday and an attendant insecurity about our own identity. The ethical and political consequences of such a humbling and strenuous realization are explored in Teju Cole's celebrated debut novel *Open City* (2011), whose narrator stumbles upon 'a kink in time and place' (Cole 2011: 191) that opens post 9/11 New York into an unfolding historical and global labyrinth. The wars, the atrocities, pile on, as do the crowds of people who have migrated to New York seeking refuge and solace. The protagonist, Julius, born of a German mother and a Nigerian father is another 'mixed-blood', a young psychiatrist who has taken to wandering the streets of the city, opening himself to encounters, stories, conversations, time warps. The book juxtaposes the ghostliness of the contemporary refugees with the reappearance of the dead that mark the twenty-first century US. Having his shoes shined in 'the underground catacombs of Penn Station' (70), Julius meets 'Pierre', a Haitian, who left the island 'when things got bad there, when so many people were killed, blacks, whites' (71–2). A later allusion to 'the terror of Boukman' which Pierre and his family, enslaved to a family named Bérard, are 'fortunate to have escaped' (72) places his flight to New York during the early years of the Haitian revolution, and, obtaining his freedom upon his masters' deaths, Pierre's sufferings during 'the years of Yellow Fever' (73), referring to the epidemics of the 1790s, places him in the same decade. He lives on Mott Street among the Irish, 'Italians, too, later on, and blacks, all working in the service trades' (72). Pierre's mention of 'our school for black children in Saint Vincent de Paul on Canal, down where the Chinese are now' (73–4), confirms that Julius is speaking to the ghost of the venerable Pierre Toussaint (1766–1853), philanthropist and patron of old St Patrick's Cathedral. As Julius ascends to the streets, images of protests against Bush's wars in Iraq and Afghanistan bleed into the New York City draft riots of 1863: 'That afternoon, during which I flitted in and out of myself, when time became elastic and voices cut out of the past into the present, the heart of the city was gripped by what seemed to be a commotion from an earlier time' (74). 'The body of a lynched man dangling from a tree' resolves itself into 'dark canvas sheeting on a construction scaffolding, twirling in the wind' (75). In such vignettes, New York, city of refugees and aspirants, is also the city of ghosts.

In this highly intertextual novel, Cole provides us with an explicit gloss of Freud's 1917 essay 'Mourning and Melancholia'. Whereas over the process of mourning a successful internment and internalization of the absent dead within the psyche is accomplished, in the melancholic, by contrast, 'this benign internalization does not happen. Instead, there's an incorporation. The dead occupy only a part of the one who has survived; they are sectioned off, hidden in a crypt, and from this place of encryption, they haunt the living' (Cole 2011: 208–9). Julius sees the city after 2001 as having botched the mourning process. It is just after he encounters an 'immigration crowd' (218) that he stumbles upon the national monument to 'the African burial ground' (219), site of up to perhaps 20,000 burials in the eighteenth century, a place forgotten until 2001, when the dead were accidentally disinterred by construction crews. The exhumation of the dead allegorizes the violence and the unacknowledged pluralism that has everywhere been disavowed by a nationalist myth and historiography, and exposes the perpetual and determining, and, yes, material present-ness of traumas of which cities, nations, empires and subjects are fabricated.

Julius suffers from historical lapses, and from memory lapses – some incidental, as in his failure earlier in the novel to remember the PIN number for his bankcard, some epic. There are hints, by the end of the novel, that Julius may be a ghost himself. 'Things don't go away just because you choose to forget them' (245), Julius is told by Moji, when his long-forgotten crimes are at last revealed to the reader and, perhaps, to Julius himself, who, like so many perpetrators, like so many of us, has found a way to gloss over his own responsibility to those whom he has hurt. Gothic compels us to acknowledge these hurts, to respond. The scholar Paul Giles has hypothesized 'that the nationalist phase of American literature and culture extended from 1865 until about 1980, and that the current transnational phase actually has more in common with the so-called early national period, between 1780 and 1860, when national boundaries and habits were much less formed and settled' (Giles 2007: 55). Giles's contention feels right; our readings of García and Cole might help us further to speculate that it makes little sense to consider contemporary literature within a 'national' framework at all. Contemporary transnational writing, much of it gothic, is best understood as the cultural production specific to imperial America, rather, even as it transgresses and subverts the claims of empire. Contemporary ethno-gothic nurtures the hybrid potentials of the genre itself, even as it bores within the available and fraudulently triumphal American narratives of limitless power, ever compelling the flagging empire to give up its ghosts.

References

Allen, Paula Gunn [1986] (1992), *The Sacred Hoop: Recovering the Feminine in American Indian Traditions*, Boston, MA: Beacon.
Anaya, Rudolfo [1972] (1994), *Bless Me, Ultima*, New York: Warner.
Brogan, Kathleen (1998), *Cultural Haunting: Ghosts and Ethnicity in Recent American Literature*, Charlottesville: University Press of Virginia.
Burnham, Michelle (2014), 'Is There an Indigenous Gothic?' in *A Companion to American Gothic*, ed. Charles L. Crow, Malden, MA: Wiley Blackwell, 225–37.
Cole, Teju (2011), *Open City*, New York: Random House.
Fiedler, Leslie, (1966), *Love and Death in the American Novel*, rev. edn, New York: Stein & Day.
García, Cristina (1992), *Dreaming in Cuban*, New York: Ballantine.
Giles, Paul (2007), 'The Deterritorialization of American Literature' in *Studies of the Planet*, ed. Wai Chee Dimock and Lawrence Buell, Princeton: Princeton University Press, 39–61.
Goddu, Teresa A. (1997), *Gothic America. Narrative, History, and Nation*, New York: Columbia University Press.
Kingston, Maxine Hong, (1976), *The Woman Warrior: Memoirs of a Girlhood among Ghosts*, New York: Knopf.
Lawrence, D. H. [1923] (1951), *Studies in Classic American Literature*, New York: Doubleday.
Morrison, Toni (1987), *Beloved*, New York: Vintage.
Morrison, Toni (1992), *Playing in the Dark: Whiteness and the American Literary Imagination*, Cambridge, MA: Harvard University Press.
Ng, Andrew Hock Soon (2014), 'Undead Identities: Asian American Literature and the Gothic', in *A Companion to American Gothic*, ed. Charles L. Crow, Malden, MA: Wiley Blackwell, 249–63.
Nora, Pierre (1994), 'Between Memory and History: Les Lieux de Mémoire', in *History and Memory in African-American Culture*, ed. Geneviève Fabre and Robert O'Meally, trans. Mark Roudebush, New York: Oxford University Press, 284–300.
Owens, Louis (1992), *Other Destinies: Understanding the American Indian Novel*, Norman: University of Oklahoma Press.
Savoy, Eric (1998), 'The Face of the Tenant: A Theory of American Gothic', in *American Gothic: New Interventions in a National Narrative*, ed. Robert K. Martin and Eric Savoy, Iowa City: University of Iowa Press, 3–19.
Selvadurai, Shyam (2013), *The Hungry Ghosts*, New York: Random House.
Silko, Leslie Marmon (1977), *Ceremony*, New York: Viking.

Silko, Leslie Marmon (1999), *Gardens in the Dunes*, New York: Simon & Schuster.
Smith, Allan Lloyd (1996), 'Postmodernism/Gothicism', in *Modern Gothic: A Reader*, ed. Victor Sage and Allan Lloyd Smith, Manchester: Manchester University Press, 6–19.
Zamora, Lois Parkinson (1995), 'Magical Romance/Magical Realism: Ghosts in U.S. and Latin American Fiction', in *Magical Realism: Theory, History, Community*, ed. Lois Parkinson Zamora and Wendy B. Faris, Durham, NC: Duke University Press, 497–550.

Part II

Gothic Genres, Gothic Sites

Chapter 4

Southern Gothic
Christopher Lloyd

National/Regional Gothic

It is perhaps a stereotype, if not an axiom, to say that the South is an inherently gothic region whose dark cultural fabric is woven by haunting, traumatic memory and lingering violence. Moreover, it seems as though the Southern Gothic is alive and well today. The South has long been depicted as the nation's other, an aberrant space within America's borders, and the Civil War's division between North and South retains much of its cultural force, if not necessarily geographical certainty. This essay posits that the Southern Gothic, in various manifestations, still defines much of the region's cultural output. While the present essay takes cinematic and televisual examples from the twenty-first century – *Trash Humpers* (2009), *True Blood* (2008–14), and *Black Snake Moan* (2006) – as evidence of this gothic focus, I will chart a brief history of the Southern Gothic in order to connect contemporary culture to canonical literature and theory.

In his wide-ranging and personal rumination on the horror genre, *Danse Macabre* (1981), Stephen King notes a particular Southern branch of this fiction. He takes the minor novel *The Beguiled* (1966), by Thomas Cullinan, as an example, the gothic story of a Union soldier 'who loses his legs and then his life to the deadly angels of mercy who dwell in a ruined girls' school that has been left behind in Sherman's march to the sea' (King 2000: 310). King immediately uses the figure of the land, longstanding in the South, to describe Cullinan's work. 'One is tempted', King writes, 'to believe that outside of the South, such an idea wouldn't raise much more than ragweed. But in this soil, it grows a vine of potent, crazed beauty' (King 2000: 310). King pushes the metaphor of rootedness further, suggesting that the most canonical (and often gothic) of Southern writers, William Faulkner, 'did more than drop a few seeds' in this soil: 'he planted the whole damn garden'

(310). Discussing Faulkner's *Sanctuary* (1931), King states: 'there is something frighteningly lush and fertile in the Southern imagination, and this seems particularly so when it turns into the gothic channel' (311). Rich in imagination, Southern soil is thus also inherently gothic. In taking Faulkner as exemplary of the Southern Gothic, King joins a litany of scholars and critics who see this Mississippian's legacy as defining the entire regional landscape (see Sundquist 1983; Williamson 1995). Suggesting that particular ideas flourish in the South in ways they would not elsewhere, King treats the region as exceptional, specific and different – unlike any other, even within the US. This notion of being 'out of place' has been long debated in Southern studies (see Gray 2000; Smith 2013; Duck 2006), but functions metonymically for American alienation more generally. By setting aside the South, the nation can displace certain gothic tendencies, which are then specifically tied to the region, despite their origin.

Teresa Goddu inverts the traditional conception of the gothic as simply concerned with otherworldliness or escape from reality, arguing that 'gothic stories are intimately connected to the culture that produces them', not 'gateways to other, distant worlds' (Goddu 1997: 2). For Goddu, the gothic needs to be historicized, rooted in the culture and time that produced it: the gothic is not only 'informed by its historical context', but 'the horrors of history are also articulated through gothic discourse' (Goddu 1997: 2). This historicization follows Leslie Fiedler's seminal *Love and Death in the American Novel* (1960), which argues that 'of all the fiction of the West, our own is most deeply influenced by the gothic, is almost essentially a gothic one' (Fiedler 1984: 142). This is, for Fiedler, because various forms of repressed guilt about past traumas have been projected onto American literature's cultural output. Such traumas include 'the slaughter of Indians' and, pertinently, 'the abominations of the slave trade, in which the black man, rum, and money were inextricably entwined in a knot of guilt' (Fiedler 1984: 143). Fiedler thus suggests that the American gothic is a symptomatic form of storytelling that is as inevitable as it is inescapable to the American mind, whether national or regional. Goddu states that 'the American gothic is most recognizable as a regional form' (Goddu 1997: 3). In a Southern context, the region's 'peculiar identity has not only been defined by its particular racial history, but has also often been depicted in gothic terms: the South is a benighted landscape, heavy with history and haunted by the ghosts of slavery' (Goddu 1997: 76). The economy that slavery supported (cotton, tobacco, sugar) was rooted both imaginatively and literally in Southern soil, with particular effects on Southern culture. To Goddu's thesis we might add the forced removal of Native Americans from the

South, the abuses of poor whites, the terrors of racial violence, the daily traumas of Jim Crow, and especially for the present essay, the racialized disciplining of sexuality and gender.

Eric Savoy argues that 'the gothic registers a trauma in the strategies of representation as it brings forward a traumatic history toward which it gestures but can never finally refer' (Savoy 1998: 11). Thus, the histories informing the gothic constitute a past that can never be fully grasped, but merely signalled or signified, often symptomatically. The traumatic event is something that is too overwhelming and unprecedented to assimilate into consciousness, and thus its presence is only felt belatedly, in flashbacks and dreams, for instance. 'It is not the event that returns', Richard Crownshaw notes, 'but rather the failure to process the event'; the trauma 'cannot be known when witnessed and cannot be known upon its insistent return' (Crownshaw 2010: 5). This theory articulates how traumas of the past become manifest, and are worked through, in the present. In this light, the gothic can be read as a genre or form that is interested in the connections between past and present. Savoy's gloss of what Fiedler calls '"the pastness of the past", the inescapable melancholy continuity between historical suffering and the visible textures of the present' (Savoy 1998: 17) is significant here. As Avery Gordon puts it, 'haunting describes how that which appears to be not there is often a seething presence' (Gordon 1997: 8). Southern culture is often interested in how the contemporary world is constituted and textured by the past, substantiated and disturbed by its presence. If the gothic is deeply rooted in the history from which it emerges, Gordon articulates a contemporary world 'seething' with ghosts. Cultural memories from the South are thus engaged by the gothic form and transformed in the process; dark traumas from the region's past are lodged in and substantiate culture. In the South, how the gothic registers trauma's lingering effects has thus produced distinctive and peculiar results.

I now want to examine these results in two films and a TV show that offer a striking and original visual imaginary of the gothic. While several cultural forms employ the Southern Gothic today, these contemporary texts delineate something of the gothic's visual aberrance, for it is in the broad reach of visual media that one often finds the Southern Gothic's most potent images and narratives. *Trash Humpers* demonstrates how the Southern Gothic story could not be told anywhere else; *True Blood* offers a contemporary take on the regional genre, with a particular emphasis on sexuality and difference; and *Black Snake Moan* ties these threads together through its long-standing gothic narrative of racial and sexual mores.

The Grotesque South

Across her writings Flannery O'Connor was interested in notions of excess, perversion, extremity, monstrousness, freakishness: what she calls 'the grotesque'. Her novels and short stories are peopled with alienated, limbless, deformed and estranged characters; we witness shocking acts of violence, such as self-blinding and cold-blooded murder; we discover, often, the darkest of human desires. Sarah Gleeson-White characterises the grotesque mode as depicting 'strange worlds of freakish outsiders placed in lovelorn barren landscapes, penetrating heat, and closed spaces, with themes of miscegenation, sexual deviance and bloody violence' (Gleeson-White 2001: 108). The Southern Gothic or grotesque has traction across literature from the region: its most notable practitioners (such as O'Connor, William Faulkner, Eudora Welty, Carson McCullers and Truman Capote, among others) repeatedly tap into this imaginary. In a famous essay on the topic, O'Connor wryly observes that 'I have found that anything that comes out of the South is going to be called grotesque by the Northern reader, unless it is grotesque, in which case it is going to be called realistic' (O'Connor 1988: 815). Here O'Connor gestures towards several issues, the first being how the nation has been constituted by its division between North and South, the South frequently signifying qualities – violence, poverty, racism – deigned other to proper national (Northern) identity. O'Connor further notes that for Northern readers, the South is inherently gothic and grotesque. As Goddu states, 'The South's oppositional image – its gothic excesses and social transgressions – has served as the nation's safety valve: as the repository for everything the nation is *not*, the South purges contrary impulses' (Goddu 1997: 76). The South functions as an 'Other' place to cast off the rest of the nation's difficult past and social problems, so that the ghosts haunting contemporary society become a regional matter that finds the South bearing all gothic burdens. Moreover, 'By closely associating the gothic with the South, the American literary tradition neutralizes the gothic's threat to national identity' (Goddu 1997: 76), so that for national literary culture a gothic associated strictly with the South cannot affect the rest of the country.

Patricia Yaeger argues that while the grotesque is not solely a Southern issue, 'grotesque bodies' especially 'provide a particularly condensed and useful figure of thought for presenting a set of problems plaguing the South' (Yaeger 2000: 25): the empty or oppressive ideals of the white South (especially womanhood); class and money; the pervasive history and memory of slavery and racial violence through displacement, marginalisation and segregation. Many of these issues emerge in O'Connor's fiction, as in her classic novel *Wise Blood* (1952), which is saturated with gothic sights and occurrences. The protagonist Hazel Motes keeps in his apartment a mummified dwarf stolen from the local museum; later, his friend Sabbath Lily clutches the corpse in a grotesque tableau that recalls the Madonna and child; a teenager with whom Motes is embroiled (Enoch Emery) stabs someone dressed as a gorilla and wears the costume around the town, shocked when people are disturbed by him. The text ends with Motes blinding himself, walking around with barbed wire wrapped around his body; he then wanders off into a thunderstorm and is found lying in a ditch by police who accidentally kill him with a blow to the head. Such grotesque bodies, materializing the novel's complex relations between religion, violence, humanity sin, and poverty, signify the regional mode of O'Connor's Southern Gothic (see Cofer 2014; Brinkmeyer 1989).

O'Connor's novel resonates with a recent experimental film from cult provocateur Harmony Korine, *Trash Humpers*. I begin with this text because it offers a way to conceive of the Southern Gothic's particularity in contemporary cinema. The film depicts a group of sociopaths (their faces covered with grotesque masks to look like elderly people) who roam the backstreets of Nashville, destroying property, 'humping' trashcans, and eventually indulging in abusive and murderous behaviour. Because they walk and move as if they are younger, but speak in a strange and affected way, we cannot tell if these characters are actually elderly or younger people disguised as elderly people. Korine's characters seem ageless, even vampiric. This disruption of developmental time, blurring youth and age, is at once disturbing and provocative. Strangely traumatic, the uncanny 'elderly masks' signify how in the Southern Gothic the present is haunted by the past. For Korine, the film's monstrosity has roots in the city where he grew up and still lives. Walking the streets of Nashville at night, he began to notice overturned trashcans, which 'began to resemble human forms to me – almost like a war zone where the trash bins had been molested and beaten up and stuff' (Ebiri 2009). He continues: 'I remembered that in my neighbourhood growing up, there were these elderly peeping toms who would stare into my neighbour's window. They lived in an old person's home down the road, and would come out at night. And I just put these ideas together' (Ebiri 2009). Tying the film's overt gothicism to the local reality from which it emerges, Korine demonstrates how such a Southern locale is implicitly aberrant. His excessive horrors merely amplify an already dark horrific Nashville, so that the cultural articulation further disfigures and reconfigures traumas already there.

The film's scenes are 'haphazardly' edited together to depict a fragmentary sense of its people's lives. Shot on distorted home video (we sometimes see on the screen 'pause' or 'play'), the film evokes a visceral realism that is alienating, bizarre and difficult to characterize – like O'Connor's grotesque. In a late scene we witness one of the group singing and shrieking into the camera, dancing in a jolting way, wearing a jumper that bears a picture of the Confederate flag. This signifier stands out in an otherwise hazy and abstract landscape, but gestures towards its regional grounding. In addition to these strange happenings, we witness the murder of a woman giving an apple to a child into which she has inserted a razor blade. The dance described above is itself interrupted by shots of the woman riding a bike in circles, dragging a child's doll around by string, set in an eerie urban environment: an empty lot, full of potholes, gravel and weeds. In the next scene, this character talks (seemingly) to God: 'I don't mean to do wrong' (Korine 2009), but this is no moment of spiritual or emotional clarity, for later she enters a home and (apparently) kidnaps a child, and in the film's last shots she takes the child for a walk through the dark streets. The film's Southern Gothic is permeated and defined by freakishness, its milieu one of urban decay and abandonment, reflecting a South that is among the poorest and deprived regions in the US. How the Tennessean locale frightens reminds us that this terrain's grotesquerie has a long history in regional culture. Just as King argues above that Cullinan's novel could not have meaning outside the South, *Trash Humpers* is obscure and unnerving precisely because of its gothicism's regional focus.

Bad Things in Louisiana

Korine's representation of the Southern Gothic bears productive comparison to the HBO television series *True Blood*, created by Alan Ball, and based on the 'pulpy' but entertaining novels by Charlaine Harris. *True Blood*, especially in its first season, rethinks the Southern Gothic within a contemporary regional setting: the Deep Southern town of the predominantly white Bon Temps. Each episode uses the steamy, nocturnal and affective Louisiana setting – and, of course, supernatural beings – to explore race, class, gender and sexuality. The show's focus on vampires, shape-shifters and fairies has its feet firmly planted on Southern soil and is the product of a regional imaginary. Caroline Ruddell and Brigid Cherry argue that the show's setting 'provides a particularly Southern context where the Gothic is negotiated and remediated within a contemporary environment (albeit one that cannot be unhinged from its past)' (Ruddell and Cherry 2012: 53). For Ruddell and Cherry *True Blood* transforms but does not dislocate or negate entirely conventional Southern Gothic tropes. Past and present are entangled, for the show cannot be understood outside of the South's history and its relationship to the gothic.

As an HBO production, the series revels in adult themes and representations, but there is more at play here than mere entertainment. As the credits open we hear the sleazy country song 'Bad Things', which lyricizes the singer's desire that 'before the night is through, I wanna do bad things with you' and thus indicates *True Blood*'s relationship not only to sex and sexuality but to its perilous connotations of deviance and violence. The song plays over a montage of images that represent a particularly Southern aesthetic: swamps, alligators, roadside bars with neon signs and dusty lots, a striking rattlesnake, a decaying fox corpse, backwoods shacks, a white 'hick' on a rocking chair, children eating berries (their mouths smeared with what looks like blood), a child member of the KKK, evangelical preachers and congregations in states of ecstasy, and the ecstasy of sexual encounters. This escalation toward climax makes clear the libidinal energy of the Southern Gothic's longstanding regional and sensational nature driving the series' narratives. As Gregory Erickson claims, the credits teach us to 'pay attention not only to the complexity of images but also to juxtapositions and transitions, and to read the space between images, the implied, the unsaid, the contradictory' (Erickson 2012: 78). Cherry notes that 'Frames have been removed from sequences so that the images sometimes appear jerky and out of time', which creates '"a beautiful kind of lunging staccato effect"' (Cherry 2012: 13). The disjointing and unsettling technique of this visual stutter, telling a story of 'heat, passion, death and the South' (Cherry 2012: 12), foregrounds a self-reflexive Southern Gothic aware of its uncanny relationship between history and representations by which it is formed – we need think only of Gleeson-White's list of attributes above.

Across the seasons, *True Blood* plays out themes of queerness, otherness, freakishness, grotesquerie, horror, trauma and the presence of the past explored by King, Fiedler, and Goddu, but is especially aware of the history of race relations in the South. Here, however, race is coded (partially) as supernatural: vampires are figures for difference and the social Other who is ostracised, feared and demonised. In the first episode, the protagonist Sookie – a waitress in a local bar – meets Bill, a vampire, who has just come to town. Everyone in the bar reacts strongly to Bill's arrival; the mainstream 'human' population rejects vampires as a threat. In this small Southern locale, stigmatisation has a particular history through which Jim Crow laws and segregation rear their ugly heads. Although as seasons go on we learn that many of the locals are supernatural in some way (fairies, shape-shifters, werewolves and so on), the series maintains its sense of a striated society. Tellingly, in the first episode, Sookie's friend Tara comments on her own name: 'Isn't that funny? Black girl being named after a plantation' (Ball 2008). Referencing the plantation at the centre of *Gone With the Wind* (1939), 'the ground zero of southern cultural reproduction' (Romine 2008: 27), Alan Ball's script immediately raises older Southern culture as a coordinate of the show's intertextual fabric. By secreting into its present this endlessly recycled image of Southern culture, *True Blood* suggests there is no way to understand its world without knowledge of how the South has been represented historically and culturally.

True Blood further references black history when in a television interview the head of the 'American Vampire League', an organisation dedicated to encouraging peaceful relations between humans and vampires, argues there is nothing to fear from her 'race'. By supporting her argument with the fact that vampires 'didn't own slaves' (Ball 2008), she thus nods to one of the South's most traumatic and traumatizing legacies. Moreover, that she says vampires want to be 'part of mainstream society' (Ball 2008) implicitly compares vampires to African Americans, and ultimately engages a larger regional past in the social relations of contemporary Louisiana, reminding us that 'Integration isn't a done deal here, and bigotry (whether covert or overt) constantly rears its ugly head' (McPherson 2011: 342). Season four of *True Blood* reveals one of this history's most traumatic lessons when the Bellefleur family – a somewhat distinguished and wealthy Louisiana dynasty – realises its genealogical connection to Bill and thus to the taint of 'vampire blood', which Caroline Bellefleur (a Southern matriarch) discovers when tracing family trees. Here the traditional association of vampires with blood and bloodlines signifies the spectre of miscegenation: the 'one drop rule' of racialized blood that could taint white familial purity, the intermixing of races through sexuality that is one of the Old South's most traumatic primal scenes.

True Blood's attention to sexuality in its various forms is given historical traction here; the first season's explicitness in particular gestures towards the structural importance of gender, sex and otherness to this Southern town. The show's explicitly queer nature yokes homosexuality and notions of cultural alterity to the show's discourse of blood. AIDS as well as miscegenation hovers at *True Blood*'s edges. The opening credits depict a roadside church sign 'God hates fangs'. Parodying the far-right-wing Christian homophobic placards 'God hates fags', this image 'blatantly foregrounds' how the show 'deploys its vampires at least partially to enter the fray over debates about gay rights' (McPherson 2011: 338). Thus, the show places the gothic's relationship to an earlier history in dialogue with the contemporary South and its associations with conservative values and religion. In this way a more recent gothic genre reflects not only older racial traumas and memories of the South but a larger network of issues that have plagued the region. Whereas *Trash Humpers* embodies and formalizes the conventions of Southern Gothic, the self-referential images and narratives of *True Blood*'s gothic play with the genre's form and content in order to engage the South's past and present.

The Chains of History

Our previous examples reveal the Southern Gothic's connection to the historical legacies of the region (particularly raced) and the ways in which this past is transmuted in the present: worked-through as a series of cultural memories that are charged with a specificity that seems to separate the South from elsewhere in the United States. These ideas find even greater emphasis in Craig Brewer's darkly comic and strangely grotesque film *Black Snake Moan*. Brewer's earlier film *Hustle and Flow* (2005) is set in Memphis and follows a hustler's journey into the world of rap music. Its treatment of race, music and regional identity flourish further in his next feature. Like *True Blood*'s revision of Southern history and its racial-sexual codes, *Black Snake Moan* transforms the region's past into a contemporary gothic tale. Older Southern narratives of black masculinity, white femininity, violence and poverty are transformed and retold through this film set against a languid Mississippi backdrop. The film centres on the characters of Rae, a poor white woman beaten and left to die on the roadside, and Lazarus, a poor black farmer who finds and rescues her. The film foregrounds Rae's uncontrollable libido: she is struck, at will, by a desire that is overpowering and intense. The film connotes her sexuality, shaped by both her history of sexual abuse and her present actions, by the sound of a rattlesnake's hiss and rattle. The danger and threat of female sexuality is nothing new in cinema, but this particularly Southern Gothic twist seems 'blatantly sensational' (Smith 2011: 327).

As Rae sleeps restlessly at Lazarus' house, recovering from her beating, Lazarus investigates her background and life. He learns about Rae's promiscuity – her boyfriend has been drafted into Tennessee National Guard and she is left sexually wanting – and upon returning decides to 'cure' her of her sins. To do so, Lazarus chains Rae to his radiator. As Rae returns to health – even chained up, Lazarus feeds and clothes her, talks to her about her life and past, instructs her about religion and sin – they form an unusual bond. As M. Thomas Inge notes, the film's connections between black men and white women follow a particular trajectory and constellation of fantasies, such as the threat of miscegenation, but also Southern Belles as paragons of purity and whiteness, an idealization contingent upon the demonization of black men as sexual threats to white women, such that blackness and whiteness construct one another. Inge writes: 'the chains invoke the entire history of slavery in the South and the subjugation of the African American', but here 'the enslaved is the white woman, that vessel of purity and virtue who, according to social tradition, was to be protected at all cost from the lustful black buck' (Inge 2011: 566). *Black Snake Moan* complicates this history, however. Here the 'predatory' black male rescues the white woman from abuse by white men, yet does so by chaining her up, symbolizing complex power relations in which Rae finds the 'connection to the security and stability' she needs as well as 'imprisonment' (Inge 2011: 568).

These relations take a particular turn when we learn that Lazarus is a blues musician who has not played in a number of years. Once he unchains Rae, and she decides to stay in his house, he plays the electric guitar for Rae, teaching her of the 'black snake moan': a certain musical quality of the blues that evokes Rae's snake-inflected sexuality. Historically, the blues is about communicating pain and heartbreak, but also for Lazarus, violence. When he first plays his guitar for Rae, a lightning storm breaks and the house is plunged into darkness, but the electricity of his guitar lights up the pair as Rae sits at Lazarus's feet, suggesting both a parental and a sexualised tableau. Here the Southern Gothic, sensational, exaggerated, even comic, evokes a steamy Mississippi saturated with sex and violence. We have already seen these themes in *True Blood*, *Trash Humpers*, and O'Connor's *Wise Blood*, but Brewer's film imagines the regional gothic, and its evocation of historical tensions, in a particularly excessive manner. When giving his blues free reign in a local club, Lazarus, singing a song about murder and revenge, whips his audience into bodily, sensual frenzy, including Rae, to whom he is still 'teaching' moral lessons. Like the convulsive edits of *True Blood*'s credits, the dancers drenched in sweat and moving in erotic contortions, shot in slow motion, visualize an affective concert that releases the town's libidinal urges, as if to unburden it from its stifling Southern milieu. Jon Smith argues that Lazarus has a 'quality of minstrelsy, even of blackface', which reduces 'the complexity of southern African American blues experience to the cardboard stereotypes available to white fantasy' (Smith 2013: 328).

Yet the film's racial representations are more complex than this. The blues is an artistic form forged in the crucible of slavery and its social organisation, borrowing rhythms and forms from African culture in order to express and even exorcise the pain and sadness of oppression. Here Lazarus's blues play out racial stereotypes but also re-imagine a profound connection to an African American past rooted in the South. As Brewer notes, 'we are doing a fable. We're not trying to do some sort of realistic portrayal of the South' (cited in Inge 2011: 571). By eschewing realism, the film risks avoiding the past, but also risks rethinking the past towards the future. This is especially true of the film's ending, which evokes a more subtle and incisive sense of the South's gothic texture. Marrying her boyfriend Ronnie with whom she has been reunited, Rae is given away by Lazarus, her new father figure. Her more destructive sexual inclinations seem to have subsided by this point, but Ronnie's masculinity remains threatened in ways he cannot control. Driving away from the wedding, likely to their honeymoon, Ronnie suffers an anxiety attack on the freeway and has to pull over as he and Rae are overtaken by a logging truck, which suggests a dominating, even racialized phallus. Rae connects her body to Ronnie's, breathing with him, alleviating some of his anxiety. As a final tableau about gender and race in the South, the film's ending asks us to probe and question the couplings – of black men and white women, white men and white women, black men and black women – as precarious and deeply entwined.

While monstrosity in *Trash Humpers* seems peculiarly Southern, and the queer identities and sexualities of *True Blood* comment on the history of the region's treatment of others, *Black Snake Moan* takes us even further into gothic territory and consciously plays out what might be the central drama of Southern life: the interrelation of white women and black men. This story has a deep and tortuous regional history, but by powerfully foregrounding its traumatic effects on gender and racial constructions, the film offers us a potential way to reconceive this history. As the film's libido threatens to spiral out of control and its central characters are pushed to their limits of sex, violence, gender and racial identification, the narrative's ending complicates the Southern dilemma of miscegenation, for as Rae calms Ronnie she clutches her belly chain, reminding us of her time spent under Lazarus's lock and key and thus that the chains of history are at once broken and remain powerful. If *Black Snake Moan* takes 'some of the traditional elements of Southern film and subject[s] them to re-evaluation by turning them inside out' (Inge 2011: 571), the Southern Gothic of its form and content reminds us that we must continually attend to ghosts of the past that continue to haunt the region's present.

References

Ball, Alan (2008), *True Blood*, HBO.
Brewer, Craig (2006), *Black Snake Moan*, Paramount.
Brinkmeyer, Robert (1989), *The Art and Vision of Flannery O'Connor*, Baton Rouge: Louisiana State University Press.
Cherry, Brigid (2012), 'Before the Night is Through: *True Blood* as Cult TV', in *True Blood: Investigating Vampires and Southern Gothic*, ed. B. Cherry, New York and London: I. B. Tauris, 3–21.
Cofer, Jordan (2014), *The Gospel According to Flannery O'Connor: Examining the Role of the Bible in Flannery O'Connor's Fiction*, New York: Bloomsbury.
Crownshaw, Richard (2010), *The Afterlife of Holocaust Memory in Contemporary Literature and Culture*, Basingstoke: Palgrave Macmillan.
Duck, Leigh Anne (2006), *The Nation's Region: Southern Modernism, Segregation and U.S. Nationalism*, Athens, GA: University of Georgia Press.
Ebiri, Bilge (2009), 'Harmony Korine on how Fatherhood Influenced his New Movie About Having Sex with Garbage Cans', <www.vulture.com/2009/10/harmony_korine_on.html>
Erickson, Gregory (2012), 'Drink in Remembrance of Me: Blood, Bodies and Divine Absence in *True Blood*', in *True Blood: Investigating Vampires and Southern Gothic*, ed. B. Cherry, London and New York: I. B. Tauris, 74–89.
Fiedler, Leslie A. [1960] (1984), *Love and Death in the American Novel*, London: Penguin.
Gleeson-White, Sarah (2001), 'Revisiting the Southern Grotesque: Mikhail Bakhtin and the Case of Carson McCullers', *The Southern Literary Journal*, 33: 2, 108–23.
Goddu, Teresa A. (1997), *Gothic America: Narrative, History, and Nation*, New York: Columbia University Press.
Gordon, Avery F. (1997), *Ghostly Matters: Haunting and the Sociological Imagination*, Minneapolis: University of Minnesota Press.
Gray, Richard (2000), *Southern Aberrations: Writers of the American South and the Problems of Regionalism*, Baton Rouge: Louisiana State University Press.
Inge, M. Thomas (2011), '*Black Snake Moan* as Postsouthern Fable', *Mississippi Quarterly*, 64: 3–4, 565–72.
King, Stephen [1981] (2000), *Danse Macabre*, London: Warner Books.
Korine, Harmony (2009), *Trash Humpers*, Alcove Entertainment.
McPherson, Tara (2011), 'Revamping the South: Thoughts on Labor, Relationality, and Southern Representation', in *American Cinema and the Southern Imaginary*, ed. D. E. Barker and K. McKee, Athens, GA: The University of Georgia Press, 336–51.
O'Connor, Flannery (1988), 'Some Aspects of the Grotesque in Southern Fiction', in *Collected Works*, New York: The Library of America.
Romine, Scott (2008), *The Real South: Southern Narrative in the Age of Cultural Reproduction*, Baton Rouge: Louisiana State University Press.
Ruddell, Caroline and Brigid Cherry, 'More Than Cold and Heartless: The Southern Gothic Milieu of *True Blood*', in *True Blood: Investigating*

Vampires and Southern Gothic, ed. B. Cherry, London and New York: I. B. Tauris, 39–55.
Savoy, Eric (1998), 'The Face of the Tenant: A Theory of the American Gothic', in *American Gothic: New Interventions in a National Narrative*, ed. Robert K. Martin and Eric Savoy, Iowa City: University of Iowa Press, 3–19.
Smith, Christopher J. (2011), 'Papa Legba and the Liminal Spaces of the Blues', in *American Cinema and the Southern Imaginary*, ed. D. E. Barker and K. McKee, Athens, GA: The University of Georgia Press, 317–35.
Smith, Jon (2013), *Finding Purple America: The South and the Future of American Cultural Studies*, Athens, GA: The University of Georgia Press.
Sundquist, Eric J. (1983), *Faulkner: The House Divided*, Baltimore: Johns Hopkins University Press.
Williamson, Joel (1995), *William Faulkner and Southern History*, Oxford: Oxford University Press.
Yaeger, Patricia (2000), *Dirt and Desire: Reconstructing Southern Women's Writing 1930–1990*, Chicago: University of Chicago Press.

Chapter 5

The Devil in the Slum: American Urban Gothic
Andrew Loman

I.

To speak of 'American urban gothic' is to yoke together three overdetermined words and use them to account for works in multiple media, produced in different places and different times. It is to imply that Charles Brockden Brown's novel *Arthur Mervyn* (1798–9) has affinities with the Hollywood film *I Am Legend* (2007), and that both have something in common with Dion Boucicault's melodrama *The Poor of New York* (1857), H. P. Lovecraft's story 'The Horror at Red Hook' (1927), and Kara Walker's installation *A Subtlety* (2014). It is to argue that adjectives routinely enlisted to characterize the gothic – 'uncanny', 'mysterious', 'horrifying', 'evil' – also frequently characterize the American city in art. Toni Morrison has remarked that 'it is striking how dour, how troubled, how frightened and haunted our early and founding literature truly is' (Morrison 1993: 35), and although her central example of Poe's *The Narrative of Arthur Gordon Pym* (1838) takes place far from any American cities, her observation nonetheless applies with special force to early American urban literature. It continues to apply now: reading Colson Whitehead's *Zone One* (2011), set in the ruins of post-apocalyptic New York, or watching *The Dark Knight Rises* (2012), with its revolutionary monster lurking in Gotham's sewers, one notes the centuries-long persistence of gothic anxieties in the imagined American city.

This chapter focuses on literature of the late antebellum period, since the two decades between 1840 and 1860 comprise a key moment in the development of American urban gothic as a subgenre. In those decades, a community of writers that was producing 'sensational pamphlet-novels aimed at a large, mainly lower-class audience' (Bell 1995: 71) organized an already extant urban gothic vocabulary into a popular and influential literary subgenre, the city-mysteries, that ostentatiously announced its link to the gothic novel. These city-mysteries were intimately intertwined with other discourses, notably the urban reportage of the so-called 'flash press', and other art forms, especially the stage. Ned Buntline's novel *The Mysteries and Miseries of New York* (1849), for instance, shares hypermasculine gender politics with the flash press and borrows two key characters, Mose the Bowery B'hoy and his lover Lize, from Benjamin Baker's 1848 stage hit *A Glance at New York*. But their most obvious debt was to the gothic novel: borrowing from Ann Radcliffe's *The Mysteries of Udolpho* (1794), these novels announced in their titles that they explored gothic mysteries in the America city. 1844 alone saw the publication of *The Mysteries of Boston*, *The Mysteries of Fitchburg*, *The Mysteries of Haverhill*, *Mysteries of Lowell*, *Mysteries of Manchester*, *The Mysteries of Nashua*, and *The Mysteries of Springfield*. Works with an urban gothic sensibility antedated these works, but these openly announced their generic lineage.

A conventional way to account for the genre's emergence is to point to the explosive growth of American cities in the nineteenth century. Between 1800 and 1850, New York's population grew from 60,515 to 515,547; Boston's grew from 24,937 to 136,881; and Philadelphia's grew from 28,522 to 121,376. Daniel Walker Howe has characterized the three decades after 1820 as 'the period of the most rapid urbanization in American history', when 'the sector of the population considered "urban" (residing in places with more than 2,500 people) multiplied fivefold and increased its share of the population from 7 percent to 18 percent' (Howe 2007: 526). David S. Reynolds has suggested that because of this growth, 'during the 1840s American city dwellers lost social knowledge and physical contact with each other for the first time. The city was suddenly an overwhelming place, filled with hidden horrors and savage struggles as fascinating as they were appalling' (Reynolds 1988: 82). This characterization of the city dweller as overwhelmed, alienated, fascinated and appalled does not account for contemporaneous representations of the city as exciting and dynamic. But it rightly suggests that dramatic urbanization fuelled American urban gothic, which was, in other words, a symptom of and a response to what Marshall Berman calls the 'maelstrom of perpetual disintegration and renewal, of struggle and contradiction, of ambiguity and anguish' (Berman 1988: 15) that characterizes modernity.

American modernization produced a general sense of cultural disintegration in the antebellum period. Nathaniel Hawthorne referred to the nineteenth century as the 'epoch of annihilated space' (Hawthorne 1962–94b: 3:195); Lydia Maria Child characterized the chaotic scenes that unfolded every 1 May, or Moving Day, in New York as 'an appropriate emblem of this country, and this age', anathematizing 'the nineteenth century, with its perpetual changes' (Child 1843: 273). Moreover, there was a burgeoning sense of class disparity in the 1840s. As Edward K. Spann has noted, while there was no European 1848 in America, nonetheless class tensions were intense enough to provoke riots, most notably in New York in 1849 and 1857. This latter riot provoked the *New York Times* to speak ominously of 'Civic Rebellion' in the city (qtd in Spann 1981: 393). The city-mysteries testify to such crises both directly and indirectly.

In this chapter I discuss the rise of American urban gothic, in three stages. First, I address the term 'American urban gothic' itself: it makes assumptions about the interrelation of nation, city and literary mode that demand attention, the better to preserve a sense of what it includes and excludes. I next survey two recurring gothic figures, the violent criminal and the confidence artist. Finally, I turn to conventional sites and abiding anxieties of early American urban gothic. These elements are richly suggestive of the tensions in the antebellum city that made urban gothic so popular a genre. And they help us to see the urban gothic as a genre or mode that expresses the fears the city provokes, whatever they may be.

II.

To speak of a specifically American gothic is to assert that nationhood has a critical influence on the gothic mode: it announces the importance of an explicitly political dimension to what might at first blush appear to be a strictly aesthetic category. Two problems emerge when speaking of a specifically American urban gothic. The first is that 'American' implies national unity, but different cities, with different histories, provoke distinct anxieties. Baron Ludwig von Reizenstein's *Die Geheimnisse von New Orleans* (1853) is different from Buntline's *Mysteries and Miseries of New York* not only because of the authors' own idiosyncrasies, nor only because one is written in German and the other in English, but also because New Orleans differs significantly from New York. Subsuming these works under a single rubric risks effacing their differences. The other problem, which in some ways contradicts the first, is that urbanization was a global process, and responses to urbanization were likewise global. The city-mysteries subgenre had an international vogue: originating in France with Eugène Sue's *Les Mystères de Paris* (1842–3), it crossed the Atlantic almost immediately. Harper & Brothers published Charles H. Town's translation of *Les Mystères de Paris* in 1843; city-mysteries set in American cities soon followed. The American city-mysteries are all derivative of *Les Mystères de Paris*, some of them extravagantly so. George Thompson's *City Crimes* (1849), for instance, follows the adventures of a wealthy New Yorker who ventures in disguise into the 'squalid abodes of the poor' of New York to offer 'relief [to] deserving poverty' (Thompson 2002: 107). *Les Mystères de Paris* follows the adventures of a German prince who ventures in disguise into the slums of Paris to 'find there some unfortunate beings he might drag from the filth' (Sue 1843: 61). Just how far the gothic representations of American cities differ from those of cities in other national literatures has yet to be mapped. In short, the adjective 'American' risks oversimplifying a complicated discursive field that operates locally, regionally, nationally and internationally.

The adjective 'urban' similarly demands scrutiny. Cities are mutable, their boundaries fluid: the New York City of 1897 was a different city from that of 1898, when Manhattan was amalgamated with Harlem, Queen's, the Bronx and Staten Island into greater New York. And where does the city stop? That it is distinct from the country is a nineteenth-century commonplace. In Hawthorne's 'My Kinsman, Major Molineux' (1832), for instance, the protagonist Robin travels from the country to a 'little metropolis of a New England colony' (Hawthorne 1962–94a: 11:210) – and thereby permanently severs himself from his country home. The story is a fable of modernity, a meditation on the urbanizing young man from the provinces. But the story's country-city opposition simplifies a more complicated historical reality of interdependence. As William Cronon has argued, 'Americans [tend] to see city and country as separate places . . . Although we often cross the symbolic boundaries between them – seeking escape or excitement, recreation or renewal – we rarely reflect on how tightly bound together they really are' (Cronon 1992: xvi). This partitioning is not trivial. Associated with the city-country opposition are competing ethico-political positions: in one version, the country is the source of virtue and the city is corrupt; in another, the city is a civilizing place and the country is primitive and stultifying. Such ethico-political positions inform all urban representation informed by the country-city binary.

Troubling above all is the noun 'gothic', particularly in relation to cities. The English works that are routinely cited as inaugurating the gothic novel – Horace Walpole's *The Castle of Otranto* (1764) and Ann Radcliffe's *The Mysteries of Udolpho* (1794) – have scant interest in the city. Although there was a lively eighteenth-century urban literature in Britain, *The Castle of Otranto* shies away entirely from urban scenes. In *The Mysteries of Udolpho*, cities play a larger role, but the novel centres on the castle of Udolpho and begins and ends in 'pastoral landscapes'

(Radcliffe 1794: 1). Gothic fiction with a serious interest in the city would appear, then, to be a belated supplement to a genre that initially shied away from it. Hence Robert Mighall is one of many critics to identify Charles Dickens's *Oliver Twist* (1837–9) and G. W. M. Reynolds's Sue-inspired *The Mysteries of London* (1844–8) as key texts in the emergence of the urban gothic novel in Britain – more than seventy years after the emergence of the gothic novel itself. The serial publication of Brown's *Arthur Mervyn* beginning in 1798 closes the gap significantly (though its American provenance and themes and its traditionally secondary stature in Brown's oeuvre alongside *Wieland* and *Edgar Huntly* have led to its marginalization in histories of the gothic novel). Even so, the claim that gothic originated elsewhere and needed to be relocated to the city; the claim too that this relocation 'involved the city itself, or at least part of it, being Gothicized' (31), as Mighall puts it: these are by and large true.

But just as Anne Williams's *The Art of Darkness* has detected 'a kind of quasi-"Gothic" tradition' (Williams 1995: 13) operative long before the publication of *Castle of Otranto*, so too can one discern an urban gothic tradition that extends at least as far back as the early eighteenth century. Works like Daniel Defoe's *A Journal of the Plague Year* (1722) or *Moll Flanders* (1722), with their focus on crime, disease and other perils of the city, pose the same challenge to Enlightenment self-congratulation that the gothic has traditionally been understood to do. John Gay's *Trivia: or, The Art of Walking the Streets of London* (1716) strikes various gothic notes, as when 'a fraudful nymph' seduces a 'yeoman' from Devon: a proto-Lucy Westenra, 'She leads the willing Victim to his Doom, / Through winding Alleys to her Cobweb Room' (Gay 1716: 45). By casting the urban gothic in terms of a discursive field rather than genre, and by appealing to eighteenth-century works that cast the city as dirty, crime-ridden, and physically and morally insalubrious, one can divine another branch of the gothic family tree.

It is a branch that challenges a critical tendency to link the gothic primarily to psychoanalysis. Williams has characterized Freud as the 'true heir of Walpole and Radcliffe' (Williams 1995: 240), and Maggie Kilgour has characterized 'psychoanalysis [as] a late gothic story' (Kilgour 1995: 221). Such an understanding of gothic will inevitably emphasize gothic novels in which familial themes predominate. And while urban gothic frequently shares this interest in family crisis, its primary setting is not the home but the street. This difference is significant, since the family romance can more readily be abstracted away from other social forces when contained behind the doors of the middle-class home. But this abstraction has its limits even in the private sphere. Peter Stallybrass and

Allon White's *The Politics and Poetics of Transgression* astutely registers how social forces intrude into dramas of the bourgeois psyche. Its critique of Freud's Rat Man case argues that the male patient's dream of a rat that bores its way into his anus 'is in need of social as well as psychic explanation. . . . [One] cannot analyze the psychic domain without examining the processes of transcoding between the body, topography, and the social formation' (Stallybrass and White 1986: 144). The Rat Man, the authors assert, '"speaks" his body through the topography of the city . . . "Rats", "sewage", "filth" are not transparent signifiers which lead directly back to some primal moment. [They] speak the unconscious . . . only through the mediation of the slum' (145). What is true of the Rat Man is likewise true of the urban gothic: Marx is as important to an understanding of its poetics as Freud.

And just as the notion of a discursive field of urban gothic challenges histories and theorizations of gothic generally, so too does it complicate notions of American gothic specifically. It challenges conventional geographies, for instance. Williams remarks that 'two regions of the United States have seemed to have a particular affinity for Gothic: New England and the South' (Williams 1995: 265n13), where, presumably, 'New England' and 'the South' are metonyms for Nathaniel Hawthorne in the first instance, and for Poe, Faulkner, Morrison and O'Connor in the second. By contrast, early American urban gothic novels cluster around Boston, New York, and Philadelphia – the major American cities of the early nineteenth century. Moreover, the genre is moveable. The vogue in the 1840s for a city-mysteries novel of one's own meant that the genre was geographically dispersed across the States, and entailed the possibility for further dispersal: if Boston merited an urban gothic, why not San Francisco? The urban gothic emphasizes the crucial link between specific strains of American gothic and specific regional histories and contexts, and expands the genre's geographies.

In other respects, however, American urban gothic is similar to the mainstream of American gothic. In the past decades a critical consensus has emerged that racial discourses are peculiarly important to American gothic. At the heart of the American gothic, Morrison sees 'American Africanism' – in her words, 'a fabricated brew of darkness, otherness, alarm, and desire' (Morrison 1993: 38). '[The] American gothic', Teresa Goddu asserts, 'is haunted by race' (Goddu 1997: 7). What is true of American gothic in general is also true of American urban gothic. I take an episode in Thompson's *City Crimes* to be highly suggestive of urban gothic's particular appropriation of signifiers of blackness. In the novel, an esteemed reverend becomes addicted to drink, and follows the conventional downward path of the nineteenth-century literary drunkard.

At his nadir, he begs for rum by delivering mock sermons in a 'low groggery' (Thompson 2002: 281) adjoining the Catherine Street Market in New York. The topographic specificity is important: Thompson notes that,

> every Sunday, [this market] was the theatre of a lively and amusing scene, wherein was performed the renowned pastime of 'niggers dancing for eels.' All the unsavory fish that had been accumulated during the week, was disposed of, being given to such darkies as won the most applause in the science of 'heel and toe.' (Thompson 2002: 282)

The toxic language distracts, but the reference to dancing for eels is significant: as W. T. Lhamon has noted, the African-American dance competition at Catherine Street Market is the likely source for Thomas Dartmouth Rice's performance style as Jim Crow.[1] The novel likens sermonizing for rum to dancing for eels, implying that the reverend, in his decline, has become symbolically black. Blackness is accordingly a marker of urban abjection.

III.

Within this complicated field of American urban gothic, certain figures recur obsessively. Surprisingly, perhaps, it is rare to find that staple of gothic literature, the ghost. There is one, of sorts, in Henry James's 'The Jolly Corner' (1908). But in James's story the ghost haunts a mansion that has escaped the 'awful modern crush' (James 2006: 466) of New York. The owner of the mansion, Spencer Brydon, has lived abroad for thirty years and has neither sold nor renovated it. It remains stubbornly the same in a city of constant change. As such, it can be the habitation of ghosts. Washington Irving's remark that 'tales of ghosts and apparitions ... thrive best in ... sheltered long-settled retreats ... but are trampled underfoot by the shifting throng' (Irving 1983: 1078) suggests that the mutability of the city is hostile to the ghost story. Urban gothic more typically focuses on different figures of Otherness, two in particular: the violent criminal and the confidence artist.

The principal antagonist in urban gothic is typically a single, male figure that embodies crime and is characteristically identified with the devil. Poe's 'The Man of the Crowd' (1840) is a case in point. The story's narrator detects a man in the London crowds who bewilders and fascinates him. He asserts that 'my first thought, upon beholding [the man's countenance], was that [Moritz] Retzch, had he viewed it, would have greatly preferred it to his own pictural [*sic*] incarnations of the fiend' (Poe 1984a: 392). But after pursuing this 'fiend' across London, the narrator declares that 'I shall learn no more of him, nor his deeds' and claims, seemingly without cause, that this *'man of the crowd'* is 'the type and genius of deep crime' (1984a: 396, Poe's emphasis). Such types and geniuses figure repeatedly in urban gothic: the Ourang-Outang that kills the L'Espanayes in 'The Murders in the Rue Morgue' (1841) and the leader of the crowd that torments Major Molineux are well-known examples, but others abound. In Lippard's *The Quaker City* (1846), the monstrous Devil-Bug presides over Monk Hall; in Thompson's *City Crimes*, the terrifying Dead Man rules over the Dark Vaults; in Charles E. Averill's *The Cholera-Fiend* (1850), the hunchback Broken Back spreads cholera through New York; in Ignatius Donnelly's *Caesar's Column* (1890), the giant Caesar Lomellini commands a 'dreaded [working-class] Brotherhood' (Donnelly 1890: 172) that destroys New York in revolution. Typically these men are working class; characteristically they are physical grotesques; often they are racially ambiguous. As Sari Altschuler and Aaron M. Tobiason have observed, while Lippard's novel declines to identify Devil-Bug by race, the playbill of his own 1844 stage adaptation of *The Quaker City* describes Devil-Bug as 'a Negro, deeply dyed in crime' (Altschuler and Tobiason 2014: 272). Donnelly describes Caesar as 'quite dark, almost negroid' (Donnelly 1890: 172), but elsewhere emphasizes that he is 'a man of Italian descent' (Donnelly 1890: 145). These figures, whatever else they symbolize, are racialized and classed personifications of urban violence.

While men such as Devil-Bug and Broken Back embody Crime as physical violence, another figure, the confidence artist, embodies a subtler, more generalized and more insidious threat. George W. Matsell's *Vocabulum; or, The Rogue's Lexicon* (1859) defines the 'confidence man' as someone who 'by means of extraordinary powers of persuasion gains the confidence of his victims to the extent of drawing upon their treasury, almost to an unlimited extent' (Matsell 1859: 20). The confidence artist is polymorphous. Reynolds describes a range of stock characters like 'the church-going capitalist, the reverend rake, [and] the pious seducer' (Reynolds 1988: 87), and other types, of all class positions, abound. Women, too, can be confidence artists. The most perfervid and misogynistic version is not the prostitute, about whom urban gothic is ambivalent, but rather the adulteress, a voluptuary of insatiable sexual appetites who maintains a veneer of middle-class decorum before the scandal she poses to domestic ideology reveals itself. What all confidence artists have in common is the profoundly threatening fraudulence of their public identities. But urban gothic rarely deploys a single figure who personifies this threat. Rather, confidence artists appear in a diverse array of identities. This diversity testifies to the paranoia of urban gothic, to the fearful prospect that no one in the city is to be trusted, that criminality is decentred and ubiquitous.

IV.

Confidence artists and urban devils, then, are key figures in urban gothic, and in them the novels embody anxieties about the city. But the anxieties exceed these figures, and vice versa. And while these anxieties are in one sense particular to the period, it is nonetheless remarkable how persistent they are: *mutatis mutandis*, fears of epidemic disease and riot underlie the contemporary zombie narrative. Antebellum anxieties play out in two registers: physical (plague; riot) and psychic (urban illegibility; ontological dissolution), and frequently crystallize around the slum, urban gothic's supplement to conventional gothic sites like cemeteries and mansions. Urban gothic focuses obsessively on the slum. Working-class poverty in the industrial city, one infers, ranks among the deepest anxieties relating to urbanization. A crucial aspect of the slum is how readily abstracted it is from any specific modern city. Literary representations of American slums – Southwark in Philadelphia, the North End in Boston, and above all the notorious Five Points in New York – correspond closely to one another, and also, often self-consciously, to representations of slums elsewhere. The slum is a transnational space, in that the anxieties it dramatizes are largely the same across American and Europe.

Accordingly, Stallybrass and White's assertion about slums in Britain and Europe is also largely true of those in America: in slums, they argue, 'the bourgeois spectator surveyed and classified *his own antithesis*' (Stallybrass and White 1986: 128; their emphasis). Stallybrass and White argue that the middle classes map and transcode the hierarchy of the bourgeois body onto the city: spaces like courts and mansions correspond with the bourgeois head – reason, spirit – while spaces like the slum and the sewer correspond with what Stallybrass and White, following Bakhtin, call the 'lower bodily stratum' – the anus, the genitals. The slum portraiture in *City Crimes* is a case in point. The novel's Five Points perch above cavernous 'Dark Vaults'. Three tableaus delineate the Vaults' 'appalling horrors': a man, 'nearly naked [and] seated upon a heap of excrement and filthy straw' (Thompson 2002: 132); an Irish wake, in which 'half-crazed, drunken, naked wretches [are] fighting with the ferocity of tigers . . . in the fury of which, the table on which [lies] the body [is] overturned, and the corpse [is] crushed beneath the feet of the combatants' (Thompson 2002: 132–3); and a 'cave . . . crammed with [men] and women, boys and girls, young children, negroes, and *hogs*' (Thompson 2002: 132; Thompson's emphasis). The Vaults are at once slum, tomb, hell, bowels and sewer.

As the stigmatizing references to the Irish and to 'negroes' suggest, American representations of the slum differ from transatlantic equivalents chiefly in the particular racial anxieties that they mobilize. The anti-Irish sentiment of Thompson's novel stems from the influx to America in the 1840s of people fleeing the Irish Famine, which markedly altered the demographic status quo of the States. The anti-black racism in these scenes derives from white fears, intensifying in the 1830s and 1840s, of 'amalgamation' or racial mixing. The narrator makes these fears explicit in describing the third tableau: 'horrible to relate! negroes were lying with young white girls, and several, unmindful of the presence of others, were perpetrating the most dreadful enormities' (Thompson 2002: 133). In keeping with the racial ambiguity of the figures personifying crime, the slum blurs racial boundaries.

That the Dead Man presides over the Dark Vaults implies something further about the symbolic force of urban devils. A personification of crime, they also personify the slum itself – conjoining, in other words, criminality and poverty. Significantly, the Dead Man lives in the Dark Vaults but frequently leaves it, often through underground passages that take him directly into middle-class urban space. The most alarming devil of the slum is therefore the one that leaves it. The Devil-Bugs and Dead Men of urban gothic threaten to infiltrate middle-class space, public and private alike, and even to overturn the state altogether. Donnelly's *Caesar's Column* describes its climactic revolution in language that emphasizes the failure of containment:

> like a huge flood, long dammed up, turbulent, turbid, muddy, loaded with wrecks and debris, the gigantic mass broke loose . . . and flowed in every direction. A foul and brutal and ravenous multitude it was, dark with dust and sweat, armed with the weapons of civilization, but possessing only the instincts of wild beasts. (Donnelly 1890: 299)

The revolution soon degenerates into chaos, but not before the mob has destroyed New York: the protagonists flee the American scene altogether.

Just as urban gothic frequently stages eruptions of violence from the slums, so too does it dwell on threats to bourgeois hygiene and the sanitary city. A major vein of urban gothic focuses on outbreaks of infectious disease. Brown's *Arthur Mervyn*, the first major American novel to articulate an urban gothic sensibility, takes place during the yellow fever epidemic that scourged Philadelphia in 1793. Hawthorne's 'Lady Eleanore's Mantle' (1837) focuses on the 1721 outbreak of smallpox in colonial Boston. Averill's *The Cholera-Fiend* focuses on a cholera epidemic in 1849 New York. Tellingly, neither *Arthur Mervyn* nor 'Lady Eleanore's Mantle' – the two earlier works – is focused on the slum, which suggests that the slum is in some respects comforting to the middle classes, a repository, albeit a fragile one, for the ills that would otherwise threaten the larger city.

Plague and riot are at root physical threats; more disturbing are the psychic stresses engendered by the city. The fear that the city is a mystery without solution appears often in urban gothic. At the conclusion of Poe's 'The Man of the Crowd', the narrator consoles himself for failing to understand the urban wanderer by remarking that 'The worst heart of the world is a grosser book than the "Hortulus Animae", and perhaps it is but one of the great mercies of God that *"er lasst sich nicht lessen"* [it does not permit itself to be read]' (Poe 1984a: 396). Figures with special urban literacy appear routinely in urban gothic, often acting as guides to the city. Their epitome is Poe's detective Auguste Dupin, who claims that 'most men, in respect to himself, [wear] windows in their bosoms' (Poe 1984b: 401). Dupin 'sees through' these men by observing how their bodies traverse the streets of Paris and thereby divining their thoughts. An urban semiologist, he detects a stable relationship between signs and meaning in the city, revealing a consoling order in the seeming chaos. The most anxious works of urban gothic, however, are the least confident of that ability, expressing pessimism about urban legibility more in keeping with 'The Man of the Crowd' than with 'The Murders in the Rue Morgue'.

But fears of ontological dissolution are arguably the most vivid. Child's *Letters from New York* (1843) generally expresses what Robert Alter has called a 'pastoral' view of the city (Alter 2010: 105), but it has moments where the tone shifts dramatically, as when Child expresses fears for her psychic integrity. 'There is something impressive, even to painfulness', she writes,

> in this dense crowding of human existence. . . . It has sometimes forced upon me, for a few moments, an appalling night-mare sensation of vanishing identity; as if I were but an unknown, unnoticed, and unseparated drop in the great ocean of human existence; as if the uncomfortable old theory were true, and we were but portions of a Great Mundane Soul, to which we ultimately return, to be swallowed up again in its infinity. (Child 1843: 57)

Child's nightmare is a recurring one in urban gothic. In *City Crimes*, the protagonist Frank Sydney is in his direst straits when imprisoned with the grotesquely malformed and cannibalistic son of the Dead Man. In a delirium Frank imagines the monstrous child's metamorphoses: first into 'a huge vulture', then into 'a gigantic reptile', then into 'the Evil One, come to bear him to perdition', and finally 'the Image and spirit of the Dead Man, appointed to torture and to drive him mad' (Thompson 2002: 249). This vision of protean monstrosity testifies to Frank's own psychic instability, aggravated by his infiltration of the slums and his contests with its presiding spirit.

V.

The frontispiece (Figure 5.1) to James Dabney McCabe's *The Secrets of the Great City*, an 1868 work of urban reportage, offers an exemplary distillation of urban gothic preoccupations. Five numbered images snake across the page to tell a Hogarthian cautionary tale about 'The Fate of Hundreds of Young Men' travelling from the country or small town to the city. Various codes inform the representative young man's path towards death. He travels downwards in class terms, from the domestic, tacitly middle-class space of the first image to the working-class space of the harbour in the fourth and fifth images. In so doing he travels from a predominantly feminine environment to an exclusively masculine one. Above all he travels from a realm of visual clarity into ones of increasing obscurity (thus even as the title promises to expose the secrets of the city, those secrets remain shrouded in darkness). Fears of confidence artists, violent crime, and psychic and physical dissolution all haunt the narrative.

The page's first two images allegorize the country-city binary with contrasting versions of womanhood. In the first image, two modestly dressed women seem to plead with the young man to remain in their domestic space. In the second, four fashionable women, alluring in their décolletage and bedecked in jewellery, welcome him to the city. The collusion of the young man in his own fall is plain in these introductory images: in the first, he obdurately leans back, as though recoiling; in the second, he leans forward with an avid smile. Together, the images signal his aversion to the tranquil domestic scene and his susceptibility to the city's blandishments. The city's supposed threat to the psyche is operative in this second image, since urban temptation figures here not only as feminine sexiness but also as liquor. The text glossing the image asserts that the setting is a 'fashionable saloon'; one of the women is bringing a glass and bottle to replace empty ones on the table before him. The juxtaposition of the women in the first two images echoes

Figure 5.1: Van Ingen and Snyder, Frontispiece, The Secrets of the Great City, 1868, Print, New-York Historical Society. Photography © New-York Historical Society.

Figure 5.2: N. Currier, Grand, National, Temperance Banner, 1851, Lithograph. Library of Congress Prints and Photographs Division.

temperance movement imagery that distinguished between the chaste domestic woman and the alcohol-temptress (for an example of such temperance imagery, see Figure 5.2). The liquor-bearing 'waiter girls' of the frontispiece are metonyms for the tempting, inebriating city itself. The self-dissolution that haunts the urban gothic appears in the frontispiece's narrative as the self-forgetting engendered by alcohol.

Having ushered the young man into the urban trap, women become supererogatory to his downward progress. In the remaining three images, he is in a homosocial world of men; the third and fourth images mark the urban gothic's preoccupation with confidence artists and violent criminals. The expulsion of women from the narrative is already underway in the second image. Across the table from the greenhorn sits a fashionably dressed, moustachioed man: the alluring women frame both men, making their relationship the crucial one in the panel. The text at the bottom of the page glossing this image characterizes the scene as 'the road to ruin'. In this metaphor the second man may be a figure for ruin itself.

Dominating the page, the third image focuses on the greenhorn's entanglement in the gamblers' confidence game – a trap in which the image also ensnares the careless reader. The scene is one of seeming good cheer: a glance at the page would suggest that the secrets of the great city involve nothing more threatening than masculine conviviality. But superimposed on the lower left-hand side of the medallion is a smaller image, veiled in shadows, that reveals the murderous intent that lurks between the gamblers' fraternizing veneer. The seeming conviviality of the third image dissolves on inspection: of the four men in this central medallion, only one holds a drink aloft – the doomed greenhorn. One of his companions is pointing to a full glass as though to enjoin him to finish the one in his hand; the bartender is preparing a further drink. The image gives the information necessary to alienate the viewer from the young man, to reveal him as the gamblers' gull.

Where the third image depicts a confidence game, the fourth and climactic image depicts violent crime, as the greenhorn, now gagged, is overwhelmed by men wearing masks. The text tells us what the formal similarity of this image to the preceding one implies: his assailants are his '"fancy" companions'. Two shifts accompany this transition from confidence game to violence. The scene is the first in the sequence to occur outdoors: until now the young man has been in interiors. It is also the first to be unambiguous in its class codes: the masts and rigging in the background and the tilting bollard in the foreground tell us plainly that the assault occurs along the waterfront, which, in nineteenth-century New York, was working-class space. Hence a conjunction of masculinity, working-class space, and violence animates this image: the assailants are figures in the vein of Lippard's Devil-Bug and Thompson's Dead Man.

The page's final image completes the graphic narrative and reveals the fate of the representative young man: he has been reduced to a sodden and disfigured corpse, the guileless face of the first three images transformed into a gaping death's head. The violation of his body begun in the fourth image is poised to continue: in the prow of the police boat, a figure in silhouette holds a hooked pole that threatens to pierce his corpse. The equation of the river and death in urban gothic is conventional. It is, in part, a function of early urban water management, which discharged waste into the rivers. In effect, the young man has become water-borne refuse – in a word, sewage.

The reportage that follows pretends to offer a prophylaxis against the dangers advertised in the frontispiece. 'This volume', McCabe writes,

> is designed to warn the thousands who visit the city against the dangers and pitfalls into which their curiosity or vice may lead them, and it is hoped that those who read the book will heed its warnings. The city is full of danger. The path of safety which is pointed out in these pages is the only one – a total avoidance of the vicinity of sin. No matter how clever a man may be in his own town or city, he is a child in the hands of the sharpers and villains of this community, and his only safety lies in avoiding them. His curiosity can be satisfied in these pages, and he can know the Great City from them, without incurring the danger attending an effort to see it. (McCabe 15–16)

It is fair to doubt the seriousness of this design. Commenting on *Les Mystères de Paris*, Poe mocked the 'cant . . . about the amelioration of society', claiming instead that Sue's 'first, and . . . sole object, is to make an exciting and . . . saleable book' (Poe 1984c: 1404). Poe's remark anticipates a longstanding critical practice of situating works of urban gothic between the poles of social amelioration (of whatever political stripe) and sensation. But no matter the expressed political project of the work, no matter how sensational its treatment of the city, the urban gothic is at root an attempt to grapple with the precipitous transformations and novel dispensations of urban modernity.

This was no easy task. Edward K. Spann prefaces his 1981 study *The New Metropolis: New York City, 1840–57* by registering conflicting attitudes towards the rapidly growing city. On the one hand, the city was 'a magnificent expression of human intelligence and enterprise at work in an age of progress' (Spann 1981: x). On the other, 'it was a disturbing example of human failure' that was 'confronted by . . . such troubles as social disorder, ethno-religious discord, mass poverty, and physical squalor' (Spann 1981: x). A sense that the nineteenth-century American city was two cities at once finds such frequent expression in urban literature that it amounts to a cliché. Hence Child opens her *Letters from New York* by mocking the 'vituperative alliterations, such as magnificence and mud, finery and filth, diamonds and dirt, bullion and brass-tap, &c. &c.' (Child 1843: 1), which so frequently structure accounts of the city. But the sense that two cities jostled in one was sincere. Spann optimistically states that 'New York must be accounted far more a success than a failure as a human society' (Spann 1981: x). The writers of urban gothic were incapable of mustering this confidence. To them, the jury was out: the profoundest mystery of the city was how it could be both magnificent expression and disturbing example all at once.

Notes

Sincere thanks to Zaren Healey White for research assistance and to Jennifer Lokash for valuable insights into eighteenth-century gothic.

1. See Lhamon's discussion (1–55) of the links between minstrelsy and the Catherine Street Market.

References

Alter, Robert (2010), *Imagined Cities: Urban Experience and the Language of the Novel*, New Haven: Yale University Press.
Altschuler, Sari and Aaron M. Tobiason (2014), 'Playbill for George Lippard's *The Quaker City*', PMLA 129.2 (March): 267–70.
Averill, Charles E. (1850), *The Cholera-Fiend; or The Plague Spreaders of New York. A Mysterious Tale of the Pestilence in 1849* in *Wright American Fiction, 1776–1850*, Boston: George H. Williams.
Bell, Michael Davitt (1995), 'Conditions of Literary Vocation', in Sacvan Bercovitch (gen. ed.), *The Cambridge History of American Literature, Vol. Two: Prose Writing, 1820–1865*, Cambridge: Cambridge University Press, 9–123.
Berman, Marshall (1988), *All That Is Solid Melts Into Air: The Experience of Modernity*, New York: Penguin.
Buntline, Ned (1849), *The Mysteries and Miseries of New York: A Story of Real Life*, Google Books, web, 1 May 2014.
Child, Lydia Maria (1843), *Letters from New York*, Google Books, web, 11 May 2014.
Cronon, William (1992), *Nature's Metropolis: Chicago and the Great West*, New York: Norton.
Donnelly, Ignatius (1890), *Caesar's Column. A Story of the Twentieth Century*, Google Books, web, 13 May 2014.
Gay, John (1716), *Trivia: or The Art of Walking the Streets of London*, Eighteenth Century Collections Online, web, 11 May 2014.
Goddu, Teresa (1997), *Gothic America: Narrative, Nation, History*, New York: Columbia University Press.
The Grand, National, Temperance Banner: Dedicated to Every Son & Daughter of Temperance, throughout the Union (1851), New York: N. Currier, *Library of Congress Prints and Photographs Division*, web, 31 October 2014.
Hawthorne, Nathaniel [1832] (1962–94a), 'My Kinsman, Major Molineux', in Hawthorne, *Centenary Edition*, 11: 208–31.
Hawthorne, Nathaniel [1852] (1962–94b), *The Blithedale Romance*, in

Nathaniel Hawthorne, *The Centenary Edition of the Works of Nathaniel Hawthorne*, ed. William Charvat, Roy Harvey Pearce, and Claude M. Simpson, Columbus: Ohio State University Press, 3:1–298.

Howe, Daniel Walker (2007), *What Hath God Wrought: The Transformation of America, 1815–1848*, Oxford: Oxford University Press.

Irving, Washington [1819–20] (1983), 'The Legend of Sleepy Hollow', in Washington Irving, *History, Tales and Sketches*, New York: Library of America, 1058–88.

James, Henry [1908] (2006), 'The Jolly Corner', in *The New York Stories of Henry James*, New York: New York Review of Books, 463–500.

Kilgour, Maggie (1995), *The Rise of the Gothic Novel*, New York: Routledge.

Lhamon, Walter T. (2000), *Raising Cain: Blackface Performance from Jim Crow to Hip Hop*, Cambridge, MA: Harvard University Press.

Lippard, George [1846] (1995), *The Quaker City; or, The Monks of Monk Hall. A Romance of Philadelphia Life, Mystery, and Crime*, Amherst: University of Massachusetts Press.

Matsell, George Washington (1859), *Vocabulum; or, The Rogue's Lexicon*, Google Books, web, 28 October 2014.

McCabe, James Dabney (1868), *The Secrets of the Great City: A Work Descriptive of the Virtues and the Vices, the Mysteries, Miseries and Crimes of New York City*, Google Books, web, 4 May 2014.

Mighall, Robert (1999), *A Geography of Victorian Gothic Fiction: Mapping History's Nightmares*, New York: Oxford University Press.

Morrison, Toni (1993), *Playing in the Dark: Whiteness and the Literary Imagination*, New York: Vintage.

Poe, Edgar Allan [1840] (1984a), 'The Man of the Crowd', in Edgar Allan Poe, *Poetry, Tales, and Selected Essays*, New York: Library of America, 388–96.

Poe, Edgar Allan [1841] (1984b), 'The Murders in the Rue Morgue', in Edgar Allan Poe, *Poetry, Tales, and Selected Essays*, New York: Library of America, 397–431.

Poe, Edgar Allan [1846] (1984c), 'Marginalia – November 1846', in Edgar Allan Poe, *Essays and Reviews*, New York: Library of America, 1404–12.

Radcliffe, Ann (1794), *The Mysteries of Udolpho, A Romance; Interspersed with some Works of Poetry*, Eighteenth-Century Collections Online, web, 30 April 2014.

Reynolds, David S. (1988), *Beneath the American Renaissance: The Subversive Imagination in the Age of Emerson and Melville*, New York: Knopf.

Spann, Edward K. (1981), *The New Metropolis: New York City, 1840–1857*, New York: Columbia University Press.

Stallybrass, Peter and Allon White (1986), *The Politics and Poetics of Transgression*, Ithaca, NY: Cornell University Press.

Sue, Eugène (1843), *The Mysteries of Paris*, trans. Charles H. Town, Esq., Google Books, web, 15 May 2014.

Thompson, George [1849] (2002), *City Crimes*, in George Thompson, *Venus in Boston and Other Tales of Nineteenth-Century City Life*, ed. David S. Reynolds and Kimberly R. Gladman, Amherst: University of Massachusetts Press, 105–310.

Williams, Anne (1995), *Art of Darkness: A Poetics of Gothic*, Chicago: University of Chicago Press.

Chapter 6

Joyce Carol Oates Revisits the Schoolhouse Gothic

Sherry R. Truffin

The history of the gothic as a counter-Enlightenment discourse, albeit an ambivalent one, suggests the suitability, if not the inevitability, of the gothic portrayal of education and educators. Previously, I have designated representations of teachers, students and academic institutions that rely on gothic tropes such as the monster, the curse and the trap as 'Schoolhouse Gothic' (Truffin 2008). This genre includes imaginative works as diverse as Edgar Allan Poe's 'William Wilson' (1839); Flannery O'Connor's *The Violent Bear It Away* (1960); Stephen King's *Carrie* (1974), *The Shining* (1977), *Rage* (1977) and 'Suffer the Little Children' (1972); Toni Morrison's *Beloved* (1987), David Mamet's *Oleanna* (1992), and Donna Tartt's *The Secret History* (1992). It also includes non-fiction representations of schools and schooling by figures such as Michel Foucault, Louis Althusser, Henry Giroux and others. Works in this mode examine schooling in relationship to such central gothic preoccupations as the tyranny of history, the terrors of physical or mental confinement, reification, and miscreation. Considered together, they suggest that schools are haunted or cursed by persistent power inequities (of race, gender, class) and, ironically, by the Enlightenment itself, which was to rescue Western civilization from the darkness of the past but which had a dark side of its own, born of its compulsion to dissect, define and dominate nature and humanity alike.

No stranger to the gothic, Joyce Carol Oates has returned more than once to the school as a source and scene of horror in novels like *Zombie* (1995) and *Beasts* (2002), which use zombification and consumption as metaphors for the effects of formal education (Truffin 2013b). *The Accursed*, published in 2013 but conceived and partially drafted in the 1980s (shortly after Oates began teaching at Princeton),[1] both exemplifies and diverges from the Schoolhouse Gothic. Like other works in this mode, *The Accursed* portrays the university as a place of mystified power, physical isolation, social stress and emotional disintegration.

Unlike these works, however, school does not leave its primary student-figure, Josiah Slade, permanently damaged, vengeful and monstrous. Josiah's most significant literary ancestor is fellow Ivy League student Quentin Compson of William Faulkner's *The Sound the Fury* (1929) and *Absalom, Absalom* (1936), and neither character experiences physical or psychological abuse at the hands of his professors, nor victimizes others in retaliation. Both are compared, implicitly or explicitly, to the most famous of literary students, Hamlet,[2] and appear more melancholy and ineffectual than monstrous. Comparing the two brings into focus the political and economic implications of the Schoolhouse Gothic, an oblique feature of *Beasts* (Truffin 2008) but more prevalent in such works as Poe's 'William Wilson' and Tartt's *The Secret History*, which portray the democratizing promise of American schooling as a grimly parodic threat (Truffin 2013a). In comparison, *The Sound and The Fury* and *The Accursed* say less about democracy than about capitalism. Harvard represents for Quentin Compson an accursed future of loss and failure that must be avoided, a capitalistic nightmare inferior to the elegant, mythic Southern feudalism he has been raised to mourn, while Princeton represents for Josiah Slade an accursed capitalist past that can be replaced with a more promising socialist future. Quentin's breakdown is permanent and irrevocable, while Josiah's makes possible the development of a new, more ethical consciousness, one in which Enlightenment values such as intellectual curiosity, unsentimental objectivity and faith in human reason are recuperated and redirected, but only after being severed from their customary but accursed educational, political, religious and economic entanglements.

Gothic U

The Accursed is a sprawling, summary-resistant tale of the so-called 'Crosswicks Curse' that plagued Princeton, New Jersey and the Ivy League university for which it is known from 1905–6. The Curse itself is named for the Crosswicks Manse, home of the fictional Slades, a privileged Princeton family whose fateful year the novel documents. Oates's narrative features a large cast of characters and weaves together the fictional and the historical, the realistic and the fantastic. Its fictitious author, M. W. Van Dyck II, eventually revealed to be the son of a Princeton philosophy professor who died trying to murder him when he was an infant, is pedantic, prudish, anxious about his authority as a historian and prone to interrupting the story to comment on the shortcomings of previous chroniclers, brag about obtaining and deciphering a wide array of often bizarre primary sources, bemoan the challenges of writing the history of such a singular event and offer his personal opinions about various figures and topics in the narrative. The tale he constructs illustrates what could be called the central gothic formula: 'a fearful sense of inheritance in time [a curse]' combined 'with a claustrophobic sense of enclosure in space [a trap], these two dimensions reinforcing one another to produce an impression of sickening descent into disintegration' (Baldick 1992: xix). While curses in the gothic can be metaphorical in nature, Oates's titular curse appears to be literal, complete with ghosts, demons, vampires and hellish alternate dimensions that may be manifestations of supernatural intervention, psychosexual repression, mass hysteria or some combination of the three. As is typical in the Schoolhouse Gothic, the trap is the claustrophobic campus, here inseparable from the equally claustrophobic town after which it is named.

Josiah Slade is the grandson of prominent and beloved minister, former New Jersey governor, and Princeton University president Winslow Slade, and heir to the Slade fortune, which came from 'railroads, real estate, manufacturing, and banking', and, further in the past, from 'the slave trade' (61). When the curse begins, Josiah has already graduated from Princeton, abandoned his studies at West Point out of restlessness and boredom and occupied himself with unknown pursuits out west before returning home with a vague notion that he might study German idealist philosophy at Heidelberg or pursue a career in law, medicine or journalism. The curse first strikes publicly at his sister's ill-fated wedding and appears to have arisen from a decades-old crime committed by his grandfather when *he* was a student.[3] During the time of the curse, Josiah inadvertently kills his favourite professor while trying to prevent him from murdering his own infant son (the author), injures one of his literary heroes, suffers a mental breakdown caused in large part by his failure to protect his sister or defend the family honour from invisible enemies, embarks on an ill-advised polar expedition to escape voices telling him to cleanse Princeton in an apocalyptic fire and takes a suicidal plunge into the icy water to rescue his phantom sister from a demonic seducer. After the curse, he repudiates his family privilege, joining (along with his sister) an agrarian socialist commune sixty miles away from Princeton and marrying an artistically inclined childhood friend known in their home town as a scandalously independent woman.

Despite their very different fates, Oates's Josiah Slade and Faulkner's Quentin Compson share a series of instructive commonalities. Both come from prominent, 'aristocratic' families (one southern, one northeastern)[4] and grow up in the shadow of legendary but morally compromised grandfathers; both are willing to endure hellfire[5] to defend the honour of their sexually fallen sisters[6] but fail in their chivalric quests and experience psychological breakdowns as a result; both hear voices and drown themselves.[7] In addition, both are students at Ivy League universities in the first decade of the twentieth century and suffer from a profound sense of guilt over this privilege. In fact, school is truly 'accursed' for each.

These similarities are unlikely to be accidental, given Oates's well-documented fascination and engagement with William Faulkner. She has described herself as being 'bowled over by Faulkner' (Milazzo 1989: 5) and reported that as a high school student, she wrote 'a bloated trifurcated novel that had as its vague model *The Sound and The Fury*' (Johnson 2006: 78). In a 1982 interview,[8] she described Faulkner as 'the most significant writer' among her contemporaries (Johnson 2006: 119). Scholars have noted Faulkner's influence on Oates; for example, Anna Sonser's *A Passion for Consumption: The Gothic Novel in America*, describes *Bellefleur* (1980), one of Oates's most famous and successful novels, as 'an imitative recasting' of *Absalom, Absalom*, 'an ironic inversion that engages the metanarrative that tells the "story" of America, its mythology, omissions, and distortions' (Sonser 2001: 54). In addition to actively imitating and imaginatively revising Faulkner's works in her own writing, she has taught at least one of the novels: *The Sound and The Fury* (Milazzo 1989: 5).

Readers will not readily connect frightening schools, teachers and students with the writings of William Faulkner, who did not complete any formal education past the eleventh grade, though he attended classes at the University of Mississippi for three semesters before dropping out (Weinstein 2010: 87, 76). Instead, Faulkner's name calls to mind the decaying houses, farms and barns of Yoknapatawpha County, Mississippi and the haunted, luckless or depraved planters, servants and criminals who inhabit them. Indeed, biographer Philip Weinstein asserts that schools 'never play more than a negligible role' in Faulkner's works (2010: 46). Nevertheless, educators and schools that do appear in those works, both within and beyond Yoknapatawpha, are typically portrayed as cruel, corrupt or incarcerating. For example, before marrying Anse Bundren, Addie, the adulterous wife and distant mother of *As I Lay Dying* (1930), had been a schoolteacher whose only pleasure in the job was whipping the children in her care (Faulkner 1930: 169–70). Hapless schoolteacher Labove attempts to sexually assault young student Eula Varner, and Houston runs away from school and the woman who pushed him through it in *The Hamlet* (1940). A date to a school dance gone wrong becomes the occasion for horrific violence for university student Temple Drake, who then condemns an innocent man to a terrible death, in *Sanctuary*. But the most gothic of Faulkner's schools is neither in nor near Yoknapatawpha: it is Harvard University, where Quentin Compson narrates *Absalom, Absalom* and commits suicide in *The Sound and The Fury*.

While *The Accursed* presents a global, multifaceted view of 1905 Princeton University, *The Sound and the Fury* portrays 1910 Harvard University exclusively through Quentin's eyes and as partially responsible for Quentin's death. For Quentin, Harvard represents at once the 'dream' of his emotionally unavailable mother (Faulkner 1929: 113), the loss of the family land particularly cherished by his mentally stunted brother Benjy (110), the place that 'form[ed] [the] character' (70) of his sister Caddy's manipulative fiancé Herbert Head, a source of guilt and humiliation, and 'a fine dead sound' (110). Quentin's obsession with his sister's purity, combined with his incestuous desire for her, cause him to behave differently from skirt-chasing classmates, who then tease him by calling his room-mate Shreve his 'husband' (50, 108). His morbid, guilty preoccupations also lead him to a quixotic fight with the strong, handsome, nouveau riche Gerald Bland. Ultimately, Harvard comes to symbolize for Quentin not a cursed past, but a (paradoxically) cursed future, the defeat of an elegant past at the hands of a crude modernity.

The section of Faulkner's novel narrated by Quentin takes place on the day of his suicide, and, although it moves unpredictably back and forth between the past and present, it remains a linear narrative punctuated by the coercive, oppressive bells of Harvard.[9] Quentin's section opens in the morning as he contemplates his watch, remembers his father's aphorisms on the absurdity of fighting time, and endures Shreve's interrogation about his plans, accompanied by the reminder that the bell indicating the start of chapel will ring in two minutes. When the bell does ring, Quentin notes that 'it stayed in the air, more felt than heard, for a long time. Like all the bells that ever rang still ringing in the long dying light-rays and Jesus and Saint Francis talking about his sister' (50). While the bells evoke in Quentin memories of Caddy's ill-fated wedding, among other things, they also symbolize time, Harvard and the whole slew of cultural expectations that Quentin strenuously resists. They also call to mind uncomfortable childhood moments in which his 'insides' would 'move ... in school when the bell rang' because his countdown to release 'never could come out even with the bell' (56), and he would lose track of his lesson and risk humiliation. Before committing suicide, Quentin embarks on a day trip designed as an escape from what Foucault's *Discipline and Punish* would suggest are the surveillance tactics of the university and of society at large – tactics known to produce the likes of banker Herbert Head – culminating in the ultimate escape of suicide, defined as the state of being 'dead in Harvard' (110). During the course of the day, he identifies with the uncatchable fish sought by the three boys at the lake and tells them that it 'deserves to be let alone' (76) and becomes agitated at the sound of the bells. Quentin's association of the bells at Harvard with the bells at Caddy's wedding makes thematic sense in that both signal the loss of the mythical past for which Quentin longs, leading him to muse, 'Somewhere I heard bells once. Mississippi or Massachusetts. I was. I am not' (110). His suicide is the concurrent denial of Caddy's wedding (his primal loss), of Harvard and, finally, of modernity itself, all of which are equivalent to non-being. Confronted by the forces of surveillance impinging upon him, he retreats into the feudal past and rejects the self and the future that Harvard offers. In the end, he grimly notes that calculating the amount of weight in flatirons required to drown himself is 'the only opportunity [he] seemed to have for the application of Harvard' (55).

Although Oates's portrayal of Princeton University is more layered than Faulkner's portrayal of Harvard, Princeton is as 'accursed' for Josiah Slade as Harvard is for Quentin Compson. The university represents, however, a blighted past that Josiah must reject rather than a cursed future he must annihilate himself to prevent. *The Accursed* depicts the Princeton of 1905 as a place of mystified but anxious white male authority characterized by a terror of encroaching modernity not unlike Quentin's. This fearful future is marked especially in Oates's portrayal by the threatening demands of 'Jews', 'Negroes', 'hysterical females demanding "rights"' and teachers of 'heretical evolutionism' and 'atheistical socialism' (Oates 2013: 662), groups whose demands are both feared and derided by every authority figure in the novel, including the ones with reputations for being politically or culturally progressive. Woodrow Wilson, the president of Princeton during the Crosswicks Curse and a central character in the novel, repeats with pride that the university will incorporate 'no new ideas' into its curriculum (213, 313), signalling the commitment of the academy to defend tradition at all costs. Oates depicts the university as inseparable from the town and its entrenched class hierarchies and as serving a critical function in preserving and perpetuating those hierarchies, replicated in a student body which, while 'naturally gracious and schooled in courtesy' (200), concerns itself less with intellectual discovery than with getting into, while cruelly banishing others from, exclusive 'eating clubs', and with perpetrating 'unspeakable' hazing practices discussed in hushed tones throughout the novel (181–6, 477–8). The university's stance of intellectual detachment enables it to give an apparently rational defence of irrational prejudices, as well as a veneer of respectability. In addition, its much-celebrated integration of learning and faith appears in the novel as pathological enmeshment, where vulnerabilities or deficiencies in one are hastily shored up by the other in an endless cycle that unleashes terror upon university and town alike.

Josiah's privileged background and family money protect him from even the (relatively light) hazing that Quentin experiences and prevent him from seeing this dark underbelly of Princeton until the curse strikes. In contrast to the narrator of *The Accursed*, who simply 'will not speak' of his undergraduate days at Princeton except to report that he would commit suicide rather than relive them (479), Josiah had been a 'sought-after' freshman (214), not unlike Quentin, whom Mrs Bland pursues as a friend for her son out of respect for the 'blundering sense of noblesse oblige' (Faulkner 1929: 58) she associates with his background. Josiah had been, in fact, 'the envy and awe of all' after receiving and 'ignor[ing], in his Slade arrogance', an invitation to join Ivy, the most exclusive eating club on campus (Oates 214). His friends, identified as 'few', came from 'elsewhere' in the school, outside the coveted cliques and clubs (214). In many ways, Josiah is an ideal student in that he 'merit[ed] high grades' and was 'at times, even a brilliant . . . student' (84) and in that 'friendship and popularity had not seemed to him the point of college' (214). After Josiah graduates, however, the curse and the suffering that it brings to the Slade family force him to rethink everything about his identity and his education.

Josiah's sense of self, deeply bound to family history and tradition, begins to disintegrate when that family and those traditions appear radically altered amidst the ravages of the Crosswicks Curse. More significant for the purposes of the current argument, however, is the part of Josiah's identity rooted in his relationship with Dr Pearce van Dyck, the narrator's father and Josiah's favourite professor. Josiah feels less 'comfortable' with his own father Augustus than with van Dyck, a long-time friend of Josiah's family and 'a specialist in Kantian idealism', who is 'taciturn by nature, scholarly and earnest' (84) and known for 'expecting a great deal of his students, and grading them severely' (312). In other words, Josiah resembles many Schoolhouse Gothic protagonists in that he strongly desires the approval of a professor who is clearly marked as a parental figure (Truffin 2008). Part of what attracts Josiah to this professor is his lack of sentimentality, which Josiah associates with van Dyck's chosen discipline, philosophy, in which 'one cuts through subterfuge . . . one goes for the jugular' (84). When a ghost appears on Slade property, Josiah picks up some unusual flowers near the sighting of the apparition and brings them to van Dyck, an amateur botanist. Van Dyck tries to identify them and explain their pungent odour and rapid decomposition. Josiah does not initially tell him where he found the flowers but basks in his professor's confident pronouncements, which 'seemed the very essence of the philosophical temperament: to wrench some sort of sense out of senselessness', an effort that 'gives the illusion of comfort' (85-86). Van Dyck's identification of the flower as a calla lily turns out to be wrong, and the flower is eventually revealed as a toxic 'Angel Trumpet' capable of producing 'a gradual deterioration' of the brain characterized by 'paranoid suspicions and rage' (426). Shortly after Josiah brings the desiccated flowers to his professor, van Dyck begins to do what so many Princetonians do in the course of the novel: he 'turns' (370). The line between 'turning' and simply having one's true self revealed is, however, never very clear in *The Accursed*.

The philosophy professor's uncompromising rationalism and philosophical detachment deeply appeal to Josiah but come to manifest themselves in horrific ways that lead to van Dyck's death and Josiah's terrible, Oedipal guilt. As disappearances, demon sightings and murders begin to happen with regularity in Princeton, van Dyck's wife Johanna becomes pregnant with a child that van Dyck tells Josiah cannot be his own (314).[10] The professor invites Josiah to observe and admire an intricate 'Scheme of Clues' (317) he has created in order to track manifestations of the curse and the activities of mysterious and possibly demonic interlopers, including Annabelle Slade's seducer. Van Dyck explains that the chart represents his attempt to bring the ratiocination of his hero Sherlock Holmes to bear on the Crosswicks Curse. When Josiah protests that the Holmes mysteries are not real, van Dyck responds with 'disapproval' at being challenged by 'a former, favorite student' (316) who should, in the professor's mind, regard him as a 'protector, mentor – savior' (403). The professor defends his fictional hero by describing the Holmes tales as 'distillations' of life's 'messy, impenetrable mysteries' that are, in fact, 'superior' to real life (316). After some time passes, and the van Dycks have temporarily relocated to an isolated and purportedly haunted property belonging to Johanna's family, Johanna invites Josiah to visit as a way of distracting her increasingly insane husband from his chart. The philosophy professor then receives a nocturnal visit from Sherlock Holmes himself, presumably a hallucination brought on by the toxic flower Josiah brought to his office. Holmes admonishes van Dyck to eschew the 'contemptible' 'life of emotion and sentiment' (408) so as to clear his mind and see that his son is 'the spawn of a demon' (414) that the professor must kill even if doing so means murdering his wife as well (415). Holmes enlists the professor's 'beloved Kant' in making his case that 'local law' must sometimes be 'transcended' (415).

Van Dyck moves to attack the child with a hot poker, and Josiah, awakened by Johanna's screams and mysteriously admonished by his sister Annabelle's voice, rushes to the nursery, grabs the hot poker with his bare hands, and knocks his professor to the floor. Van Dyck soon dies from a head injury, adding to Josiah's considerable burden of accumulated guilt and filling him with despair for betraying a man who had 'trusted' him 'as a son' and for turning from van Dyck's 'admiring pupil' to his 'executioner' (424). Although Josiah does not publicly admit to bringing the poisonous flowers to van Dyck's office (426) and is found 'blameless' in his professor's death (434), Josiah becomes increasingly paranoid that 'all of Princeton [is] observing him, and passing judgment', as though he bore the 'mark of Cain' (434). Killing the professor he most loved and admired, even in defence of a helpless baby, irrevocably alters both Josiah's self-concept and his relationship to Princeton.

The Curse of the Gothic Self

Unlike Quentin Compson, for whom a 'Harvard self' is a contradiction in terms, Josiah Slade flails helplessly as his Princeton identity slowly disintegrates. His violent encounter with Dr van Dyck, whose philosophical detachment had become both a mask and a justification for murderous impulses, is paradigmatic of his relationship to Princeton. The Crosswicks Curse exposes a nightmare world that reveals the worst in everyone he has been trained to respect and exposes the dark side of everything that Josiah has been trained to be – proud, refined, paternalistic, detached.

The Crosswicks Curse destroys the complacency and pride that came with Josiah's wealth, status and elite education. During his sister Annabelle's absence from Princeton, she appears to have been suffering in a hellish alternate dimension, the 'Bog Kingdom', where servants have overthrown aristocrats and subjected them to degrading, deadly service and horrific abuse (261–78). Instead of interpreting her experience as a nightmare revolution and an affirmation of the inherited order, she resolves to 'consecrate' herself 'to freeing ... fellow-sufferers' (277) and after she returns (and dies giving birth to a deformed and possibly monstrous child, who also dies), Josiah begins to read the works of socialist writers like Jack London and Upton Sinclair. Josiah is alarmed to discover that Sinclair's most famous work, *The Jungle* (1906), exposes the unsanitary conditions and shocking labour practices in meat-packing plants owned by Slade family friends. After reading *The Jungle*, he realizes with great mortification that his expensive education has left him wholly ignorant of basic realities such as the sources of his own wealth as well as the wealth of the rest of his set (292). Although he experiences 'envy' and 'a yearning for his lost youth' (289) while watching Princeton undergraduates go about their studies, Josiah feels an increasing 'revulsion for his Slade-self, seeing this individual through the eyes of others, as one of privilege and shame in equal measure' (293).

The Crosswicks Curse also brings religious disillusionment. Although Josiah is sceptical by nature and has 'long abandoned the hope of acquiring his grandfather Winslow's combining of faith and intelligence' (294), Winslow's reasonable, moderate, post-Enlightenment Presbyterianism is an integral part of Josiah's upbringing and sensibility. As a young child, he had even 'imagined' Winslow to be 'God himself' (36). By the end of the novel, however, Winslow has confessed to murdering a young girl and allowing another man to be executed for the crime, an old injustice that appears to have triggered the Crosswicks Curse. This blatant hypocrisy, however, represents only the simplest part of the novel's commentary on institutional religion and its enmeshment in industry, politics and education. The novel's epilogue suggests that Winslow regarded the curse as God's punishment for experiencing true love for his grandchildren and failing to live up to a dark 'Covenant' (649). In a bizarre final sermon that Winslow spoke about but died before he could deliver, a sermon the author claims to have acquired years later at an estate auction, Winslow declares that after his crime, God revealed to him that he treasures men most 'WHEN THEY GROVEL IN DESPAIR' and 'TAKE NO SOLACE IN HUMAN LOVE' (665, capitalization in original here and following). At this time, God also agreed to protect Winslow from disgrace and punishment if he would 'PREACH DISCORD WHILE EMPLOYING A VOCABULARY OF LOVE' (659) and 'DISGUISE THE WORKINGS OF EVIL ON EARTH WITH A PACIFIST SMILE' (657). In other words, just as the novel presents Dr van Dyck's philosophical detachment in a horrific light, it also highlights the role religious moderates of the period played in perpetuating injustice. The epilogue also adds to the novel's commentary on class by intimating that Winslow's nightmarish vision of God may be a product of the distortions that come with pride and privilege. Winslow writes in his sermon, 'I AM A SLADE, AND ORDAINED BY GOD; AND GUILTY OF NO CRIME; FOR ALL THAT FALLS FROM MY HAND MUST BE GOD'S OWN DESIRE, AND CANNOT BE DEEMED SIN' (654). *The Accursed* simultaneously indicts religious moderates whose reasonableness and caution mask a deeper complicity with institutional evil and a wealthy class whose extreme sense of entitlement allows for no distinction between its behaviour and God's will. Neither identity remains an option for Josiah.

Given the hypocrisy and violence lurking within Josiah's 'dreamlike' town and 'enchanted' university (291), it is little wonder that he becomes increasingly 'altered and strange' (287) as the 'jeering voices' in his head instruct him to 'purify' Princeton with a 'torch' (305). Like Quentin Compson, he is plagued by fantasies of suicide. Unlike Quentin, he struggles mightily against them rather than calmly and quietly succumbing (521–2). To escape Princeton, he joins an ill-conceived and under-resourced expedition to the South Pole reminiscent of Poe's *The Narrative of Arthur Gordon Pym* (1838), explaining in a letter to his parents that 'the Southern sky has no history, . . . & no memory; no mind' (538). Early in the journey, he obtains a brief respite from the voices, but they eventually return, urging him to commit all manner of heinous and self-destructive acts, from seducing and murdering the captain of the ship (provocatively named 'Oates') to plunging into the arctic waters so that he might investigate the sea like a proper 'man of science' (540–1). Increasingly, he sees the 'Ice Kingdom' as his own 'Scheme of Clues', and he is visited by visions of his grandfather, his philosophy professor and many other figures from his past. When he finally plummets into the sea, he does so in the belief that he is rescuing Annabelle from the ice (548–9), marking even his suicide as a gesture of hope. That hope is fully realized when the Crosswicks Curse is lifted, an event that coincides with the moment that Josiah's recently deceased cousin Todd defeats Annabelle's demonic seducer in a game of draughts in the Bog Kingdom, as well as the moment that Winslow Slade dies at the front of a crowded church eager to hear the simultaneously esteemed and cursed Princetonian deliver a sermon. At this time, all of Winslow Slade's grandchildren are miraculously restored to life (641). Having experienced a complete breakdown of identity, however, Josiah leaves his Princeton self behind forever.

Despite the myriad similarities between Quentin Compson and Josiah Slade, their stories imply quite different views of history, modernity, gender, class and learning. Quentin, incapable of empathy and lost in a world of abstractions (family honour, southern womanhood, *noblesse oblige*) rendered meaningless by history, succumbs to narcissism and madness. His story dramatizes the pathos of losing a cherished, though untenable and defeated, way of life that Harvard, 'a fine dead sound' (110), cannot replace. He neither sees nor desires a future, particularly one exemplified by the crass ways and tastes of nouveau riche Harvard classmates like Gerald Bland. In contrast, Josiah 'discover[s] that a traditional way of thinking, whether of theology, intercollegiate sports, or the eating clubs on Prospect Avenue, was disagreeable to him' (313) and rejects the 'accursed' customs and habits of his upbringing and education. Instead of surrendering to religious fatalism or melancholy, adopting a narrow and imperious but acceptably 'masculine' rationalism, clinging to fantasies of racial superiority and inherited privilege or pursuing success on bourgeois capitalist terms, Josiah embraces an agrarian socialism and takes his place in a community committed to promoting social justice and caring for (rather than dominating) one another and the earth (646–8).

Although the novel concludes on a decidedly anti-capitalist note, Oates does not canonize the socialists who play a role in the tale. In fact, she depicts Upton Sinclair as earnest but pedantic and devoted to an asceticism that is destructive to his own health as well as that of his young wife, who contemplates suicide and eventually leaves Upton and returns with their son to her well-to-do family (141–58, 239–55, 460). Worse, she portrays Jack London as a narcissistic, hyper-masculine alcoholic whose socialism is compromised by fantasies of racial superiority (487–529). When Josiah meets the very drunk London in a restaurant after a socialist rally planned by Sinclair, London wrongly accuses Josiah of sending covert 'signals' to his lady-friend, and a fight ensues in which Josiah ends up knocking London to the floor just as he did to his beloved professor, though London does not die from his head injury (526–7). Despite the failings of these characters, as well as the fact that 2013 is hardly a historical vantage point from which the socialist vision of the early twentieth century can be portrayed without irony, that vision is presented within her novel as the only real alternative to a sordid and corrupt Princeton.

Significantly, Oates presents Josiah's new socialist consciousness as one that recuperates certain aspects of the Enlightenment humanist tradition typically rendered horrific in the Schoolhouse Gothic. The qualities that made Josiah Slade an ideal student – his curiosity, his earnest but unsentimental bookishness, his habits of observation and analysis, his sceptical nature, his Enlightenment faith in the human mind – do not destroy him and the people around him, as they do in most works of the Schoolhouse Gothic. Instead, those qualities enable him to play a significant role in making the 'Helicon Home Colony' a success, 'self-sustaining, and even profitable', as he and his comrades teach themselves 'such disciplines as agronomics, organic agriculture, animal husbandry, and greenhouse-horticulture' (647). His Enlightenment frame of mind is, however, divorced from the corrupting influences and interests of Princeton society and its esteemed university. The end of the novel provides scant details but paints an idyllic picture marred only by 'an arson-set fire' (648) targeting the colony, a fire survived by all of the principals. The novel proper ends with the 'double wedding' of Josiah and Wilhelmina and Annabelle and Yaeger Ruggles,[11] at which Upton Sinclair proclaims, 'It is the dawn of a new day! *Revolution now!*' (648, italics in original). Although an epilogue containing Winslow's disturbing sermon follows this exultant scene, Josiah is left secure and happy. Instead of continuing his prestigious formal education, as he once seemed destined to do, he chooses to join a community of learners devoted to one another and to nature. As such, he represents a new development in the Schoolhouse Gothic: the student who escapes the curse of institutional schooling and breaks its cycle of terror.

Marianne Juhl and Bo Hakon Jørgensen have described the Gothic novel as 'a protest against bourgeois rationalism which claims that human reason can master nature as well as itself' (Juhl and Jørgensen 1993: 90). Such a formulation identifies the dark underbelly of the Enlightenment not as human reason itself, but as human reason enmeshed in capitalist exploitation, bent on domination and unchecked by the equally human capacity for respect or empathy. It is precisely this type of 'bougeois rationalism' that Josiah rejects. We could attribute his achievement to hero worship on the part of an unreliable narrator who owes Josiah his very life and may wish to remove his rescuer, ideologically and physically, from a town and university he regards as hopelessly compromised. We could also credit Josiah's renunciations to the fantastic elements of the novel in which he appears, a novel unbound to strictures of realism that might render his choices implausible. While these formal considerations do ironize Josiah's portrayal, the fact remains that in *The Accursed*, Joyce Carol Oates has granted a student character an uncharacteristically happy ending that sharply contrasts with the bleak fates suffered by most of his fellow Princetonians and by other students in her own Schoolhouse Gothic canon (Truffin 2008, 2013b). By imagining an alternative socialist future for this character, she foregrounds political and economic considerations that gothic and Schoolhouse Gothic texts typically incorporate but sometimes downplay or obscure. At the novel's conclusion, Josiah has embraced not the familiar, seductive *posture* of neutrality that masks a deeper complicity with the capitalist status quo, but rather a healthy rationalism directed towards achieving harmony with the environment and with others. He has repudiated the inherited wealth, corrosive elitism, destructive competition and mystified institutional power of his time – and challenged students and educators alike to imagine how we might do the same in our own.

Notes

I would like to thank Reed Lawson, who aided in preliminary research on *The Sound and The Fury* while serving as an undergraduate Research Assistant at Campbell University.

1. See Smith 2013.
2. For references to Hamlet in descriptions of Josiah, see Oates 73–4, 137, 288, and 462. For commentary on Quentin as 'the Southern Hamlet', see Brooks 1952, Taylor 1963: 137–40, Sykes 1990. For an examination of the role of the university in Shakespeare's *Hamlet* and the ways in which the 'gentrification of learning' (207) in the early modern period destabilized concepts of nobility and helped facilitate Hamlet's tragedy, see Hanson 2011.
3. During a period of great personal and academic stress, the young Winslow Slade walks miles away from Princeton, drinks heavily at a pub, and is lured by a thief into a sexual encounter with a young, poor, mixed-race woman, whom he strangles to death and abandons. The thief is subsequently hanged for the crime. This episode emerges in two different confessions, the second of which announces that the first was only partially true (Oates 2013: 441–8, 649–57).
4. For discussion of *The Sound and The Fury* as a commentary on the Southern 'aristocracy', see Hanson 1994 and Bauer 2000. *The Accursed* identifies the Slade family as American 'aristocracy' (ironic as the term may be) by placing George Washington and other founding fathers at the family home, Crosswicks Manse, and going as far as to say that 'It was in the Manse . . . that the fate of the young Republic was determined' (49).
5. See Faulkner 1929: 50–1, Oates 174.
6. Further, the sexual impurity is symbolized in both cases by a pair of muddy drawers, though the young Quentin carefully observes young Caddy's soiled pants, while the adult Josiah is not present for the muddying of the bride-to-be Annabelle's petticoat (Faulkner 1929: 25, Oates 126). To defend the family honour, both Quentin and Josiah plan to confront their sisters' seducers with pistols, though Josiah never actually finds Annabelle's (possibly supernatural) despoiler (Faulkner 1929: 101–2, Oates 167–79).
7. See Roberts 1995: 117–88 for a consideration of Quentin's similarities not only to Hamlet, but also to Hamlet's lover, Ophelia. Such a comparison could be usefully considered in relationship to Josiah as well.
8. This interview took place around the time that Oates first conceived and drafted *The Accursed* (Smith 2013).
9. Quentin's narrative, which obsessively returns to the problematics of time, has been particularly instrumental in instigating and sustaining the long critical tradition – from Jean Paul Sartre on – of theorizing Faulknerian time in terms borrowed from Henri Bergson, who argued that time measured rationally or scientifically interfered with authentic, experiential human time and thus represented an artificial hindrance to the direct intuition of knowledge (Benét 1965: 99)
10. This child is the fictitious author of *The Accursed*.

11. Yaeger, a distant cousin of Woodrow Wilson, had been a Latin preceptor (teaching assistant) at Princeton until he pressed the university president to speak out against lynching, revealing his own mixed-race heritage in the process. Wilson, shocked at discovering black blood in the family line, quietly arranged to have Yaeger dismissed from his post at the university.

References

Baldick, Chris (1992), *The Oxford Book of Gothic Tales*, Oxford: Oxford University Press.

Bauer, Margaret D. (2000), '"I have sinned in that I have betrayed innocent blood": Quentin's Recognition of His Guilt', *Southern Literary Journal*, 32:2, 70–89.

Benét, William Rose (1965), 'Bergson, Henri', *The Reader's Encyclopaedia*, 2nd edn, New York: Thomas Y. Cromwell Company.

Brooks, Cleanth (1952), 'Primitivism in *The Sound and The Fury*', *English Institute Essays*, 13–14.

Faulkner, William [1930] (1985), *As I Lay Dying*, New York: Vintage International.

Faulkner, William [1929] (1994), *The Sound and The Fury*, 2nd edn, ed. David Minter, New York: Norton.

Hanson, Elizabeth (2011), 'Fellow Students: Hamlet, Horatio, and the Early Modern University', *Shakespeare Quarterly*, 62:2, 205–29.

Hanson, Philip J. (1994), 'The Logic of Anti-Capitalism in *The Sound and the Fury*', *The Faulkner Journal*, 10:1, 3–27.

Johnson, Greg (2006), *Joyce Carol Oates: Conversations, 1970–2006*, Princeton: Ontario Review Press.

Juhl, Marianne and Bo Hakon Jørgensen (1993), 'Why Gothic Tales?' *Isak Dinesen: Critical Views*, Columbus: Ohio State University Press, 88–99.

Milazzo, Lee (1989), *Conversations with Joyce Carol Oates*, Jackson: University Press of Mississippi.

Oates, Joyce Carol (2013), *The Accursed*, New York: HarperCollins.

Roberts, Diane (1995), *Faulkner and Southern Womanhood*, Athens, GA: University of Georgia Press.

Smith, Wendy (2013), 'Joyce Carol Oates is at Her Gothic Best in *The Accursed*', *LA Times*, 29 March 2013.

Sonser, Anna (2001), *A Passion for Consumption: The Gothic Novel in America*, Bowling Green, OH: Bowling Green State University Popular Press.

Sykes, John (1990), *The Romance of Innocence and the Myth of History: Faulkner's Critique of Southern Culture*, Macon, GA: Mercer University Press.

Taylor, William R. (1963), *Cavalier and Yankee*, New York: Anchor Books.

Truffin, Sherry R. (2008), *Schoolhouse Gothic: Haunted Hallways and Predatory Pedagogues in Late Twentieth Century Literature and Scholarship*, Newcastle-upon-Tyne: Cambridge Scholars Publishing.

Truffin, Sherry R. (2013a), '"Gigantic Paradox, . . . Too Monstrous for Solution": Nightmarish Democracy and the Schoolhouse Gothic in "William Wilson" and *The Secret History*', *A Companion to American Gothic*, ed. Charles L. Crow, Malden, MA: Wiley Blackwell, 164–76.

Truffin, Sherry R. (2013b), 'Zombies in the Classroom: Education as Consumption in Two Novels by Joyce Carol Oates', in *Zombies in the Academy: Living Death in Higher Education*, ed. A. Whelan, C. Moore and R. Walker, Bristol: Intellect Press, 203–15.

Weinstein, Philip (2010), *Becoming Faulkner: The Art and Life of William Faulkner*, Oxford: Oxford University Press.

Plate 1: Washington Allston (1779–1843), *Tragic Figure in Chains*, 1800. Watercolour on paper mounted on panel. 31.3 x 23.5 cm (12 7/8 x 9 5/8 inches). Addison Gallery of American Art, Phillips Academy, Andover, Massachusetts.

Plate 2: Jackson Pollock (1912–56), *Gothic*, 1944. Oil on canvas. 215.5 x 142.1 cm (7 5/8 x 56 inches). Museum of Modern Art, New York. Gift of Lee Krasner.

Plate 4: Cindy Sherman (b. 1954), *Untitled #308*, 1994. Colour photograph. 176.5 x 119.4 cm (69 ½ x 47 inches). Courtesy of Metro Pictures, New York.

Plate 3: Bruce Conner (1933–2008) *The Bride*, 1960. Wood, nylon, string, wax, paint, candles, costume jewellery, marbles, paper doily, etc., 92.7 x 43.2 x 58.4 cm (36.5 x 17 x 23 inches). Walker Art Center, Minneapolis. Braunstein/Quay Gallery and T. B. Walker Acquisition Fund, 1987. © Conner Family Trust, San Francisco / Artists Rights Society (ARS), New York.

Plate 5: Robert Gober (b. 1954), *Untitled Leg*, 1989–90. Beeswax, cotton, wood, leather and human hair. 28.9 × 19.7 x 50.8 cm (11 3/8 × 7 3/4 × 20 inches). The Museum of Modern Art, New York. Gift of the Dannheisser Foundation.

Plate 6: Kara Walker (b. 1969), *Grub for Sharks: A Concession to the Negro Populace*, 2004. Cut paper. Dimensions variable. Tate Gallery. Acquisition presented by the American Fund for the Tate London, 2009.

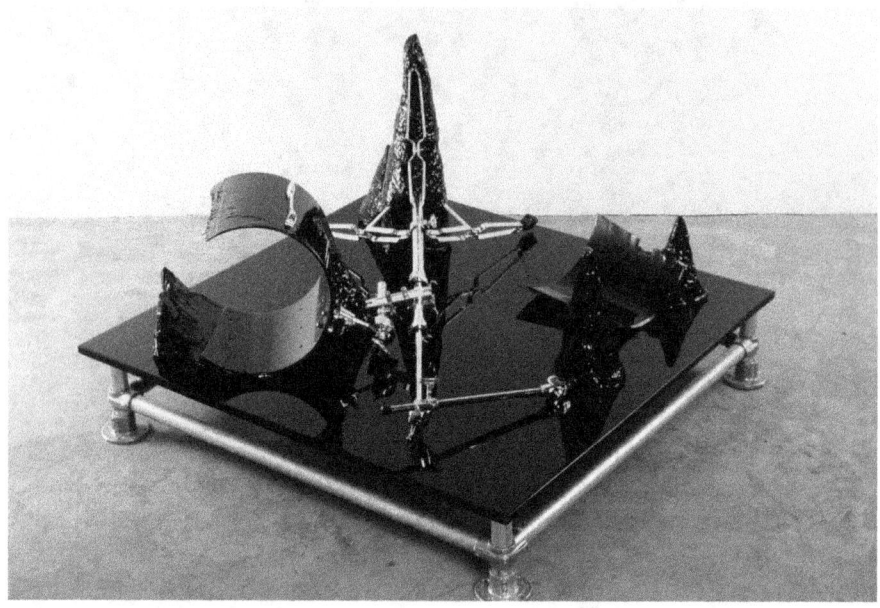

Plate 7: Banks Violette (b. 1973), *Untitled (model for a future disaster)*, 2003. Steel, drum hardware, polystyrene, polyurethane and tinted epoxy. 83.8 × 121.9 × 121.9 cm (33 × 48 × 48 inches). Over Holland Collection. Courtesy Team Gallery, New York.

Part III

Gothic Media

Chapter 7

American Gothic Television
Julia M. Wright

'Gothic television' is a contentious category, not least because it has no currency in the industry structures which organize, produce and market television series in the United States.[1] In scholarship, the term is better established but controversial because it appears to be an oxymoron at the level of form: the gothic is associated with the fantastic, and television with verisimilitude (see Robson 2007: 242). In one of the earlier essays to wrestle with the subject, Lenora Ledwon suggests that gothic television grafts together these competing rubrics:

> television's heavy reliance on 'reality programming' would seem to tip the scales in favour of common life, drying up television's potential for 'fancy'. Lynch's *Twin Peaks* can be seen as a twentieth-century reconciliation of common and uncommon, home-like and uncanny, domestic and Gothic. (Ledwon 1993: 268)

What such discussion overlooks, however, is the ways in which the gothic has, from its inception, responded to realism and its cognates: as David B. Morris notes of the first gothic novel, '*The Castle of Otranto* actively subverts the prosaic vision of the world implicit in novelistic conventions of probability and verisimilitude' (Morris 1985: 301). Such arguments as Morris's paint the gothic as reactive, even formally parasitic, but they do provide context for the interdependence of gothic television series and realist forms: most American gothic series follow dramatic series convention in centring either on a home or a workplace, for instance. But the gothic is also focused on reaction in another sense – the response of characters and, tacitly by extension, audiences to the completely improbable and excessive. In what follows, I shall focus on these three aspects of American gothic television: first, the entwined relationship between realism and the gothic in early television; second, the focus of gothic series on probable characters in improbable situations; and, finally, the division of gothic television into conventional dramatic domestic and workplace forms, and their challenge to that dramatic division.

Realism, the Gothic and Production History

Gothic is, in formalist parlance, a mode, not a genre. It is a mood, a style (like the pastoral or the comic), rather than a structure (like the sonnet or the novel), and as a mode it can be deployed in combination with other modes and across genres. Drop a moment of terror arising from obscurity (in Edmund Burke's famous terms) or 'a vertiginous and plunging – not a soaring – sublime' (Morris 1985: 306) into the middle of a police procedural, and the moment is as gothic as if it were in the middle of a horror movie. Recognizing it as a mode helps to situate the transplantation of the gothic from fiction, to poetry and drama, to film, television and music. *Frankenstein* alone has cut across myriad such forms, from nineteenth-century plays based on Mary Shelley's 1818 novel to early film, television and even cereal brands. The great gothic parodies of early sitcoms, *The Munsters* and *The Addams Family* (both 1964–6), and, in more muted ways, *Bewitched* (1964–72), were all based on other media: *The Munsters* alluded to gothic literature and film (the cuckoo clock featured a Poe-esque raven crying 'Never more!' and the major characters were all drawn from horror-movie classics), *The Addams Family* was based on a *New Yorker* comic and *Bewitched* drew centrally on two films, *I Married a Witch* (1942), an adaptation of a novel, and *Bell, Book, and Candle* (1958), based on a play. In more recent gothic television, adaptation has given way to dense allusiveness: the late-season episode of *Buffy, the Vampire Slayer* (1997–2003), 'Buffy vs. Dracula' (2000), for instance, ranges from Bram Stoker's novel to early films to *Sesame Street*'s 'Count' Muppet and Anne Rice's vampire novels; *Supernatural* (2005–) frequently references not only contemporary film and television, and literature from Homer's *Odyssey* to Kurt Vonnegut's novels, but also fanfic, LARPing (Live Action Role Playing), conventions, and other elements of twenty-first-century fan culture.

This sort of cross-media transfer is also at the very foundation of television as a medium: most directly, much early television built on the adaptation of plays and radio serials. Two of the first gothic television series identified by Helen Wheatley (Wheatley 2006) in her comprehensive list were adaptations of radio anthology series, namely *Lights Out* (1946–52) and *Suspense* (1949–54). As anthology series, the more famous gothic series before colour television – *Alfred Hitchcock Presents*

(1955–62) and *The Twilight Zone* (1959–64) – are part of a larger television trend that predates the earliest of these by over two decades, and predates by nearly as much the sitcoms and dramas that have come to define television as a realist medium. But the usual candidate for the very first dramatic series in North America predates even *Lights Out* by over a decade: *The Television Ghost* (1931–3) featured gothic storytelling in which a single actor (George Kelting) assumed the personae of victims recounting their own murders. Reportedly (the show predated recording technology, so no episodes survive), Kelting wore white make-up and a towel or cloth on his head and was shot only from the shoulders up. The very title of *The Television Ghost* registers the spectral shock of the new medium (see, for example, Sconce 2000), with its flickering black and white images, while Kelting's costume is the series' only concession to the medium's visuality. Television, then, from its earliest decades, engaged gothic conventions, both in form (adaptation, allusion) and in content (ghosts and all that goes bump in the night).[2]

Broadly speaking, televisual realism emerged as the technology improved, the other-worldly effects of early cathode ray tubes no longer embedded in the medium: dramatic serials centred on suburban families became prominent in the final years of black-and-white television when the quality improved significantly; social realism emerged with colour television, with series such as *All in the Family* (1971–9) beginning just as colour sets became more widely affordable; and reality TV, though its rapid growth was in part a response to the 2001 writers' strike, stayed on screens as new high-definition quality led to significantly sharper, 'realistic' images. The gothic transformed along with the medium: instead of using shadow to conceal what it could not represent, later technologies made possible special effects that could create the illusion of probability, of what might be seen on screen if vampires or ghosts existed. This is neither televisual similitude nor the hyperreal (Baudrillard 1995): it is purely aesthetic. The puff of dust after staking a vampire in *Buffy* fits the aesthetic of the tamely represented sexuality and violence of a series aired on the WB, a youth-focused network, while the gory blood and guts of *True Blood*'s vampire deaths is consistent with the HBO aesthetic of grittier representations of violence and straining against the boundaries of network television's self-censorship. 'Gothic sublimity does not depend upon judgments concerning the truth or reality of supernatural agents and events', as Morris notes, and as Steven Bruhm has extensively discussed, early gothic literature is centrally concerned with the representation and production of affect (Morris 1985: 309; Bruhm 1994).

Televisual realism was largely developed in the 1950s, and television historians usually point to *Father Knows Best* (1954–60, but derived from a radio series) and *Leave it to Beaver* (1957–63) as the groundbreaking series in this vein. But, as critics note, these series were more ideological than accurate: Mary Beth Haralovich, for instance, identifies the 'verisimilitude' of *Father Knows Best* with 'the promises that suburban living and material goods held out for' the white, middle-class nuclear family, and addresses *Leave it to Beaver*'s elisions of class and race in this context (Haralovich 2003: 72, 78). There are striking similarities between the parameters of these early series and the core precepts of the 1954 Comics Code, instituted to cultivate the morals of America's youth: authority figures had to be represented in ways that fostered respect, the word 'crime' could not be prominently displayed and criminal acts could not be depicted in any detail, 'in every instance good should triumph over evil', and so on (Nyberg 1998: 166). Such carefully controlled representations, as Haralovich notes, market an ideal present rather than accurately depict reality.

Moreover, in the 1950s and 1960s, television's first decades as a mass medium, American gothic was multimedia, and not only in the availability of new material in film, television and various kinds of print, but also in the insistent cross-media and cross-genre activity of its creators. Richard Matheson, for instance, in this period published gothic novels (including his vampire novel, *I am Legend* (1959)) and wrote extensively for gothic television, including the script for the television adaptation of *House of Usher* (1960) and episodes for *The Twilight Zone*. Other writers regularly moved back and forth between gothic and putatively realist series. Ed James, the creator of *Father Knows Best*, co-wrote the first episode of *The Addams Family*; Paul West, a frequent writer for *Father*, wrote an episode of *The Ghost and Mrs. Muir* (1968–70). *Leave it to Beaver* has similar crossovers: Joe Connelly wrote for *The Munsters*, Phil Leslie wrote for *The Addams Family*, and Richard Baer wrote for *Bewitched* and *The Munsters*. Such exchanges were not all realist-to-gothic, either. There was also considerable migration of writing staff from gothic series to the early feminist series of the late 1960s and early 1970s, such as the career-woman series, *That Girl!* (1966–71; Baer again), *Mary Tyler Moore* (1970–7; Allan Burns, who wrote for *The Munsters*), and *Julia* (1968–71), centring on a widowed African-American mother working as a nurse (with writers such as Harry Winkler and Phil Leslie from *The Addams Family*), and other socially minded series, such as *Room 222* (1969–74; also Burns, and, for example, Joanna Lee, who wrote for *Bewitched*). The significant role of gothic writers in the progressive series of the post-1966 television era points to the ways in which the apparent realism of the latter was itself a kind of fantasy. It is worth considering *The Ghost & Mrs. Muir* particularly in this context, a series contemporary with the feminist series but deploying the gothic. In juxtaposing old-style patriarchy through the grumpy ghost of a nineteenth-century sea captain and more modern views of women's independence through Carolyn Muir, a professional writer and the widowed head of a household that includes a housekeeper and two children, the series played out on screen the ideological tensions of 'women's lib' in the late 1960s. That the ghost often fumes ineffectually is part of its political message – his world is dead and gone.

Gender was pushed even further by gothic innovations on the domestic forms it parodied in the mid 1960s. *Dark Shadows* (1966–71) returned the gothic to its traditional interests in class and gender, and made the gothic serious again precisely by avoiding what the parodies had mocked. Instead of a nuclear family (like the Addams, Munsters and Stevens), *Dark Shadows* features a protagonist who grew up in an orphanage; she works for Elizabeth Collins Stoddard, apparently abandoned by her husband and raising a daughter on her own. The other family units of the first season are a father-son and a father-daughter pair, both without mothers. There are no happy lustful couples like Gomez and Morticia Addams here. Instead, *Dark Shadows* precedes a flurry of series that centre on women-run families, from *Julia* and *The Ghost & Mrs. Muir* to *The Partridge Family* (1970–4) and the slightly later *Alice* (1976–85) and *One Day at a Time* (1975–84). In other words, 1960s gothic television arguably first parodied and then rewrote domestic conventions, which were then picked up by realist series. Such threads of influence and innovation, along with the exchanges of writers and creators noted above, register the synergetic rather than contradictory relationship between realist and gothic television.

The Character's the Thing: The Gothic as Psychological Thought-Experiment

The gothic has, from its inception, been interested not in describing what is, but in imagining what might be under other circumstances – and how universalized human subjects might react. In his Preface to the second edition (1765) of *The Castle of Otranto* (1764), Walpole wrote that he had sought to combine 'the boundless realms of invention' while 'conduct[ing] the mortal agents in his drama according to the rules of probability, in short, to make them think, speak, and act, as it might be supposed mere men and women would do in extraordinary positions' (Walpole 1996: 9–10). Half a century later, Samuel Taylor

Coleridge closely echoes Walpole in Chapter XIV of the *Biographia Literaria* (1817) in describing the gothic verse he wrote for *Lyrical Ballads* (1798): 'the incidents and agents were to be, in part at least, supernatural; and the excellence aimed at was to consist in the interesting of the affections by the dramatic truth of such emotions, as would naturally accompany such situations, supposing them real' (Coleridge 1951: 264). The focus, then, in the early decades of the gothic is the probability of the characters' reactions rather than the probability of what provokes those reactions. The gothic, in short, is a space for psychological thought-experiments – and this, I shall suggest here, continues in recent American gothic television.

J. J. Abrams's series *Lost* (2004–10) draws extensively on realism, but also on touristic aesthetics and the gothic mode. Filmed in Hawaii, the series often lingered on the sublime landscapes and it became something of a tourism draw for the islands; tours even offered to take visitors to shooting locations for *Lost* episodes. In a recent essay, Jordan Lavender-Smith suggests the attraction of the series and others like it lies in their aesthetic coherence, 'ask[ing] their audiences to identify symmetries and echoes, to revisit the past and connect it to the present, to map out and be familiar with countless plotted events, to treat the shows, in other words, as unified texts, as solvable puzzles' (Lavender-Smith 2012: 64). The Blu-ray release reinforces the series' status as puzzle, with splash screens of still shots with what would, in a textbook, look like study questions. In this view, *Lost* not only depicts mysteries but is itself a mystery – a mystery, however, that requires certain formal cultural parameters (from unity to conventions of character) to decode. Its connections to the gothic are direct from the start: Abrams is on record as saying the opening credits were created 'in the vein of' *The Twilight Zone* (Malcom 2006).

The series centres on the survivors of a plane crash on a tropical island: they use wreckage to build shelter, adjust to a different diet, improvise medical treatment, wear increasingly bedraggled clothes, and so on, in terms consistent with realism. But the series punctuates that realism with gothic moments: in the first season, for instance, the lead character has a *Hamlet*-like vision of his dead father, a boy has supernatural abilities and the group is terrorized by unseen monsters and 'the others' who whisper in the dark but are never seen, while the second season returns again and again to ghosts as well as other gothic topoi such as incest (the episode 'What Kate Did', for instance, has both); later seasons have a guilty wanderer who cannot die (see the episode 'Meet Kevin Johnson') and a medium, Miles Straume. The series is not coy about its gothic roots, either. In the third-season episode, 'Not in Portland', during a flashback scene, the new recurring character Juliet confronts her tyrannical ex-husband, the camera panning briefly over the nameplate on his desk: 'Edmund Burke'.

What unites the two modes of the series, moreover, is a very Burkean lynchpin, that is, fear in relation to the unknown; surviving on a desert island and dealing with monsters are alike unfamiliar and terrifying to the almost exclusively urban, Western characters at the centre of the series. The whispering of 'the others' suggestively echoes the constant stream of background conversation and noise in the segments that depict the characters in the modern world before the fateful flight, and the monsters arguably symbolize a threatening natural world that they do not know or understand. And certainly there is much to suggest this. But the series is also fundamentally about character: most episodes focus, one by one, on a single character, interweaving flashbacks with the present into a study of motivation, trauma and personality traits that situate their responses to events on the island. After the first season, the construction of episodes around developing single characters required a significant infusion of character fodder: for the second season, characters from another section of the plane that crashed on another part of the island; for the third, 'the others' whose organization and scientific interests make their story something of a cross between William Golding's *Lord of the Flies* (1954) and H. G. Wells's *The Island of Dr. Moreau* (1896); for the fourth, a freighter; and so on.

Lost, then, not only has supernatural machinery but also shares a fundamental concern of early gothic literature – putting realistic characters into unrealistic situations to explore what we might now term psychology. It, too, is about *effect* rather than informational content. In *Lost*, this gothic interest is explicitly interwoven with psychological experiments, particularly through the Dharma Initiative and 'the others'. Early in the series, the survivors find an underground facility that requires someone to type in a sequence of numbers every 108 minutes to prevent some sort of catastrophe, and after various debates about whether the threat is real they find another underground facility that has a bank of monitors surveilling the first along with documentation suggesting it is a psychological experiment. Now that there is evidence that it is a psychological test, the veracity of the threat is even more hotly disputed – to the point that belief in the threat is rendered analogous to religious faith. But this is just the thin edge of the wedge, as more and more episodes and story arcs turn on such experimentation. The series roots these experiments in the settling of the island in the 1960s, an era when psychological experiments with significant ethical dimensions, and problems, were common, from the notorious Milgram experiment to the

Harvard Psilocybin Project to groundbreaking work on the bystander effect. In the third season, three lead characters are captured and kept separated, monitored by video cameras, and then provoked in various ways: one is told he has been given an implant that will make his heart explode if his pulse exceeds a certain moderate level; another is shown videotape of the other two having sex, aggravating the love triangle that has run through the seasons to date; at various points one character is taken away and then returned, driving another character into anxious terror about what has been done. The characters who administer this testing appear to be scientists – they use technology, carry around files of notes, and often have advanced scientific training, and they sometimes keep their human subjects in animal cages. But, as the characters are introduced in detail, this scientific veneer is stripped away to reveal a community as shaped by power and thwarted sexual desire as any other gothic ensemble. In the third-season episode 'Left Behind', Juliet wryly remarks of their leader and apparent scientific director, 'Ben has a thing for mind games.'

The early seasons of *Lost*, then, use psychological experiments to modernize the gothic device of putting conventional characters into extreme conditions (later seasons add unconventional characters, such as the guardian Jacob who is in a mythic struggle with the Man in Black). I have stressed this aspect of *Lost* because this focus on characters in unusual, even impossible, situations extends not only back to Walpole but also forward through most gothic television series. Over and over again, gothic series in the United States – whether the anthology series of early television or the serial narratives of more recent decades – have centred on ordinary people, like Coleridge's Ancient Mariner, who have been thrown into extraordinary situations: Darrin in *Bewitched*, Victoria in *Dark Shadows*, Buffy the suburban teenager called to be the Vampire Slayer, the middle-class nuclear family of the first season of *American Horror Story* (2011) that moves into a haunted house, the blue-collar hunters of *Supernatural* cast from quiet, small-town lives into the realm of monsters by some extraordinary act of violence in their lives, and so on. In some rare instances, series reverse the lens, so that the central characters are extraordinary but thrown into relief by the reactions of the ordinary characters around them. *The Munsters* and *The Addams Family* relied heavily on the comic potential of this reversal of gothic convention: instead of screaming with the ordinary people who are shocked by Herman Munster, viewers, familiar with Herman as sweetly harmless, were cued to laugh at them. This deployment of character is a further extension of the production and formal history traced in the previous section: realism and the gothic work in tandem with each other. The extraordinary effect of the gothic only works against a realist ground, and that realist ground tacitly defines itself in opposition to the gothic. Gothic television pivots on the question, 'Is this the real life? / Is this just fantasy?' (Mercury 1975).

Genres are Not to be Mixed

So, if gothic television is not a violation of televisual realism, but the condition of its possibility, and vice versa, then how does this play out in more recent series? Over the last twenty years, the use of the gothic to comment on dominant television genres has led to two lines of gothic series: the domestic gothic (discussed by Wheatley and others), drawing on soap opera, sitcoms and suburban dramas, and what I term 'workplace gothic', responding instead to mystery-oriented realist series, such as police dramas, journalism series, and profiling series. Domestic gothic generally has female protagonists and extends from the 1960s to *Buffy the Vampire Slayer*, *Charmed* (1998–2006), *Point Pleasant* (2005–6), and two seasons of *American Horror Story* (2011, 2013–14); workplace gothic typically centres on male protagonists and began with *Kolchak, the Night Stalker* (1974–5), and is perhaps the more popular subgenre, with examples including *Twin Peaks* (1990–1), *X-Files* (1993–2002), *Angel* (1999–2004), the reboot of *Kolchak* as *Night Stalker* (2005), *Supernatural*, *Grimm* (2011–), and the second season of *American Horror Story* (2012–13), as well as less popular series such as *American Gothic* (1995–6) and *The Chronicle* (2001–2). Both subsets of US gothic television are parasitic on realist genres in the sense that parody is, but these often directly critique the institutions and ideologies promulgated by that realism – as *Dark Shadows* did when it rethought the gothic family. *Supernatural*'s various television-parody episodes include critiques of game shows, police procedurals, celebrity culture, and hospital dramas – particularly one of the latter, the series points out, which has a ghost in it, despite its apparent realism.[3]

Chris Carter's *Millennium* (1996–9) brings the two streams together. The series focuses on Frank Black, an ex-profiler with a professional wife, Catherine, and a preschool daughter, Jordan: they live in a bright yellow house with lots of windows and spacious rooms, and a walled front yard. Frank works as a consultant for various law-enforcement groups, regularly working at night in the seedier parts of town dealing with serial murders, often sexually violent, and returns to the FBI in the third season. As Samira Kawash notes, the lighting alone presents a simplistic picture: 'Within the visual vocabulary of *Millennium*, the yellow house is the explicit and exact opposite of danger, violence, and disorder. *Millennium* maps security directly onto the yellow house; we might say that in the world imagined by *Millennium*, the signifier house signifies security' (Kawash 2000: 185). In this sense, argues Kawash, the series registers a larger social angst in millennial America, so that 'the ambivalent signifying function of *Millennium*'s yellow house suggests [that] the safe house is and is not the dream house; it is less an opposite than an uncanny double, refiguring the possibility of domestic happiness as the necessity of freedom from danger' (Kawash 2000: 193). The danger is real, and omnipresent: Frank has had a nervous breakdown and quit his job with the FBI, and he regularly confronts the same violence in his new job as a consultant for the Millennium Group, a private organization that originally defines itself as assisting public law enforcement.

But this understanding of the house as a refuge from the working world of the ex-profiler situates the gothic as psychological symptom rather than formalist strategy. Within the well-established conventions of gothic (and its grisly cognate, horror), the house is quite obviously dangerous from the first episode. It is a narrative cliché. A family with a difficult past buys a house in another city or region and hopes to make a fresh start, erasing history – always a losing game in the gothic – and looking eagerly forward to the fantasy of an ideal domestic future. From *Amityville Horror* (1979) to the opening episodes of *Buffy, the Vampire Slayer* and *American Horror Story*, it is a conventional starting point – and has roots in such earlier gothic topoi as the governess starting a new life with a post in a large house, from Charlotte Brontë's *Jane Eyre* (1847) to the first weeks of *Dark Shadows*. The new-house-fresh-start device is also conventional in domestic sitcoms, from *The Brady Bunch* (1969–74) to *One Day at a Time*, where that fantasy of an ideal domestic future is generally delivered. In other words, the saturated images of the yellow house are, from the outset, ironic. The effect is doubled, like the gingerbread house in the old fairy tale: it is both attractive in a literal sense and threatening because it is *too* attractive in cultural context. It is precisely in such ways as this that the gothic challenges realism at the levels of both form and content.

Various episodes of *Millennium* further develop this foundational irony. Take the second-season episode, 'Somehow, Satan Got Behind Me' (1998), written and directed by Darin Morgan, known for such offbeat episodes as this. The episode begins with four stooping, white-haired men who meet in a doughnut shop late at night to reminisce nostalgically about boxing and the old days – reminiscent of the recent *Grumpy Old Men* (1993) – but are revealed to be four devils who, in their true guise, have horns and scorched wing-stumps. As the episode unfolds, they tell each other stories of their attempts to destroy souls, especially by driving their targets to suicide. Morgan peels back the realism of the opening moments to return to an old gothic device, offering the same narratives of demonic temptation and human desperation that can be found in Matthew Lewis's *The Monk* (1796) and, in a similar frame narrative structure, Charles Robert Maturin's *Melmoth the Wanderer* (1820). The temptation here, however, is not a Faustian overreaching for power but the acceptance of defeat – one by one, the devils' victims accept the impossibility of improving their lives. The first devil, Blurk, tells of his encounter with a young man who reads a lot of 'true crime books'. Blurk encourages him to turn fiction into reality:

> 'you, yourself, possess so many characteristics of the prototypical serial killer ... Inability to hold a steady job or relationship with women; spending all your free time dreaming about turning your masochistic, mutilation, sex fantasies into reality – to say nothing of the fact that you drive a van, and keep a roll of duct tape in your glove compartment. . . . Play the hand you've been dealt'.

Another devil expresses surprise:

> GREB: Good Lord, don't tell me that's all it took?
> BLURK: You know, we were so envious when Man was given free will. But what has it brought them? The belief that their lives are determined by everything other than their own will.

Then it is Abum's turn:

> 'The trouble with serial killers is they're too evil. . . . Their evil is too conspicuous. When people hear about some psycho killer, it can lead them to thinking about the nature of evil, which leads to thoughts about right or wrong, bad or good'.

He drives his target to suicide by simply allowing a modern life ruled by alarm clocks, exercise contraptions sold on TV, boring jobs, and petty annoyances like impossible parking regulations: 'When not at work, their free time is spent in servitude, performing menial chores, none of which could be called life-affirming.' So, the first two devils work through two particular aesthetic modes: serial-killer narratives (like *Millennium* itself; Dyer 1997: 16),[4] and the tedious, irritating story that realism will never tell. As Toril Moi sarcastically notes in her trenchant critique of critical readings that require literature to 'be measured against "real life"', 'leg-shaving' and 'toe-nail clipping' 'seem neglected as fictional themes' (Moi 1988: 45). The third makes the metacommentary of the first two narratives even more apparent as Greb torments a television censor. Clearly invoking an *X-Files* episode written by Morgan, 'War of the Coprophages' (1996), the television executive, with the resonant name 'Waylon Figgleif', complains on the phone:

> On page seven of the script, your use of the word 'crap' is unacceptable to Broadcast Standards. No, it is acceptable to use the word 'crap' but only when not referring to defecation. No, the use of the word 'defecation' is not acceptable either. We suggest that you do not use any word to describe it, and simply cut the scene entirely. Now that word is completely unacceptable! Oh, you were just reacting, not suggesting, I see. Well, my next objection begins on page eight.

The devils consider the subject of the censor:

> GREB: You can imagine the weight they must bear – the burden of maintaining a nation's morality on their very shoulders.
> BLURK: What are you talking about? It's just TV!
> GREB: But you're forgetting how humans regard everything in their lives now as a matter of life and death. Under that constant pressure, making them crack is a snap.
> [*change of scene to television studio office*]
> FIGGLEIF: Unacceptable. If you are going to show a pile of dung, it must be dry dung, not moist. Why? Because I am Broadcast Standards and Practices and I bear the burden of maintaining a nation's morality on my very shoulders!

Blurk and Greb here mock the mistaking of television for the real – 'It's just TV!' Figgleif's remarks on the phone then undercut the realism further by using the same wording as Greb in the coffee shop: 'the burden of maintaining a nation's morality on their very shoulders' (it is repeated a third time in this segment, as Greb says it directly to Figgleif). The Figgleif-Greb narrative, in other words, centres on the ways in which television censorship both mistakes the medium and drives it further from realism. As the script indicates, crap, in Figgleif's world, is only ever figurative and can have no signified. Figgleif gets more and more confused about the line between fiction and reality, sorting through a woman's underwear at the laundromat to divide it into 'acceptable' and 'unacceptable', and critiquing a script for failing to recognize that aliens 'are an intelligent, superior race'. The Figgleif-Greb narrative ends with Figgleif entering a television studio with a gun and shooting people on set, while declaring that the violence is 'unacceptable' as the division between the 'real' and the censored fiction completely collapses. His last words address the technician behind the television camera: 'Is that thing still rolling?' The censor then kills himself on tape.

Such 'meta' episodes are now conventional for gothic television, that is, episodes in which the television industry is itself thematized and protagonists interact with it diegetically: *Angel*'s 'Smile Time' (2004) features a demon-run children's show that is sapping the life from its viewers, and in *Supernatural*'s 'The French Mistake', the lead characters are thrown into an alternate reality in which they are actors playing the leads in a television show called *Supernatural*. At issue here is less the gothic resistance to realism than the ways in which that resistance makes it amenable to more postmodern critiques of form and medium. But beyond such direct critiques of the industry and its rigid formal structures are more integrated critiques. In the first season of *American Horror Story*, there is little comedy and less parody, but the season's setting in Los Angeles in a house built by a 'surgeon to the stars', with at least three failed actors among the leading characters, and myriad discussions of media, celebrity murders, the tourism industry around Hollywood, and so on, the season regularly presses against the same naturalizing of Hollywood (self-)representation as 'Smile Time' and 'The French Mistake'.

'Somehow' is not a typical *Millennium* episode: those begin with some sort of crime or mystery and then follow Frank and his colleagues as they try to solve it. But 'Somehow' is an illustrative episode for calling attention to the series' ongoing interest with the ways in which culture responds to and sometimes shapes, but does not simply reflect, the real. Quite apart from the serial killer who reads 'true crime books', episode after episode depicts killers who focus their mania on cultural materials. The first episode, 'Pilot', focuses on a man killing sex workers, his fantasies of the women on fire matched to passages from W. B. Yeats's apocalyptic 'The Second Coming'. In 'The Mikado', the serial killer uses Gilbert and Sullivan's operettas, and a final-season episode, '. . . Thirteen Years Later', centres on an actor who takes method acting one step too far to perform famous horror-movie parts in the real world. Extra-diegetically, many episodes are interleaved with epigraphs, mostly from the Bible, but also quotations of historical figures and work by such writers as W. H. Auden, Friedrich Nietzsche, Johann Wolfgang von Goethe and George Eliot. The epigraphs are presented, amidst silence, in damaged white typewriter font on a black screen, an explicitly literary, and lettered, intervention, an archaism at the dawn of the millennium: 'Do you ever find yourself talking with the dead? Since Willie's death, I catch myself every day, involuntarily talking with him, as if he were with me. Abraham Lincoln – upon the death of his son' ('The Curse of Frank Black'). The lettering for this epigraph is time lagged, so that one sentence partially fades as the next is revealed, making the attribution, the third piece to emerge on screen, something of a punchline in reframing the preceding sentences: this is not fiction but presidential biography and the point here is not ghosts but a parent coping with profound grief. The epigraph dramatizes the interpretive codes at work in the kind of puzzling out that Lavender-Smith refers to in *Lost*. The next episode opens with a character taking notes based on television, the Bible and other sources to weave together a pattern of events from which he believes he can predict the future. It is in this context that we might reconsider the analysis of the 'cinematic' quality of the series, its overt 'stylishness' at a visual level (Wheatley 2006: 75–8, 181). The realism of the series, in which evidence is collected and scientifically examined and detectives have home lives that include chores and worrying when someone comes home late, is reframed through the series' relentless attention to textuality and aesthetic surfaces ('stylishness') – a key feature of the gothic mode.

Gothic television is not only uninterested in representational accuracy or verisimilitude, but also continues to question the very possibility of such representation. The history of censorship in US mass media, industry-administered from the Comics Code to television's Broadcast Standards and Practices and the Motion Picture Association of America's rating system, has shaped these cultural materials and the ideologically determined vision of the 'reality' that they present. The gothic, as a non-realist mode, operates aslant such dictates; by its very nature, and especially in its focus on aesthetics and affect, it often pushes against the limits of these rigid paradigms not only by representing violence but also by challenging the representational credibility of realism. From parodies of realist televisual genres, from *The Munsters* to *Supernatural*'s 'Changing Channels', to overt critiques of the constructedness of media representations such as the Figgleif narrative in *Millennium*'s 'Somehow', the gothic both predates television self-censorship and challenges the illusion that the censored and highly formalized narratives are somehow 'the real life'.

Notes

1. Helen Wheatley makes this point about 'industry professionals' (Wheatley 2006: 2), but we can add television publications and websites, Netflix and various other affiliated businesses. Information here about series – writers, producers, dates – are taken from the Internet Movie Database (www.imdb.com). All dialogue from television episodes here are my own transcriptions.
2. Wheatley discusses the 'long tradition of using the supernatural Gothic to demonstrate ... innovations in audio-visual media' (Wheatley 2006: 172).

For a discussion of radio gothic, and the challenges of sound, see McCracken 2002.
3. In the fifth-season episode of *Supernatural*, 'Changing channels' (2009), the writers thinly veil a sustained reference to *Grey's Anatomy* (2005–), in which the actor Jeffrey Dean Morgan (who played the protagonists' father in the early seasons of *Supernatural*) plays a character who dies and then reappears as a ghost.
4. On the general subject of the television serial killer, see also Maier 2004; for further discussion of television gothic and realism, see Wright (2016).

References

Baudrillard, Jean (1995), *Simulacrum and Simulation*, trans. Sheila Faria Glaser, Ann Arbor: University of Michigan Press.
Bruhm, Steven (1994), *Gothic Bodies: The Politics of Pain in Romantic Fiction*, Philadelphia: University of Pennsylvania Press.
Coleridge, Samuel Taylor [1817] (1951), *Biographia Literaria: Or, Biographical Sketches of My Literary Life and Opinions*, in *Selected Poetry and Prose of Coleridge*, ed. Donald A. Stauffer, New York: Modern Library, 109–428.
Dyer, Richard (1997), 'Kill and kill again', *Sight and Sound*, n.s. 7:9, 14–17.
Haralovich, Mary Beth (2003), 'Sitcoms and suburbs: positioning the 1950s homemaker', in *Critiquing the Sitcom: A Reader*, ed. Joanne Morreale, Syracuse: Syracuse University Press, 69–85.
Internet Movie Database, www.imdb.com
Kawash, Samira (2000), 'Safe house? Body, building, and the question of security', *Cultural Critique*, 45, 185–221.
Lavender-Smith, Jordan (2012), '"It's not unknown": the loose- and dead-end afterlives of *Battlestar Galactica* and *Lost*', in *Time in Television Narrative: Exploring Temporality in Twenty-first Century Programming*, ed. Melissa Ames, Jackson: University of Mississippi Press, 56–68.
Ledwon, Lenora (1993), '*Twin Peaks* and the television gothic', *Literature/Film Quarterly*, 21.4, 260–70.
Lost (2004–10), created by J. J. Abrams, Jeffrey Lieber, and Damon Lindelof, ABC.
Maier, Sarah E. (2004), 'John Doe reads: interrogating the postmodern serial killer in *Millennium, Se7en* and *Profiler*', in *Crime Time – Prime Time – Global Time: Intercultural Studies in Crime Serials*, ed. Ute Fendler and Susanne Fendler, Aachen, Germany: Shaker, 171–86.
Malcom, Shawna (2006), '*Lost* Boss Tackles *Star Trek* Enterprise', interview with J. J. Abrams, *TV Guide,* 11 August 2006. http://www.tvguide.com/news/lost-boss-tackles-37613.aspx (last accessed 28 July 2015).
McCracken, Allison (2002), 'Scary Women and Scarred Men: *Suspense*, Gender Trouble, and Post-War Change, 1942–1950', in *Radio Reader: Essays in the Cultural History of Radio*, ed. Michele Hilmes and Jason Loviglio, New York: Routledge, 183–207.
Mercury, Freddie (1975), 'Bohemian Rhapsody', perf. Queen, in *A Night at the Opera*, EMI.
Millennium (1996–9), created by Chris Carter, FOX.

Moi, Toril (1988), *Sexual/Textual Politics: Feminist Literary Theory*, New York: Routledge.
Morgan, Darin, 'Somehow, Satan Got Behind Me', in Chris Carter, *Millennium*, FOX, 1 May 1998.
Morris, David B. (1985), 'Gothic sublimity', *New Literary History*, 16, 299–319.
Nyberg, Amy Kiste (1998), *Seal of Approval: The History of the Comics Code*, Jackson: University Press of Mississippi.
Robson, Eddie (2007), 'Gothic television', in *The Routledge Companion to the Gothic*, ed. Catherine Spooner and Emma McEvoy, New York: Routledge, 242–50.
Sconce, Jeffrey (2000), *Haunted Media: Electronic Presence from Telegraphy to Television*, Durham, NC: Duke University Press.
Walpole, Horace [1964] (1996), *The Castle of Otranto: A Gothic Story*, ed. W. S. Lewis, intro. and notes E. J. Clery, Oxford: Oxford University Press.
Wheatley, Helen (2006), *Gothic Television*, Manchester: Manchester University Press.
Wright, Julia M. (2016), *Men with Stakes: Masculinity and the Gothic in US Television*, Manchester: Manchester University Press.

Chapter 8

American Gothic Art
Christoph Grunenberg

The gothic in American art looks back on a long tradition which is almost as old as the gothic novel itself. However, gothic art as a pronounced tendency that can be identified and labelled as such is a relatively recent phenomenon. This essay will survey the characteristics of the gothic in American art and trace its history from its earliest manifestations to a boom of the gothic in late twentieth- and early twenty-first-century art. As a trend in art, the gothic is intrinsically linked not only to the phenomenon of goth subculture as it emerged in the 1980s but also to a wide variety of forms of expression in the popular arts, in particular film and music but also fashion, design and architecture. In this productive cross-pollination between art, literature and the more ephemeral manifestations of the gothic in popular culture, it is a typical product of the postmodern era. In recent decades it has become a potent and pervasive, almost ubiquitous signifier for dark moods in times of change and crisis as expressed in a contemporary mordant mindset, the liberal indulgence in horror, macabre images and flirting with disaster.

The gothic is traditionally circumscribed through various related aesthetic phenomena such as the sublime, the uncanny, the ugly, the grotesque, formlessness and, most recently, the abject. I will attempt to classify the gothic as an independent aesthetic category that integrates elements of the previous but also stands alone. In defining the gothic, one needs to balance literary and other cultural influences with trends and traditions specific to the visual arts. Images of horror existed before the gothic – such as the grotesque goblins of medieval cathedrals, Renaissance paintings of saintly martyrdom and the Baroque celebration of the body or Piranesi's fantastic architectures of horror. However, over the 250 years of its existence, the gothic has evolved as a unique combination of terror and fantasy that materializes dark atmospheric moods and challenges moral and social trends. The gothic has always led a marginal existence, subverting the status quo from the outside and eroding commonly held ethical assumptions and accepted conventions of normality through shocking words, images and rituals. It presents, on a superficial level, a battle between good and evil, between progressive and reactionary forces, between purity of soul and tainted disposition. These simple antagonisms are particularly pronounced in American society with its strong Puritan heritage and taste for clear moral divisions, manifesting far deeper and complex conflicts, more often than not racial by nature. The gothic thus functions as kind of moral valve, releasing repressed memories and revealing the traumas that haunt American society throughout its history and presence.

The Gothic in Art

Formally the gothic manifests itself in a wide range of stylistic languages reaching from the exuberant dissolution of form in the grotesque to reduced objects and situations that produce horror through subtle allusions and sentiments. The gothic as an aesthetic category thus is characterised by its flexibility and mutability, making it such a prominent and enduring strand in art and culture. The gothic is more a state of mind than a distinct style, defined by a plurality of expressive modes and presentational strategies. Ultimately, the origins of the gothic can be located in the upheavals of the French Revolution and its reverberations across the European continent, producing a fierce reaction to the cold rationalism of the Enlightenment. Although the emergence of the gothic can be traced back to the neoclassical period, it is foremost a child of the Romantic age, dramatically manifesting anxieties about the effects of the industrial revolution and increasing urbanisation as well as the radical transformation in social relations and power structures.

The emergence of the gothic as a trend in art and architecture developed in parallel with the rediscovery of medieval gothic architecture and a full-blown gothic revival in all creative disciplines from the mid eighteenth century. Before this time, 'gothic' still denoted 'barbarous' and 'primitive', derived from the low estimate of medieval architecture and its disproportionate emphasis on vertical movement, crude and abundant ornamentation and reliance on dramatic light effects. The Romantics rediscovered what they termed the 'picturesque' qualities of the medieval gothic, admiring both its expressive beauty as well as projecting a Romantic ideal of the still unbroken harmony of religious belief, art and life. John Ruskin – 'always speaking as a Goth' (Ruskin 1959b: 167) – established in the mid nineteenth century that 'the characteristics or moral elements of Gothic are the following, placed in the order of their importance: 1. Savageness. 2. Changefulness. 3. Naturalism. 4. Grotesqueness. 5. Rigidity. 6. Redundance' (Ruskin 1959a: 230). Reversing the negative connotation of these attributes, Ruskin encouraged his contemporaries to 'examine once more those ugly goblins, and formless monsters, and stern statues, anatomiless and rigid; but do not mock at them, for they are signs of the life and liberty of every workman who struck the stone' (234). These formal categories continue to offer a useful guide to the circumscription of the gothic in art and the authenticity and force of its expression, born out of assumed genuine creative integrity (then) and the attempts at its recuperation respectively (now).

Gothic America

While the gothic as a creative genre first manifested itself in British literature, a distinctive tradition of the gothic developed in the United States as a vital expression of a continuing fascination in American society with horror and violence, moral ambiguity and the disintegration of personal identity and social cohesion.[1] The young American Republic's image of itself as an enlightened, liberal and progressive society seemed to distance it from the dramatics of the gothic. However, the gothic is a genre of 'borderlands', at home in contested moral, social and political territory and therefore 'naturally suited to a country that has seen the frontier (as shifting geographical, cultural, linguistic and racial boundary) as its defining characteristic' (Crow 2009: 2). Throughout the eighteenth and nineteenth centuries Americans were confronted with the truly unknown, unfamiliar and at times mysterious in their exploration of the West while projecting a conception of the Other onto American natives and slaves. The gothic is particularly active where underlying moral ambiguities, ideological contradictions and social tensions fail to enter public discourse and therefore manifest themselves in other forms – literature, art, music and popular culture. As Sarah Burns has argued, 'Gothic pictures are meditations on haunting and being haunted: by personal demons, social displacement (or misplacement), or the omnipresent spectre of slavery and race' (Burns 2004: xix). Through monsters, nightmares and ambiguity, these images 'grapple with the terror of annihilation by uncontrollable forces of social conflict and change', invert or subvert 'the status quo', 'threaten the social construction of the normal', 'dissolve boundaries designed to segregate social and cultural space, crisscrossing between high and low, elite and popular, painting and caricature' (xix). The gothic thus found a particularly fruitful ground in the United States, nurtured by a deep schism between the pretensions of social harmony and moral propriety and the realities of the social, political and racial conditions.

The emergence of the gothic novel in Britain in the 1760s was accompanied by an increasing preoccupation in the arts with horror and the supernatural, with fallen heroes, witches and fairies, most prominently in the visionary work of Henry Fuseli (1741–1825), William Blake (1757–1827) and their contemporaries. The gothic movement in America has frequently been labelled as 'Dark Romanticism', a pessimistic version of Ralph Waldo Emerson's and Henry David Thoreau's influential mid-nineteenth century Transcendentalism with its emphasis on idealism, inner-directed self-realisation and natural mysticism. It was this more introspective and spiritual form of the 'new sublime' championed by Emerson and Thoreau that defined landscape painting of the mid to late nineteenth century. The landscapes of the so-called Luminists after 1850 projected a pastoral serenity of untouched wilderness that was mostly too peaceful and ordered to contain any traces of evil. Even the second generation of the Hudson River School and in particular the monumental canvases of Albert Bierstadt (1830–1902), which capture the majestic grandeur of Western mountain ranges, lakes and canyons, were ultimately more concerned with man's insignificance in the face of nature's greatness than with the terror of supernatural forces.

The Dark Romantics in contrast detected a destructive tendency in nature, explored inexplicable metaphysical phenomena and suspected an inherent malevolence in man's essential disposition that manifested itself in 'images of anthropomorphized evil in the form of Satan, devils, ghosts, lamia, incubi, succubi, vampires, and ghouls' (Thompson 1974: 6). Rather than aberration or eccentric sideline, the gothic constitutes a prominent tradition in nineteenth-century American art that reaches from the Romantic period to the Realism of Winslow Homer (1836–1910) and Thomas Eakins (1844–1916) (Burns 2004). Fuseli's and Blake's most prominent counterpart in the United States was the painter Washington Allston (1779–1843), who displayed a similar Romantic predilection for the supernatural and the sublime. Allston, who studied with Fuseli at the Royal Academy in London and spent many years in Britain and Europe, can be seen as founding in American art a Romantic tradition concerned with a 'feeling for shadow, antiquity, mystery, and picturesque and gloomy wrong', acting as a counterpoint to the more dominant American preoccupation with realism (Novak 1979: 45). His early *Tragic Figure in Chains* (1800) echoes Blake's and Fuseli's despondent characters and gives form to an anti-rationalist sentiment, the enlightened mind torn by madness, uncontrolled temperament and suspension of liberty (Plate 1). In his attempts at 'pathetic fallacy' Allston also infused classical landscapes with a sense of sublime drama, overwhelming emotion and heightened terror. After his permanent return to the United States in 1818, the endless expanses and awe-inspiring grandiosity of American nature moved him to create atmospheric paintings of limitless landscapes amplified by dramatic light effects, so that, as Allston writes in *Lectures on Art and Poems* (1850), 'the very thought of [nature's] vastness darkens into wonder' (cited in Novak 1979: 48). His contemporary Thomas Cole (1801–48) similarly employed dead trees, cartilaginous roots, stormy seas and ruined castles to depict landscape as 'a gothic space where that inner world of doubt and dread tangled with the outer world of haunting history and foreboding change' (Burns 2004: 3).

Allston's direct spiritual descendants can be found in Symbolism at the end of the century, especially in the landscapes of Albert Pinkham Ryder (1847–1917), also known as 'Poe of the Brush' (Burns 2004: 222). His stormy seascapes, gloomy landscapes and architectural fantasies, painted with a rough textural expressiveness, introduce a dark visionary element that translates dream imagery into atmospheric miniature scenes of dread and doom. *The Flying Dutchman* (painted before 1890) combines a representation of the elemental forces of the sea with the tragic myth of a seaman's eternal limbo between life and death. Ryder's coarse, built-up surfaces, his eccentric personality and even his lack of personal hygiene conjure associations of living membranes and decaying matter, generating feelings of disgust which suggest how death 'must be fended off and kept at a distance, lest identity collapse and dissolve back into nothingness' (Burns 2004: 240).[2] We can thus establish a direct lineage from Ryder to early Abstract Expressionism, via John Marin and Marsden Hartley, and especially to Jackson Pollock, as in his closely related *Seascape* (1934).

American Gothic

The flexible nature of the gothic makes its appearance unpredictable, surfacing in the twentieth century in a variety of different stylistic guises. It is not necessarily attached to avant-garde idioms but emerges in times of profound disorder and uncertainty and manifests itself as much in Surrealism's exploration of the nether regions of the unconscious through dreams and sexual perversions as in more conservative stylistic modes re-emerging after World War I. A powerful vein of the gothic in the twentieth century can thus be found in the urban melancholia of Edward Hopper and the exacting realism of American Regionalism, establishing a familiar dynamic between quotidian normality and hidden passions and buried secrets. A prime example is Grant Wood's iconic *American Gothic*

(1930), its title alluding to the house in the background constructed in the so-called Carpenter Gothic style popular in the nineteenth-century United States. Wood composed the architecture and two protagonists as a unity, imagining 'American Gothic people with their faces stretched out long to go with this American Gothic house', famously asking his sister and his dentist to model as a farmer and his daughter (*Art Institute* 2013: 56). 'American Gothic' here does not evoke horror but rather a certain strict Protestant piety and virtuousness associated with simple and clean-living folks in the rural Midwest. However, the painting has also been interpreted as 'an old-fashioned mourning portrait', the closed curtains indicating a Victorian funeral custom, the theme of death creeping in through the backdoor (Solomon 2010: 16). This tension between restrained realism and the outward demonstration of propriety and the painting's darker subtext makes *American Gothic* an intriguingly mysterious and therefore essentially 'gothic' image. Behind the appearance of respectability lurk the unresolved conflicts of American society – the insistence on simple living versus the celebration of material accumulation; the prevalence of a Protestant work ethic versus conspicuous consumption; the celebration of individualism versus the rigid social conformity proscribed by a pervasive religious and moral conservatism; the principles of moderation and temperance versus the spectre of sexual desire and deviance. On a more general level, the work alludes to the Depression, widespread unemployment, the increasing ideological confrontation of left- and right-wing politics with the rise of fascism and a looming world war as its most extreme threat.

In his powerful photographic variation on Wood's painting, *American Gothic, Washington D. C.* (1942), Gordon Parks revealed another, ever-present spectre – that of racism. The bespectacled and stern-looking farmer has been replaced by a black cleaning woman, now holding a broom and a mop instead of a pitchfork. The verticality of the gothic architecture is replicated by the stripes of a hanging American flag, as an accusatory symbol of the gap between political pretension and the harsh realities of racial discrimination in wartime America. The appropriation of the title of the already iconic painting questions the formalized display of decency in the original and uncovers a sinister aspect of American society.

Apocalyptic Gothic

In the establishment of an independent modern American art that could compete with the creative products of the Old World and Paris in particular, the 'gothic' usually was seen more as an unnecessary diversion than a genuine form of indigenous expression. In 1947 Clement Greenberg characterized the post-cubist paintings of Jackson Pollock (1912–56) from the mid 1940s as 'gothic' and 'morbid', inscribed with 'paranoia and resentment', establishing a proximity in spirit to Poe and even detecting a sadistic and scatological sensibility (Greenberg 1986b: 166). Greenberg here employed gothic as a negatively charged synonym for Surrealism, a movement he vehemently condemned. 'Surrealism has revived all the Gothic revivals and acquires more and more of a period flavour, going for Faustian lore, old-fashioned and flamboyant interiors, alchemistic mythology, and whatever else are held to be the excesses in taste of the past', he wrote in 1944, the same year Pollock painted *Gothic* (Greenberg 1986a: 226; Plate 2). Retroactive nostalgia, formal fragmentation and biomorphic remnants for Greenberg dangerously obstructed the forward thrust of modernist painting and tainted the purity of artistic means and expression.

For Pollock the title is both literal and evocative. On the one hand, he references the luminosity of stained glass windows of gothic cathedrals, dancing dark outlines framing copper-green, grey-blue and clay-red patches of colour in pointed shapes. On the other hand, *Gothic* also seems to denote elemental forces and an underlying threatening energy emanating out of the dark. According to Greenberg, the 'gothic' with its backward orientation towards the 'transcendental, romantic, subjective' continued to exert a particularly strong and diversionary influence on creative production in America (Greenberg 1986b: 164). It illustrated the failure to develop an art that successfully translates 'the "positivism" and "materialism" of industrial modernity into culture' (Duve 2010: 32). The gothic nature of Pollock's art thus reveals a conflict between internal formal and wider social and political concerns, between tradition and progress, between irrational fears and the immediacy of expression.

Although Greenberg acknowledges the authenticity of emotion that characterizes Pollock's foundation in urban culture, something else disturbs Greenberg in the gothic: its indulgence in a dark apocalyptic outlook that was so essential to Abstract Expressionism in the wake of World War II and the Holocaust. For Greenberg this was a redundant ambition: 'In the face of current events painting feels, apparently, that it must be more than itself: it must be epic poetry, it must be theater, it must be rhetoric, it must be an atomic bomb, it must be the Rights of Man' (Greenberg 1986c: 133–4). The gothic thus contains traces of the deep neurosis of 'Organization Man' of 1940s and 50s America, grappling with the existentialist fear of disempowerment in a conformist capitalist society and mass culture and, on a more global level, with the very real threat of mankind's extinction. Maybe, then, Greenberg's objection was to the hyperbole of the gothic as an overly dramatic and therefore 'vulgar' evocation of angst, as T. J. Clark has pointed out: 'Death makes a bad metaphor. Pictures that summon it up too readily . . . get to look Gothic before their time. . . . Death is enlisted to make vulgarity look deep' (Clark 1997: 60). This familiar accusation is almost as old as the gothic itself, deriving from its delight in formal immoderation, convoluted dramatic plots and exaggerated ghoulish spectacles.

Kalifornia Gothic

Mostly, however, these manifestations of the gothic in America remained confined to the margins of cultural discourse, violating the demands for monolithic statements, stylistic integrity and easy consumption. Significantly, it was on the West Coast – far away from the reigning capital of modern art – that the gothic once again manifested itself most forcefully from the 1950s onwards. The sculptures of San Francisco 'Beat' artist Bruce Conner (1933–2008) – constructed from old furniture, dolls, cloth, string and other found objects, his assemblages are covered in dirt and cobwebs – display all the features of a gothic sensibility. Disjunctive, decaying and soiled, they are everything that contemporary Minimalist objects were not, defying the anonymity of industrial production, the purity of simple geometric objects and the rhetoric of pure thought. Conner's sculptures offer a powerful antidote to California's eternal sunshine of the mind, repressively good humour and the superficiality of its ubiquitous entertainment industry. Conner's 'fetishized American gothic thrift-store creepiness' (Hoberman 2012) was translated into dramatic spatial tableaux by his Los Angeles contemporary Ed Kienholz (1927–94). His *mise en scènes* feature dark and dingy bars, empty corridors in cheap hotels and squalid bedrooms fitted with ill-matched and out-of-fashion furniture – metaphors for urban isolation, failed relationships, social downfall and mental instability. These scenarios are always tinged by a sombre gloom, some slightly repulsive patina of age that evokes loneliness and desperation (Plate 3).

The Los Angeles gothic is particularly complex, or even 'schizophrenic', as fact and fiction blend into one reality and the fabricated landscape of film noir merges with the city as ready-made movie set. The proverbial 'sunshine and noir' of California; the dream world of Hollywood and the dark side of LA gothic; the city's hedonistic life style and celebration of the perfect, youthful body; and the art world's indulgence in the abject, decadent and perverse, should not reduce California art to a simplistic 'Edenic/dysopic dualism' (Barron 2000: 35). However, the gothic does like to feed on these opposites, on lingering conflicts and moral and cultural ruptures. Capitalism's discarded detritus composed into Beat culture objects and assemblage art of the 1950s and 60s provided a stark counterpoint to the state's economic boom, rapid population growth, sprawling suburban housing developments, pervasive consumer culture and sanitized cultural mainstream. Beat art offers reminders of a less civilized past, the displacement of its indigenous inhabitants and of a less glorified reality behind the facade of glamour. It then should not come as a surprise that California, and Los Angeles in particular, would provide a particularly fertile territory for a gothic sensibility in the United States during the gothic decades of the 1980s and 90s.

The End is Nigh: Pre-millennial Gothic

Powered by the destabilizing effects of widespread deindustrialization and the moral conflicts of the so-called 'culture wars', the gothic made a compelling return in the final decades of the twentieth century. With the apparent dissolution of common values and standards resulting from the student revolution; the disruptive demographic and social shifts as a consequence of the Civil Rights movement, in parallel with the United States' traumatic experience of the loss of the Vietnam War and resulting decline in international stature; and the disintegration of confidence in politics in the wake of Watergate, the 1970s can be seen as a typical moment of national uncertainty and moral confusion, laying the foundation for a violent eruption of the gothic. In an uncompromising backlash against this perceived moment of fundamental national crisis, the Reagan 1980s saw a pronounced shift to the right and emphasis on conservative values in combination with a laissez-faire capitalism. In addition to the existence of a pronounced apocalyptic mood, pre-millennial fears of a total collapse of technological and, by extension, of economic and political systems, a perceived rapid disintegration of all ethical certainties, in combination with a dark aesthetic that perfectly captured these fears, made the 1980s and 90s particularly fruitful decades for the gothic. It now was much more than a creative genre or emerging subculture: the gothic became a powerful indicator of a pervasive moral malaise and pessimistic outlook as the twentieth century crawled to the new millennium. An obsession with the paranormal and fantastic, evil deeds and distorted minds, serial killers and psychopaths once again occupied a central place in the popular imagination. As Mark

Edmundson writes, 'A Gothic spirit much like Poe's now infuses a great deal of our film and popular fiction – and other, less predictable zones of the culture as well' (Edmundson 1996: 48).

'Gothic' became a byword for sombre and disturbing moods, sites, events and cultural by-products of latter-day America: from 'Gothic capitalism' to the 'Day of the Locust "Gothic"' of Los Angeles, 'Ghetto-Gothic', the 'Southern Gothic' of true crime in Georgia, the *Batman* films' 'dime store gothic gloom', the definition of the successful TV programmes *X-Files* and *Millennium* as 'mod-gothic melodramas' or *Melrose Place* as a 'gothic serial for the cyberage', and finally to the ubiquitous 'American Gothic', embracing everything from daytime TV talk shows to O. J. Simpson, satanic ritual murders, Timothy McVeigh's New York state home town and the television series of the same name.[3] The ghosts of the gothic seemed to have returned to haunt the American soul with its images and ideas, holding up a mirror to the nation's sacred principles: 'Unsentimental, enraged by gentility and high-mindedness, sceptical about any progress in any form, the Gothic mind is antithetical to all smiling American faiths. A nation of ideals, America has also been, not surprisingly, a nation of hard disillusionment, with a fiercely reactive Gothic imagination', as again Edmundson described the mood in 1996 (Edmundson 1996: 48).

The United States of the 1980s and 90s seemed to be entering a second Victorian age, with all its aberrations of repressive social codes, moral terrorism, sanctimonious ideals and double standards. It was Satan who revealed himself in false splendour, grotesque exaggeration and insolent ostentation:

> We are in the midst of one of those periodic moments of repression, when the culture, descended from the Puritans, imposes its hysterical visions and enforces its guilty constraints on society, legislating moral judgments under the guise of public health, all the while enlarging the power of surveillance and the reach of censorship to achieve a general restriction of freedom. (Klein 1993: 3)

Abject: The Postmodern Gothick

In the wake of goth music and subculture, which first surfaced in the late 1970s and early 80s in England, the gothic emerged in America and internationally as a phenomenon in the visual arts. On the eve of the millennium, it could be argued, the gothic grew up, supported by a theoretical superstructure which addressed the disintegration of the body, open sexual identity and the self's invasion by technology. Its desire to shock and provoke, its delight in excess and exaggeration, however, remained undiminished. Accordingly, the gothic has been defined as a typically postmodern phenomenon, obsessed with the 'deviant, exotic and grotesque', assuming that truth lies in the extreme rather than the boringly mundane: 'Everyday life is now felt to be irredeemably alienated, so that only what violates or estranges can be valid. For Post-Modern thought, the normative is inherently oppressive' (Eagleton 1999: 7).

For the first time the gothic was explicitly named and recognised as a pervasive trend in contemporary art and culture, most prominently in an exhibition which I curated at the Institute of Contemporary Art in Boston in 1997 (Grunenberg 1997).[4] Here the gothic arrived in the shape of formless, horrendous, shocking images of mutilated and rotting bodies with limbs covered in boils and wounds. It also entered consciousness quietly – almost hesitantly – via the slow realization of terror, as evoked in Robert Gober's reductive reconfiguration of simple everyday objects or body parts into nightmarish scenarios disturbing the illusion of domestic comfort. The traditional gothic themes of the uncanny, the fantastic and pathological and the tension between the artificial and organic were infused in contemporary art with new potency as they addressed concerns about the body, disease, voyeurism and power. Gothic art was fascinated exactly by those subjects that transgress society's vague definitions of normality, discreetly peeling away the pretences of outmoded conventions and transversing the amorphous border between good and evil, sanity and madness, erotic desire and repulsion, disinterested pleasure and visual offensiveness. The internal characteristics that unite the contemporary gothic were defined as a preoccupation with 'paranoia' ('the "implicated" reader is placed in a situation of ambiguity with regard to fears within the text'), 'the notion of the barbaric' (bringing us up 'against the boundaries of the civilised' and 'fear of racial degeneracy'), and 'the nature of taboo' (addressing 'areas of socio-psychological life which offend, which are suppressed') (Punter 1996: 2.183–4).

In the 1980s and 90s, the future monsters of technology created by man were no longer contained in clean boxes with blinking lights and dematerialized mechanical voices (as Hal in *2001: A Space Odyssey*), but once again occupied 'gothicized' bodies as cyborgs, aliens and endless variations on the mythical figures of the Golem, Frankenstein or Dracula: 'Like the bolt through the neck of Frankenstein's monster in the modern horror film, the technology of monstrosity is written on the human body' (Halberstam 1995: 106). One of the key obsessions of the decade became 'abjection', as manifested most prominently in the unsettling work, amongst others, of Gregory Crewdson, Robert Gober, Mike

Kelley, Paul McCarthy, John Miller, Cindy Sherman and Kiki Smith. It continues a distinctive American tradition in Surrealism (foremost Ivan Lorraine Albright and Pavel Tchelitchew) in which the parallel dissolution of the physical and psychological self figures prominently. The human body's repugnant physiological functions and emotional traumas became a particular focus in contemporary art at a moment when nudity, sexual pleasure and explicit language became increasingly taboo subjects. Abjection is evident in Mike Kelley's accumulations of soiled and worn-out dolls, sad objects of unfulfilled affection, or in his scatological drawings that exemplify contemporary art's 'fixation not simply on sexual organs but, as well, on all bodily orifices and their secretions' (Krauss 1996: 90). The concept of abjection has also been associated with the 'monstrous-feminine' as manifested in Kiki Smith's flayed figures or in Cindy Sherman's photographs of incongruous composite bodies. In Sherman's images of grotesque demons and masked faces, the artist returned to her earlier investigations into female identity as an enactment of codified roles, combining contemporary ideas of beauty with horror film props (Plate 4). Here the abject, which Julia Kristeva defines as the 'in-between, the ambiguous, the composite', manifests itself through the literally dismembered, 'monstrous' female body put on display in a museum (Kristeva 1982: 4, 9–10).

Beyond the confrontation with remnants of sexual intercourses, scatological substances and symptoms of disease, the abject can be located in the confrontation with base materials – earth, dirt, grunge. The earth, according to Deleuze and Guattari, is a body without organs, which in Cindy Sherman's 'abstractions' and Crewdson's tableaux of the American small-town picturesque erupt into a formless mass of internal organs without body (Deleuze and Guattari 1988: 40). In Sherman's almost abstract landscapes of the so-called 'Vomit Pictures' (1987–91), the human figure is absent (or hidden, only occasionally visible in a reflection), represented by vomit, excrement and rotting food. These are highly attractive, almost seductive images – large-scale, colourful and glossy as in fashion and advertising photography – which play with the fetishization of the exterior facade of the female and the concealment of the interior of the woman's body. Both the pictures of externalized bodily substances and identities disguised behind frozen masks are concerned with the mechanics and pressures of constructing and destroying feminine identity, raising 'the spectre of the anorexic girl, who tragically acts out the fashion fetish of the female as an eviscerated, cosmetic and artificial construction designed to ward off the "otherness" hidden in the interior' (Mulvey 1991: 146).[5]

Abjection in art produces disgust and repulsion and severs 'the identificatory bonds of between the viewer and the image', breaking down the border between imagined reality and truth, regression and consciousness, inside and outside (*Abject* 1993: 62). However, the frisson of horror and repulsion is never the ultimate objective of abjection, our reluctant attraction founded in the desire to glimpse into another, more inclusive, reality. The state of schizophrenic confusion triggered by disgust and transgression suspends programmed inhibitions and conditioned responses to create a state of moral uncertainty. Gothic art skilfully negotiates the ambivalent territory of beauty and disgust, providing as much pain as it gives pleasure through the beauty of an art that is ecstatic in its intensity.

The Return of the Uncanny: Memory and Repression

Over the last decades, small-town and suburban America – the last refuge of the middle classes – has become the preferred site for encounters with strangers, serial killers and the supernatural. Since George Romero's *Night of the Living Dead* (1968), horror fiction and movies have situated the bloody clash of the normal and pathological into a pastoral and idyllic America, ignorant of social, urban or technological change. In Wes Craven's *A Nightmare on Elm Street* (1984) suppressed communal crimes haunt the protagonists in a pleasant suburban neighbourhood, adolescents paying for their parents' deeds. This classic gothic trope exemplifies the conflict between interior and exterior world, individual and society, the intra- and inter-subjective. It further signifies the disintegrating institution of the bourgeois nuclear family which, unlike in the European gothic, remains a primary site of conflict exemplifying 'the destructive power of families' deriving 'from America's puritan heritage, "the old violent vindictive Mysticism", as Faulkner called it' (Davenport-Hines 1998: 267). Economic realities, demographic changes and the break-up of traditional gender roles are 'the monsters' that have descended on common citizens since the late 1960s. As Judith Halberstam has pointed out, the gothic monsters that threaten and terrify us are never 'unitary but always an aggregate of race, class, and gender' (Halberstam 1995: 88).

The domestic sphere is a primary site of the inversion of assumed normality into a battlefield of the monstrous. Robert Gober's miniature models of ordinary American homes or his suggestive *Untitled (Closet)* (1989) revive childhood memories of playful fantasies and secrets explored in locked cupboards or closets, which present an open and empty space, apparently stripped of any traces of past inhabitants.

However, as one enters the small claustrophobic room, it becomes permeated with the visitor's own memories and responses. The closets, similar to Gober's other transformations of furniture, doors or sinks, are

> objects you complete with your body, and they're objects that, in one way or another, transform you. Like the sink, from dirty to clean; the beds, from conscious to unconscious, rational thoughts to dreaming; the doors transform you in the sense . . . of moving from one space through another. (Simon 1992: 20)

These staged scenes are essentially uncanny situations, describing the return of repressed events, memories and fantasies, and the encounter with one's own most intimate fears: 'something, which is secretly familiar, which has undergone repression and then returned from it', as Freud described it (Freud 1955: 245).

In Gregory Crewdson's panoramic, high-definition photographs of small-town America and bland suburbia, the peaceful idyll is disturbed by inexplicable supernatural events, lost souls wandering empty streets and strange rituals being performed by deranged men and women. As Terry Eagleton states, 'The transgressions of Gothic are dependent on the sobrieties of realism, just as the "bad" body of Gothic – monstrous, mutilated, libidinal – represents the guilty yearning of the "good", sanitised body of the suburbs' (Eagleton 1999: 7). Crewdson's images are carefully composed, spectacular and theatrical, and at the same time project an eerily still and disturbing atmosphere. Artifice and illusion are key instruments in the gothic toolbox, attracting the viewer through an abundance of detail, opulence of colour and sophistication of workmanship only to repulse us through the evocation of the real that is death and decay, the loss of control and sanity.

A similar tension exists between the perfect illusion of reality and its disturbance through the dubious nature of the human figure caught between the animate and inanimate – as in wax mannequins, shop-window dolls, puppets, automatons or hyperrealist sculptures and, on an even more real level, doubles, doppelgängers and cyborgs. The exhibition *The Uncanny*, curated by artist Mike Kelley (1993 in Soonsbek and restaged 2004 at Tate Liverpool), was initially organized within the context of the revival of polychrome figurative sculpture in contemporary art. It explored 'the Greek prejudice' which has banned illusionary and hyperrealist depictions of the human figure from most of art history but allowed them in 'functional' figures such as fetishes, religious statues, mannequins, stuffed animals, anatomical models and puppets, all of which were included in the show (Kelley 1993: 25). Since the 1980s many artists have returned to the realist depiction of 'anthropomorphic forms' to express concerns about medical advances in reconstructive and plastic surgery, genetic manipulation, prescriptive media constructions of beauty as well as the harrowing effects of the AIDS epidemic. These include Gober's fragmented body parts (Plate 4), John Miller's and Charles Ray's mannequins, Judy Fox's naked children, Tony Oursler's 'techno-grotesque' (Welchman 2001: 123), Paul McCarthy's battered and traumatised victims and Tony Matelli's sleepwalkers (Plate 5). Their human scale and illusionistic rendering force an intense physical confrontation with the *objet d'art* rare in a contemporary art often more concerned with abstract ideas and concepts. Like the original gothic monster, Frankenstein, these figures conjure a gothic state of flux that disrupts old certainties about the self, expose the vulnerability of the human body and ultimately raise the dark spectre of death. It is most extreme and truly uncomfortable when the illusion verges on the perfect, crossing the 'uncanny valley' where robots and animatronic figures become too human and the pleasurable shiver of uncertainty turns into real fear.

The history of slavery and racial division provides a powerful and disturbing subtext in American history and art that manifests itself in the 'Southern Gothic' as a major subcategory in literature, film and the arts. As Leslie Fiedler argues, 'the proper subject for American gothic is the black man' (Fiedler 1997: 397), and Sarah Burns notes that 'a continuum of blackness bearing all the connotations of evil, danger, and mystery' defines much of nineteenth-century art and beyond (Burns 2004: 102). Kara Walker plays with the traditions and topoi of the Southern Gothic, creating dramatic tableaux of grotesque bodies and exaggerated violence set in swamp landscapes with overgrown trees and dying vegetation (Plate 6). The artist appropriates extreme racial stereotypes that are part of the Southern Gothic mystique and makes them her own through the two-dimensional technique of the silhouettes which, in itself, employs blackness as its primary formal means. The landscape itself becomes a kind of vegetable gothic architecture in dissolution, its liquid structure returning us to the origins of gothic architecture in the soaring verticality of proud trees and primordial huts. Walker's American South is a place of hopeless backwardness, sexual permissiveness, racial degeneration, inbred misogyny, rampant racism and licentious exploitation, a dark and brutal world which is made bearable only through the collapse of horror in an overstated representation of humorous vulgarity. Her characters perform unspeakably obscene deeds, delight in lewd sexual acts and scatological escapades, represented through the distancing abstraction of the silhouette technique.

Gary Simmons similarly uses black and white contrasts to comment on racial stereotypes and the blending of historical fact and fiction in black history. Since the late 1980s Simmons has erased chalk drawings on slate painted walls or charcoal drawings on white walls or paper, thus 'obliterating' the images in order to reveal the grey areas between 'black' and 'white'. His monumental *Ghost Ship* (1995) dissolves into the atmospheric background, evoking mythical stories of sunken slave ships and images from black-and-white pirate adventure movies. *Light House* (1996) places a tumbling building into a swallowing fog of sublime nothingness. The practice of erasure changes and negates historical images while radically modifying their formal consistency and original meaning. Both artists address the issue of race through the specifics of their artistic medium, conjuring still repressed ghosts of slavery and questioning the association of 'darkness' with evil, immorality, obscurity and gloom.

New Gothic Art

The gothic continues as an influential strand in the visual arts until today, periodically entering public consciousness without having ever really disappeared. The resurgence of what has been termed 'new gothic art' can be seen as an extension of the last, pre-millennial gothic wave of the 1990s (Kennedy 2005; see also Egan 2005). It shows all the signs of the 'mainstreaming of a trend that was once the exclusive domain of societal outcasts and freaks', having established itself firmly in Hollywood films, television series, romantic novels as well as becoming a major influence in fashion and interior design: 'These days Goth is "an Upper East Side way of being edgy without actually drinking anybody's blood"' (La Ferla 2005).

The 2004 Whitney Biennial included a number of younger artists whose continued fascination with death, horror and the macabre manifested itself in a 'gothic sensibility that revels in a voluptuous, sensual materiality. Decay and fragmentation, ruin and dissolution describe both the specific forms as well as their allegory of moral, corporeal, emotional, or socio-political state' (Momin 2004: 47–8). Banks Violette's installations of cold steel, mirrors and neon combined with shiny black, drooping epoxy can be seen as pure gothic opposition of glamour and dread (Plate 7). Violette draws inspiration from the extremes of Norwegian death metal music and real-life dramas of teenage murder and arson to implicate the viewer and question received notions of normality. David Altmejd's installations are no less macabre though more poetic, constructing complex fantasy castles and elaborate sculptural displays of werewolves and sleeping giants from glass, mirrors, crystals, jewellery, fur and hair that blur the boundary between the real and the fantastic, the architectural and the morphological. Both artists touch on elements of the cybergothic and its fascination with a bygone industrial aesthetic and the incorporation of 'the pretechnological "biological" body and the posttechnological "golem" body' (Elferen 2009: 107). The painter Mark Ryden displays a true gothic sensibility in the Los Angeles tradition that finds inspiration in art history, Gay Nineties illustrations and fairy tales. Ryden combines old-master technique with over-the-top artifice to depict strange characters (preferably cute girls with oversized heads and big doll's eyes, but also historical figures such as Jesus or Abraham Lincoln), scenes of mutilation and abundant displays of meat.

'Forever Young'

What seemed like a short-lived surfacing of the dark and macabre has entered the mainstream and continues to make periodic reappearances, like a spectre refusing to die. Some feel that gothic horror has spent itself through endless repetition and excessive commercialisation, resulting in what Fred Botting termed 'Candygothic', 'in which transgressions, repressions, taboos, prohibitions no longer mark an absolute limit in unbearable excess and thus no longer contain the intensity of a desire for something that satisfyingly disturbs and defines social and moral boundaries' (Botting 2001: 134). Proclamations of the demise of the gothic, however, have proven premature. Despite the penetration of the gothic into the mainstream, it remains changeable enough to re-emerge like some bad dream in unexpected forms and unlikely locations. The gothic in American culture has led a perpetually marginal life because it has always been a little too dark and too strange to warrant full integration into mainstream tastes. But this same peripheral existence is what makes it a seductive way to express revolt against bourgeois norms, test moral codes and explore alternative identities. The gothic thus also speaks powerfully to an age tired of politics, one that has lost any real enthusiasm for or genuine belief in grand utopias. Yet by challenging moral norms and exploring sexual proclivities it necessarily also acquires a distinct political dimension.[6]

As art continues to search for intense feelings and authentic modes of expression distinct from an often uniform, bland mainstream entertainment, the gothic reacts against a persistent and protective 'anti-intensity emotionology' that challenges 'the requirement of a corporate, service-oriented economy and management structure; small-family size, with emphasis on leisure and sexual compatibility between spouses; consumerism; and anxiety about hidden forces within the body that might be disturbed by emotional excess' (Stearns 1994: 289–90). Oscillating between attraction and repulsion, recent art continues to explore the concentrated negative pleasures of the sublime, which in the eighteenth century Edmund Burke better defined as 'productive of the strongest emotion which the mind is capable of feeling. . . . I am satisfied the ideas of pain are much more powerful than those which enter on pleasure' (Burke 1987: 39). No longer concerned with the production of grand and majestic terror, however, the contemporary version of this elevated aesthetic sentiment evokes what Violette has called 'a glue-sniffer's apotheosis of Burke's sublime' (Kennedy 2005).

So momentous, shocking and visually powerful a spectacle were the terror attacks of 9/11 that art recognises its own inability to represent adequately such events. Some creative products captured the initial outpouring of shock, grief and anger, serving 'useful purposes – cathartic commemoration, therapeutic expression, public rallying – but in retrospect, many of them now feel sentimental or heavy-handed' (Kakutani 2011). The gothic, however, never was an art that felt comfortable with serving the mainstream or fulfilling some vague redemptive function. Fact is stronger than fiction and frequently the most 'powerful works to emerge about 9/11 and its aftermath have been documentary or fact-based' (Kakutani 2011). Already before 9/11 Andrew Delbanco recognized a metaphorical vacuum in American society:

> Our culture is now in crisis because evil remains an inescapable experience for all of us, while we no longer have a symbolic language for describing it. . . . It leaves us in our obligatory silence, with a punishing question: 'How', in the words of one literary critic, 'is the imagination to compass things for which it can find no law, no aesthetic purpose or aesthetic resolution?' (Delbanco 1995: 11, 224)

Artists had to find a visual language that resists 'the new kitsch of post-9/11 America' and the 'subtle blackmail' and not so subtle moral coercion it exerts (Foster 2005: 225). Allegory and 'overt symbolism', as in the work of Violette, have made a surprising return, providing a convincing way of dealing with dark subject matter, unexplainable events and the continuing paranoia that haunts twenty-first-century America (Kakutani 2011). Gober, for example, resorted to 'broken allegory that both elicits and resists our interpretation' (Foster 224). The gothic provides a powerful visual and symbolic language to deal with feelings of calamity and uncertainty without drifting into illustrative depictions or worn clichés – a ready-made style for the perpetual state of crisis that now defines our culture.

Notes

1. For a discussion of the relationship between the gothic in British romantic literature and American gothic art and architecture, see Carso 2015.
2. Burns here paraphrases Julia Kristeva.
3. Halberstam 1995: 102–5; Bessman 1995, 8; *Time*, 3 April 1995, 79; Allen 1994: 107; Wolcott 1997: 76; Martin 1997: B2; Edmundson 1996: 48-55; Oates 1995: 35–6; Elias 1995: H37, H42.
4. Other important exhibitions were *Post-Human*, curated by Jeffrey Deitch 1992; *Helter Skelter: L.A. Art in the 1990s*, Museum of Contemporary Art, Los Angeles 1992; *Belladonna*, Institute of Contemporary Arts, London 1997; and *Apocalypse: Beauty and Horror in Contemporary Art*, Royal Academy of Arts, London 2000.
5. For a discussion of the 'monstrous-feminine' see Creed 1993.
6. 'If working-class militancy is dead, Marxism discredited and revolutionary nationalism on its uppers, then the field of sexuality can provide the forms of power-struggle, symbolism and solidarity which are less and less available elsewhere, along with a greater chance of political gains' (Eagleton 1999: 5).

References

Abject Art: Repulsion and Desire in American Art, New York: Whitney Museum of American Art, 1993.
Allen, Henry Southworth (1994), *Going Too Far Enough: American Culture at Century's End*, Washington: Smithsonian Institution Press.
The Art Institute of Chicago: The Essential Guide, Chicago, 2013.
Barron, Stephanie (2000), 'Introduction: The Making of *Made in California*', in *Made in California: Art, Image, and Identity 1945–2000*, ed. Sheri Bernstein and Ilene Susan Fort, Berkeley: University of California Press, 27–47.
Bessman, Jim, 'Capitol's Melvin Van Peebles issues first album in 20 years', *Billboard*, 107.9, 4 March 1995, 8, 86.
Botting, Fred (2001), 'Candygothic', in *The Gothic*, ed. Fred Botting, Cambridge, MA: D. S. Brewer, 133–52.
Burke, Edmund [1757] (1987), *A Philosophical Enquiry into the Origin of Our Ideas of the Sublime and the Beautiful*, ed. James T. Boulton, Oxford: Basil Blackwell.
Burns, Sarah (2004), *Painting the Dark Side: Art and the Gothic Imagination in Nineteenth-Century America*, Berkeley: University of California Press.
Carso, Kerry Dean (2015), *American Gothic Art and Architecture in the Age of Romantic Literature*, Cardiff: University of Wales Press.
Clark, T. J. [1994] (1997), 'In Defence of Abstract Expressionism', in *October: The Second Decade, 1986–1996*, ed. Rosalind Krauss, Cambridge, MA: MIT Press, 50–77.

Creed, Barbara (1993), *The Monstrous-Feminine: Film, Feminism, Psychoanalysis*, London: Routledge.
Crow, Charles L. (2009), *American Gothic*, Cardiff: University of Wales Press.
Davenport-Hines, Richard (1998), *Gothic: Four Hundred Years of Excess, Horror, Evil and Ruin*, New York: North Point Press.
Delbanco, Andrew (1995), *The Death of Satan: How Americans Have Lost the Sense of Evil*, New York: Farrar, Straus and Giroux.
Deleuze, Gilles and Félix Guattari (1988), *A Thousand Plateaus: Capitalism and Schizophrenia*, London: Athlone Press.
Duve, Thierry de (2010), *Clement Greenberg Between the Lines: Including a Debate with Clement Greenberg*, Chicago: University of Chicago Press.
Eagleton, Terry (1999), 'Allergic to Depths', *London Review of Books*, 21:6, 18 March 1999, 7–8.
Edmundson, Mark (1996), 'American Gothic', *Civilization: The Magazine of the Library of Congress*, 3, May/June 1996, 48–55.
Egan, Maura (2005), 'The Remix; School of Ghoul', *New York Times*, 18 September 2005, <http://query.nytimes.com/gst/fullpage.html?res=9801EED8113CF93BA2575AC0A9639C8B63> (last accessed 24 August 2014).
Elferen, Isabella van (2009), 'Dancing with Spectres: Theorising the Cybergothic', *Gothic Studies*, 11:1, 99–112.
Elias, Justine (1995), '"American Gothic" Settles In on the Dark Side', *New York Times*, 22 October 1995, H37, H42.
Fiedler, Leslie [1960] (1997), *Love and Death in the American Novel*, Champaign: University of Illinois Press.
Foster, Hal (2005), 'American Gothic: Hal Foster on Robert Gober', *Artforum International*, 43:9, May 2005, 222–5.
Freud, Sigmund [1919] (1955), 'The "Uncanny"', in *The Standard Edition of the Complete Psychological Works of Sigmund Freud*, vol. 17, trans. and ed. James Strachey, London: Hogarth Press, 219–52.
Greenberg, Clement [1944] (1986a), 'Surrealist Painting', in *The Collected Essays and Criticism. Volume 1: Perceptions and Judgments, 1939–1944*, ed. John O'Brian, Chicago: University of Chicago Press, 225–31.
Greenberg, Clement [1947] (1986b), 'The Present Prospects of American Painting and Sculpture', in *The Collected Essays and Criticism. Volume 2: Arrogant Purpose, 1945–1949*, ed. John O'Brian, Chicago: University of Chicago Press, 160–70.
Greenberg, Clement [1947] (1986c), 'Review of Exhibitions of the Jane Street Group and Rufino Tamyo', in *The Collected Essays and Criticism. Volume 2: Arrogant Purpose, 1945–1949*, 131–5.
Grunenberg, Christoph (1997), *Gothic: Transmutations of Horror in Late Twentieth-Century Art*, Cambridge, MA: MIT Press.
Halberstam, Judy (1995), *Skin Shows: Gothic Horror and the Technology of Monsters*, Durham, NC: Duke University Press.
Hoberman, J. (2012), 'Looking for "Looking for Bruce Conner"', *Movie Journal*, 12 November 2012, <http://blogs.artinfo.com/moviejournal/2012/11/12/looking-at-%E2%80%9Clooking-for-bruce-conner%E2%80%9D/> (last accessed 24 August 2014).
Kakutani, Michiko (2011), 'The 9/11 Decade: Outdone by Reality', *New York Times*, 1 September 2011, <http://www.nytimes.com/2011/09/01/us/

sept-11-reckoning/culture.html?pagewanted=all> (last accessed 24 August 2014).
Kelley, Mike (1993), 'Playing with Dead Things', in *The Uncanny*, exhibition catalogue, Arnhem: Sonsbeek, 4–27.
Kennedy, Randy (2005), 'Master of the Dark Arts', *New York Times*, 15 May 2005, <http://www.nytimes.com/2005/05/15/arts/design/15kenn.html?oref=login&_r=0> (last accessed 24 August 2014).
Klein, Richard (1993), *Cigarettes are Sublime*, Durham, NC: Duke University Press.
Krauss, Rosalind (1996), '*Informe* without Conclusion', *October*, 78, Fall 1996, 89–105.
Kristeva, Julia (1982), *Powers of Horror: An Essay in Abjection*, New York: Columbia University Press.
La Ferla, Ruth (2005), 'Embrace the Darkness', *New York Times*, 30 October 2005, <http://www.nytimes.com/2005/10/30/fashion/sundaystyles/30GOTH.html?pagewanted=all> (last accessed 24 August 2014).
Martin, Douglas (1997), 'Step Right Up to the Cyberhustle: A New Breed of Barker for the New Times Square', *The New York Times*, 31 January 1997, B1–2.
Momin, Shamim M. (2004), 'Beneath the Remains: What Magic in Myth?', in *Whitney Biennial 2004*, ed. Shamim M. Momin and Chrissie Iles, New York: Abrams; Göttingen: Steidl, 49–55.
Mulvey, Laura (1991), 'A Phantasmagoria of the Female Body: The Work of Cindy Sherman', *New Left Review*, 188, July/August 1991, 137–50.
Novak, Barbara (1979), *American Painting in the Nineteenth Century: Realism, Idealism and the American Experience*, New York: Harper Row.
Oates, Joyce Carol (1995), 'American Gothic', *New Yorker*, 71, 8 May 1995, 35–6.
Punter, David (1996), *The Literature of Terror: A History of Gothic Fictions from 1765 to the Present*, 2 vols, London: Longman.
Ruskin, John [1853] (1959a), 'The Nature of Gothic', in *The Lamp of Beauty: Writings on Art*, ed. Joan Evans, London: Phaidon, 228–34.
Ruskin, John [1883] (1959b), 'Classic and Gothic', in *The Lamp of Beauty: Writings on Art*, ed. Joan Evans, London: Phaidon, 167–70.
Simon, Joan (1992), 'Robert Gober and the Extra Ordinary', *Robert Gober*, Madrid: Museo Nacional Centro de Arte Reina Sofia.
Solomon, Deborah (2010), 'Gothic American', *The New York Times Book Review*, 31 October 2010, 16.
Stearns, Peter N. (1994), *American Cool: Constructing a Twentieth-Century Emotional Style*, New York: New York University Press.
Thompson, Gary Richard (1974), 'Introduction: Romanticism and the Gothic Tradition', in *The Gothic Imagination: Essays in Dark Romanticism*, ed. G. R. Thompson, Pullman, WA: Washington State University Press, 1–21.
Time, 3 April 1995.
Welchman, John C. (2001), *Art After Appropriation: Essays on Art in the 1990s*, Amsterdam: G+B Arts International.
Wolcott, James (1997), 'Too Much Pulp', *New Yorker*, 72, 6 January 1997, 76–7.

Chapter 9

Doppelgamers: Video Games and Gothic Choice
Michael Hancock

In Fred Botting's study of the gothic, horror and technology, he touches briefly on video games, noting that video games have much in common with the early gothic novel: both are the centre of moral panics and controversy; both are known for their somewhat formulaic and mechanical structure; both emphasize intense emotion and violent shock (Botting 2008: 79). But though he cites gothic-oriented games such as *DOOM* (1993) and *Silent Hill* (1999), Botting's focus is not on the narrative of video games themselves, as he mainly wishes to use them to illustrate how their play reinforces the notion of the gothic as counterfeit, as an empty circulation that 'haunts and affirms the boundaries of cultural formations' (83); to that end, he concludes that there 'is little difference . . . between figures on the screen and figures twitching in front of it' (137). The connection Botting draws between video games and the gothic is worth further study, however; indeed, video games as a medium can be usefully thought of as inherently gothic in the way they are predicated on doubling and repetition. Even when the games' narratives don't rely on gothic mechanics, this doubling is still inherent in the game play itself. While the act of a player controlling an avatar would seem to follow an Enlightenment model of rational self-fashioning, in which the player gains in knowledge, skill, and self-assuredness with each iteration of the experiment, still the gothic doubling inherent in the game play calls into question notions of the stable Enlightenment self. The simulacrum of the game, with its complex engines of choice and consequence, serves as a paradoxically unstable but grounded real, one that highlights control only to suggest that the world 'outside' is more chaotic, less governed by reason, and more gothic in its own right. However, as I argue below, players are so used to this doubling, that this apparent potential for gothic destabilization of self is left somewhat unrealized. Through the encoding of gothic elements into the narrative, and importantly into the very act of choice that governs video games, these games both reinforce and simultaneously call attention to the lie of rational choice that undergirds the very neo-liberal economic market that saw games rise to media dominance. In other words, video games may be simulacra, but not in the way we usually think: not just 'virtual reality', video games are the uncanny symptom of the neo-liberal subject's recognition of its own lack of self.

Digital Doubles

As Michael Fuchs has persuasively argued, the gothic tropes of doubling and repetition are primary aspects of both Freud's theory of the uncanny and of postmodern theory (Fuchs 2012: 64). In Fuchs's argument, the pronounced intertextuality of the gothic is expanded in the new multimedia landscape. This hyperextended intertextuality creates, for Fuchs, its own uncanny digital doubling and repetition. In his reading, gothic doppelgängers become metatextual analyses of the way in which 'the contemporary mediascape is defined by convergence and the blurring, if not disappearance, of media borders' (Fuchs: 68). Likewise, 'In this contemporary digiculture', he writes, 'we constantly construct virtual doubles of ourselves through which we communicate with other people, among many other things that are oftentimes similar yet different to our "true" selves – an uncanny, if not to say "gothic", kind of human existence' (Fuchs: 73). In this reading, the multiplicity of repetition allowed by digital and other mass media narratives leads to an inescapable simulacrum of experience: we have met the doppelgänger, Fuchs would suggest, and it is us. Digital gothic narratives, with their always present uncanny doubles, allow for metatextual analyses of the postmodern world, one that Fuchs identifies with the American simulacra analysed by Baudrillard, and as discussed in the introduction to this volume.

Fuchs's analysis focuses on specific episodes of the television show *Supernatural* (2005–) and the video game *Alan Wake* (2010), and takes a narrative approach to the latter. With regard to doubling, however, as Botting's discussion above makes clear, game play itself is a form of doubling. In many video games, the player's chief representation in the game world comes about through the manipulation of a gamepad or keyboard that is then translated into some action performed on-screen by a representation commonly called the player-character (PC),[1] or avatar. To varying degrees, the game pushes the player to identify with the avatar, to accept its actions as a surrogate for the player's actions within the game world, making it a candidate for the gothic double, or doppelgänger. In his working definition of doppelgänger,

Webber identifies nine premises, four of which are particularly relevant in the case of video games: double vision, double talk, performance, and repetition (Webber 1996: 3–4). Double vision is the case where 'the subject beholds its other self as another, as visual object, or alternatively is beheld as object by its other self' (3). And indeed, the player's relationship with the avatar invokes this visual blur between subject and object, as the game prompts the player to think of the avatar as both an extension of self and an object to manage. Any player using lagging voice-chat technology in a game has experienced double talk, when the doppelgänger 'echoes, reiterates, distorts, parodies, dictates, impedes, and dumbfounds the subjective faculty of free speech' (3). More generally, whenever an avatar utters a preprogrammed statement that does not coincide with the player's own opinion, the player's attention is drawn to the gap between self and avatar. The performance of a doppelgänger draws attention to how identity is a performance rather than something embedded within the subject (3). In video games, every action of the avatar could then be considered a performance, but the doppelgänger is most noticeable when the avatar is caught up in a glitch, when it moves contrary to the player's wishes or clips into the environment around it, creating a momentary, disturbing meld of object with avatar. An appreciation of the gothic tradition draws out the gaps and ellipses in the hyphen between player and character, gaps normally only noticed in brief moments of failure or error.

But of the traits Webber associates with the doppelgänger, the one most prevalent in video games may be the one less associated with the error of the game and more with that of the player: repetition. In a video game, a player tends to progress until she fails to pass some sort of obstacle, often resulting in the avatar's death. The player will then be returned to a previous point in her play and forced to repeat the experience over and over until she performs acceptably.[2] The performance of a particular act over and over need not require failure either; hence the term 'grinding' to refer to 'the act of playing in a repetitive, unexciting, or otherwise un-enjoyable fashion in order to make faster progress' (Sorens 2007). In exploring the repetitions of gothic ghosts, Arno Meteling comments that they 'seem to be specific figures of anachronism, or more precisely, of asynchronicity, representing a static moment of the past haunting the present' (2010: 187). In this sense, the player is faced with ghosts of repetition coming and going: the ghost of the future, flawless performance and the ghost of the past failure, both moments that no longer exist in the game's memory, but persist in the player's mind.[3] The notion of the skilled player – the gamer – depends on the erasure and elimination of these ghosts of past failure; this tendency is evident in the many speed runs and strategy guide videos available on the Internet for virtually any video game. In order to create the authority to showcase their playing skills to others, players edit and present only their successful play as the model form. Like the avatar, repetition is an intrinsic part of video games that lends itself to gothic interpretation.

However, players are so accustomed to the use of avatars and the repetition of play that any potential for gothic-like destabilization, for the double and repetition to be used to draw the player's attention to the constructed nature of video games, is muted. Instead, it falls to video games that deliberately and explicitly court the gothic in video games to de-familiarize these elements and make players again appreciate the gothic qualities of the video game medium. A gothic perspective on the 1999 computer game *Planescape: Torment* and the 2011 X-box 360 and PS3 game *Catherine* demonstrates how traditional gothic tropes within the games destabilize the roles of the avatar and repetition. And in the process, the games illustrate what video games have to offer the gothic, that by granting players choices within a traditional gothic story, they can decide for themselves whether they wish to explore their avatar double's monstrous potential through repeated play. But such a choice is one already constrained by the gothic mechanics of the games. And so what video games highlight is that choice – that marker of the Enlightened and rational subject – is itself a simulation. In this reading, video games are themselves the gothic double of the Enlightenment self; they are the prime image of the American neo-liberal consumer's hollow self, the mass-marketing of self-fashioning. The 'gothic' of gothic video games has thus less to do with shooting zombies and more to do with 'being lost in the supermarket', to quote The Clash. The gothic mechanics – the zombies, corpses, succubi, etc. – are merely the symptoms of the larger counterfeits, in Jerrold E. Hogle's terms, of the larger society, the global(ized) but often American(ized) demographics targeted by the video game industry. After a brief summary of both games and accounts of the main gothic tropes they employ, I will illustrate how the unit operation of choice within the game play becomes the prime location of this gothic counterfeiting.

Black Isle's *Planescape: Torment* is notorious for being not only a long game, which is not unusual for an RPG (Role-Playing Game), but a long game famous for focusing mainly on plot and conversation over fantasy battles; it is a commonly cited statistic that the game contains 800,000 words of text (Griliopoulous 2009; Gillen 2007; Miller 2010), and as such, any summary of its plot should be considered an extreme abridgement. With that in mind, the game's plot can be read as a movement of five parts. The game begins in the Mortuary, a massive facility run by a faction commonly called the Dustmen for storing and animating corpses. The player controls the amnesiac immortal known as the Nameless One, and his first task is to escape the Mortuary, where he has been brought after being mistaken for the dead. In the second portion of the game, The Nameless One (hereafter abbreviated as TNO) searches for Pharod, a leader of a local gang, and for TNO's missing journal, as he believes both to contain knowledge of his lost past. In the third part, TNO must discover a way to reach Ravel, the night hag who rendered TNO immortal. From this point on, the player is periodically set upon by shadow beings that attack on sight.

Though the eventual meeting with Ravel results in her attack and subsequent death at TNO's hands, she reveals that TNO sought immortality to avoid facing up to the crimes he committed in the afterlife, and she brought about that immortality by physically tearing his mortality from him. The separation has come at a cost: every time TNO now dies, a life near him is taken, and becomes one of the shadows that hunt him. Further, dying erases his memories, and his mind is breaking under the strain. To survive, he must seek out the leader of the Shadows and regain his mortality. The fourth stage of the game sees TNO leaving the city to free and best the deva (an angel, but one particularly dedicated to goodness through order and show of force) who knows how to get to the shadow leader's lair, the Fortress of Regrets. And in the game's final stage, the player reaches the Fortress and confronts the Shadow's leader, The Transcendental One, who reveals itself to be his long-shorn mortality, which has gained sentience and its own will to survive, its ruthless drive for self-preservation echoing TNO's own decision to pursue immortality, making it his de facto double. In the game's climax, the player must decide to merge back with TNO's mortality, or kill it or TNO, destroying both. Preoccupied with death and mortality from its beginning to end, *Planescape: Torment* is a gothic exploration of identity through monstrosity.

Atlus's *Catherine* is more straightforward in its story, in comparison to *Planescape: Torment* at least, though its plot also has more than its share of twists and turns. The game places the player in the role of unambitious 32-year-old office worker Vincent Brooks. After his long-term girlfriend Katherine McBride presses him about his views on marriage, Vincent begins to have nightmares wherein he has to climb a strange staircase, moving blocks to allow access to the next level before the current level falls away. Shortly after the nightmares begin, Vincent blacks out at the bar the Stray Sheep and wakes up the next day in bed with a 22-year-old named Catherine (her name being the first of many of the game's doublings). A pattern emerges, as the next several days unfold, with Vincent, during the day, dodging (with variable enthusiasm) this second Catherine's pursuits, while dealing with the increasing suspicions of the first Katherine and her revelation that she may be pregnant. At night, the nightmares repeat with Vincent being chased by a parade of monstrously warped doubles from his daily life, including a cadaverous Katherine in bridal apparel (Doom's Bride), a skinless demonic Catherine, and a giant chainsaw-wielding infant (Child with a Chainsaw).

Long story short, Catherine is actually a succubus. This revelation ushers in a final set of block-climbing levels spent evading the succubus's employee and his monstrous permutations. At this point, the game ends, with the player receiving an ending based on the choices made in-game. While there are over half a dozen endings, they break down into three main variations: Vincent and Katherine reconcile and marry; Vincent rejects both women to assert his personal independence; or, in a fairly absurd twist, Vincent becomes a demon in order to dwell in Hell with Catherine and the game concludes with a demonic orgy atop the back of Catherine's father, the lord of Hell. *Catherine*, then, is relatively straightforward patriarchal wish-fulfilment, with variations of what R. W. Connell refers to as 'hegemonic masculinity', but narrativized within several mechanical gothic tropes, from the succubus, to demons, to murder, and all the way to Hell.

Even in relatively broad strokes, it should be clear that *Catherine* and *Planescape: Torment* have strong gothic overtones, based on their relative preoccupations with death, dreams and demons. But it is their specific engagements with different aspects of the gothic that allow them the stability of repetition and of the avatar: specifically haunting and a gothic sexuality. In *Planescape: Torment*, the Nameless One is haunted not only mentally by past selves and decisions but also physically, his escape from death turning his visage monstrous and death-like. In *Catherine*, the primary gothic element comes not from within the avatar's past, but by the dual threat and temptation presented by the sexuality of the succubus. Examining the specific gothic engagement of each game grants a better understanding for how the games individually lead players to make and repeat choices, emphasizing the gothic nature that haunts video games. The next section explores these mechanical elements of gothic game play in order to lay the groundwork for an exploration of the ways in which these games, and video games in general, both necessarily participate in and simultaneously call attention to the unreality of the myth of 'rational choice' that governs not only Enlightenment humanism and American democracy but also neo-liberal formulations of freedom within the market.

Death, Desire, and the Monstrous Self

Though *Planescape: Torment* is not known as a gothic game, it is certainly filled with gothic characters and scenarios. To offer three among many, there is a Dustman who is secretly a wererat working for a rat hive-mind that seeks to undermine a society of undead zombies, ghouls and skeletons; at one point, TNO must negotiate with the Pillar of Skulls, the tormented resting place for sages, liars, traitors and anyone who betrayed their friends; the game's two potential love interests are both unrequited, as one is a succubus with a lethal kiss and the other is a half-fiend whose blood starts to boil when she is aroused. The following should not be taken as an exhaustive examination, then, but as a quick overview of its most important gothic themes: death and monstrosity.

That *Planescape: Torment* is focused on death should be evident from the description of its plot; it begins with an immortal in a mortuary, and ends with him confronting a living form of his mortality and regaining his ability to die. In a very literal way, *Planescape: Torment* could be described as a game in which the player searches for a way for the player avatar to commit suicide. Most video games feature what amounts to an essentially immortal protagonist, as the player can reload from a save point or start a new game upon dying; death is almost always just a temporary setback. *Planescape: Torment*, then, is taking the process of repetition already present in video games and drawing the player's attention to it, to the uncanny consciousness that a series of constant deaths and rebirths would create. By incorporating this repetition directly into its plot, the game forces the player to consider that immortality, what sorts of sacrifice are justifiable in the pursuit of such a goal.

In particular, *Planescape: Torment* strongly suggests that The Nameless One's efforts to live forever and avoid punishment for his previous, unremembered crimes have transformed him into a monster. Even his lack of a name suggests as much: in horror, it is common for a monster to be unnamed in order to suggest such beings do not fit any standard categories (Carroll 1990: 220) and TNO's strange state certainly sets him apart in similar fashion. In discussing the shift in gothic vampires starting in the 1970s and culminating in *Twilight*'s Bella, Victoria Nelson argues that the vampire has shifted from a figure of death to a figure of immortality and the divine (Nelson 2012: 124-47). TNO has performed the reverse operation, his immortality rendering him more like the dead. The reminders are constant: other characters remark on TNO's pallid appearance, calling him 'corpse', 'the dustie's deader', 'scarred vampire', 'cryptcrawler'. Like a skeleton or zombie, many of his body parts appear to be detachable; the bartender at The Smouldering Corpse Bar keeps his old eyeball as collateral until he pays his old tab, and Marta, an old woman who searches corpses for items, is willing literally to root around TNO's guts in order to see if there are any items of interest. Though these scenes are played in part for laughs,[4] they further reinforce the monstrous aspect of The Nameless One's nature. A typical use of monsters is to act as a disruption in the natural order of things, and the story moves towards the restoration of that order. Diane Carr argues that *Planescape: Torment* transcends this typical unfolding, in that its monsters are presented as normal, and *Planescape: Torment* is not about restoring a dualistic moral order (Carr 2003). One of the notable things about *Planescape: Torment* is that it is indeed not about an epic, world-saving struggle between good and evil; instead, it is primarily a story of TNO coming to terms with his own being. But there is still a disruption of natural order and a restoration, as TNO's unnatural immortality comes to an end. The difference is that, unlike traditional gothic stories, the disruptive element and the protagonist that must challenge it are one and the same.

Catherine is an unusual game for a North American market, given its blend of horror themes, reliance on the Japanese genres of anime and visual novels, and puzzle-based platforming; even its primary action is unusual, given that Vincent's only possible response to the game's monsters is to run away. But its connection to the gothic is fairly traditional, given its use of a gothic mainstay, the succubus. In the context of Jacques Cazotte's 1772 occult romance *Le Diable amoureux*, Joseph Andriano argues that succubus is generally an anima figure, wherein men cast their own anxieties or desires onto women (Andriano 1993: 5). In particular, to qualify as an anima, a succubus figure must satisfy a number of traits: 'she should at least appear to originate in the mind of the haunted man'; she must be a part of him or 'an unconscious projection onto a real woman'; she must energize his actions and instigate change; 'she must be bipolar, like a magnet, having one pole that attracts and one that repels', be both fascinating and repulsive (24). Though these guidelines were constructed with a 1772 French romance in mind, they amply describe Catherine's relation to Vincent within this 2011 video game.

It is suggested in the game that Catherine's appearance does indeed arise out of Vincent's mind; Mutton, the local bartender in the game who is working with Catherine, admits that 'She appears at will and seduces men under the curse . . . [b]y appearing as their ideal woman.' Moreover, Vincent's uncertainty over Catherine's existence late in the game creates an uncanny possibility – albeit one later dispelled – that she is a projection of his mind. Vincent starts questioning if he dreamed up Catherine entirely, which further blurs the line between his waking world in the Stray Sheep bar and the dream world of his nightmares. In fact, a discussion of Catherine's dreamlike nature leads Vincent and his friends directly to discussing their dreams, speculating uneasily that the dreams are a result of the stress of everyday life, again furthering the idea that the boundaries between dream and reality are breaking down as one seeps into the other.

Catherine also acts as an energizing force to spur Vincent into action. Mutton lays out the problem he and Catherine are meant to address:

> 'When there are people like you who spend a long amount of time with a partner without commitment . . . It impedes the population model . . . The rate of population growth is less than optimal . . . Wasting a woman's time of greatest fertility is a hindrance to the future of the species.'

Catherine's entire purpose in the game is to tempt Vincent into bringing his arrested relationship to a conclusion, one way or the other, so that Katherine is 'free' to pursue a more traditional path of marriage and children with a more willing partner. As a further consequence, Catherine's part in preventing that which 'impedes the population model' means that the role of the succubus in *Catherine* is less about avenging wronged women, and more about furthering their role as breeding stock for further demonic plans.[5] Consequently, Catherine is simultaneously a symbol of sexual promiscuity and monogamous heterosexual coupling, fulfilling – within the game's gendered logic – the final condition of a 'bi-polar' nature designed to attract and repel. In *Catherine*, the succubus is, as much as the constantly collapsing staircase, an engine to force Vincent towards resolution, a character born out of his own conflicting desires. The story is reasonably stock for gothic tales and at worst reinforces negative gender roles. But given that video games in general are awash in unrealistic, sexualised depictions of women that avoid any actual exploration of sexual desire while simultaneously revelling in its exploitation,[6] *Catherine* can be viewed as a positive first step towards at least acknowledging the existence of more mature relationships.

When it comes to gothic doubling, Catherine is most obviously Katherine's double rather than Vincent's, representing the youthful, impulsive free spirit that Katherine – to Vincent, at least – does not. But as a personification of Vincent's sexual desires, Catherine draws on another trait of the doppelgänger, that the doppelgänger's challenge to identity creates a '*double bind* between cognitive and carnal knowledge' (Webber 1996). Catherine is a double of Katherine, but also a physical double of Vincent's secret ideal of a sexualized woman, and it is entirely adhering to the game's characterization of Vincent that when faced with the necessity of acknowledging his desires, his first impulse is to flee.

Both *Catherine* and *Planescape: Torment* thus draw on traditional gothic tropes to tell their stories. But to focus on story is to miss significant elements not only of the games themselves, but of what makes them gothic. Put simply, a video game is more than a story. Reading these two games as case studies, one can see that the ways in which the players are positioned to make and repeat the choices of their avatars is crucial to the overall engagement between gaming and the gothic.

Choice as Gothic Self-fashioning

In a recent paper, Tanya Krzywinska addresses the overlap between American gothic and video games through a close study of two games, the Stephen King-inspired *Alan Wake* and the MMO (massive multiplayer online) 2012 game *The Secret World* (Krzywinska 2013). Like *Catherine* and *Planescape: Torment*, these games draw overtly on a gothic aesthetic and have clear gothic influences in their narratives. Krzywinska argues, however, that it is necessary to further consider how the game play for both games embodies a sense of the gothic. In *Alan Wake*, this embodiment occurs through the use of flashlights and other light sources to combat the darkness-infused enemies attacking Wake (508). In game studies, the divide between narrative and game is long-entrenched,[7] to the point where even definitions of games that attempt to meet both sides halfway can be interpreted as exacerbating that divide by distinguishing between 'fictional worlds' and 'real rules' (Juul 2005: 1). In light of that history, Krzywinska's consideration of gothic game play is a useful, perhaps even necessary, step.

Unfortunately, such a consideration works poorly for *Planescape: Torment* and *Catherine*, as neither game contains game play that is explicitly gothic. For *Planescape: Torment*, the main actions are combat, conversation and exploration. The exploration portions unfold in a manner similar to *The Secret World*, and as such, a case could be made that its game play is gothic on those grounds. However, I would argue that a more theoretical approach to the gothic shows how the game play is essential to how the gothic works in both games, because of the way both games are centred around the continual assertion of choice. While there are many different formal and generic differences between video games and other forms of media, two in particular are relevant here: unit operations and player avatar. Coined by Ian Bogost, 'unit operations' refers to the 'general instances of procedural expression' that form a 'configurative system, an arrangement of discrete, interlocking units of expressive meaning' (Bogost 2006: ix). Further, while these unit operations can potentially exist in any medium, video games in particular use them in procedural rhetoric: persuasive arguments that present themselves to the user through the user's experience of the process at hand (Bogost 2010). In essence, if repetition is a basic part of video game play, the unit operations of a game are what actions are most commonly repeated, and what this repetition implies. For example, the 2013 video game *Papers, Please!* presents a rhetorical argument about the nature of bureaucracy by assigning the player the role of an immigration officer for a fictional country, and so demanding the player perform specific unit operations related to such bureaucracy.

As stated earlier, performance is a key feature in another aspect of game play, as the means by which the player avatar functions as the player's doppelgänger. In terms of creating a doppelgänger, video games can differentiate themselves from other fiction by virtue of the fact that the other forms generally do not address the user directly (Choose Your Own Adventure novels being a notable exception). Further, video games not only address the players, they call on them to perform, through their avatars, a role within the confines of the game's fictional world. In their analysis of *Final Fantasy VII* (1997), Andrew Burn and Gareth Schott contrast this performance with oral narrative, stating that Cloud, the main player avatar of the game, is both 'heavy hero', in the mould of the oral narrative, and 'digital dummy', as a collection of unit operations the player moves through:

> The engagement with character is in many ways developed as in conventional narratives, in response to the guise of the game, which offers a narrative statement through an unrestricted semiotic of visual design, animation, text and music, to compose the character as visible, audible presence, his narrative role and affective appeal drawing on the provenance of popular narrative, both folk and mass media. The immersive experience of role-play, by contrast, is engaged through the specific rule-based demands of the game, and the player's improvisatory deployment of the restricted set of actions offered, although this is infused by the imaginative engagement with the character and game-world, so that a highly-restricted set of actions become elaborated and deepened by a semiotic merger with other modes. (Burn and Schott 2004: 230)

While this distinction draws somewhat on the narrative/game split in game studies, it is an accurate description of the complex negotiation that many games ask of their players. In *Planescape: Torment*, the player must balance the narrative presentation of The Nameless One as an eldritch being of strange, unearthly strength with his strength statistic, which will determine actual performance during battle. In *Catherine*, players can only bring Vincent to his narrative catharsis if they have the skill to make their way quickly through the puzzle stages. Digital dummy meets heavy hero, and some sort of compromise generally ensues.

These games are therefore gothic in both mechanics and structure. From their basic stories and themes through to the construction of the avatar and relationship to the player, they highlight gothic elements in repetition and doubling. But they go beyond this, to highlight a gothic uncertainty of self that lingers in the Enlightenment structures of (rational) choice and self-fashioning, and neo-liberal structures of consumer freedom and identification within the market. It is at this point that unit operations meets player-avatar, in the form of repeated choice. Both *Planescape: Torment* and *Catherine* feature *choice* as a primary unit operation, in that both predominately ask the player to choose among several options regarding how to respond to the queries and situations thrust upon them. In both cases, these choices register how their player avatar is situated in the larger game. In both games, choice is measured in a more overt manner as well, in a way that exposes video games' general reliance on doubling and repetition. Other media forms can depict, through representational means, a monstrous main character. The video game, however, can take another approach to the monstrous protagonist: by virtue of the player/avatar relationship, the players not only observe a monstrous hero, they perform it as well. Building on Noël Carroll's concept of 'art-horror' to describe the mixture of 'fascination and repulsion' that arises upon viewing situations of horror that are simultaneously threatening and imaginary (Mäyrä 2012: 113), Frans Mäyrä coined the phrase 'art-evil' to refer to 'actions that are carried out within the fictional frame of a game, and which involve simulated acts that are commonly considered morally wrong, particularly of intentionally causing other beings harm, pain or death' (119). Mäyrä focuses on games where the evil nature of the player avatars are foregrounded in a clear, even exaggerated manner: managing a stable full of monsters in *Dungeon Keeper* (1997), playing as an undead Warlock in *World of Warcraft* (2004), engaging in Monster Play as a giant spider in *Lord of the Rings Online* (2007). However, the definition he provides is much more far-reaching, potentially encompassing any action ranging from plunging the world into a nuclear holocaust, as in *DEFCON* (2006), to impishly kicking a chicken in *Legend of Zelda* (2006). Virtually any action performed in the context of a video game that, if it occurred in the outside world, would have legal or social repercussions, could arguably fall under art-evil.[9] In essence, through playing art-evil, players can establish their avatars not just as their doubles, but their overtly evil doubles.

By choosing to act – or not to act – in an art-evil manner in games with strongly gothic themes, players are in effect positioning their player avatars in response to those themes. In *Planescape: Torment*, there is a wide variety of potentially art-evil choices, ranging from slaying poor Angyar on sight, to selling other party members into slavery, to intentionally exploiting a ghost whose 'between-life-and-death' status makes her functionally useful. For *Catherine*, the concept of art-evil becomes more complicated, as the player has, in general, fewer choices (regardless of the player's wishes, Vincent will end up doing some very foolish things), and it is up to the player to decide how to convey those choices to others. Further, the harm and pain that Vincent's actions can bring about mostly involve inflicting emotional rather than physical pain, making it something of an oddity for a video game.

One of the factors involved in determining the nature of art-evil for a game is how that game frames the player's actions, which can be a result of aesthetics or game play; a game that rewards you for killing asks for a different approach to art-evil actions in comparison to one that punishes you, as does a game that adopts a splatter porn aesthetic over an abstract one where defeated enemies vanish. Katie Salen and Eric Zimmerman state that meaningful play – that is, game play designed to convey some sort of a meaning – must fulfil two categories: first, it must be discernible, in that the result of the action is conveyed to the player in a perceivable way. Second, it must be integrated, in that the action must have some effect on play at a later point as well (Salen and Zimmerman 2003: 33–5). Under those conditions, then, a unit choice that allows the player to act out in an art-evil manner must have some sort of effect on game play and the consequence of the immediate choice must be conveyed as art-evil to the player.

For its part, *Planescape: Torment* uses the alignment system from *Dungeons & Dragons*, which means the player avatar is placed along two axes: good–neutral–evil; and lawful–neutral–chaotic, resulting in nine combinations in all. Many, though not all, of the choices made in the game push the alignment in a specific direction, though not all choices are weighed equally; lying to someone changes The Nameless One's alignment to slightly more evil and chaotic, but turning over a world of innocent robots to the care of a sentient weapon created by Entropy to bring about the unmaking of the multiverse changes the alignment towards evil and chaotic in a much greater way. In terms of meaningful play, the designers partially obscured the feedback for such decisions. *Planescape: Torment* does inform the player what The Nameless One's current alignment is, but it keeps the exact level of the alignment hidden, and only makes it discernible when the avatar changes from one alignment type to another. That is, it performs checks based on alignment, but does not inform the player it is doing so: an individual choice may accumulate points towards order or evil, but the game does not inform the player about the points accrued unless there is a shift in overall status.[10] Consequently, in terms of playing art-evil (or any other alignment), the players will only be informed overtly that their actions are art-evil when the scales are first tipped in that direction. Presumably, the assumption is then that the players will either immediately correct their course back to the side of the angels (or at least the side of neutrality) or aim to engage fully with art-evil.

Again, *Catherine* is the more complicated case, thanks largely to the coy way the game deals with its own gauge. Like *Planescape: Torment*, *Catherine* measures the player's choice through a red and blue gauge. Unlike *Planescape: Torment*, however, any change to the gauge is made immediately visible to the player, a shift towards discernible play that may at first make it seem the simpler of the two. The complication, however, is twofold. First, the game never informs the player exactly what the gauge is measuring. Even the manual is deliberately vague: 'This strange red-and-blue meter will appear when you direct Vincent to make particular decisions or actions throughout the game. Whatever you do will have an effect on . . . something . . .' The image is also somewhat misleading: on the red side of the gauge, there is a devil and on the right side, a cherubim, leading the player to expect an evil-good measurement accordingly. Instead, the gauge measures compatibility with the two women; rejecting Catherine's advances and her general viewpoint moves the gauge right, and the same rejection of Katherine moves it left, while being cruel to both keeps the gauge in the centre. Where this gauge sits during the final level of the game determines which sets of endings are then available to the player.

Players who do not wish to acknowledge Vincent as their avatar-double may choose to interpret the gauge as a measure of the repeated decisions they make on his behalf rather than a reflection of their own selves. And the game could be viewed as supporting that interpretation, were it not for the other complication: the Confessionals. The Confessionals serve as the transition point between a Landing and the next part of a stair-climbing challenge. Combined with the angelic choir that sings when a level is completed and the pews present in many of the Landings, they are clearly meant to be interpreted in the Catholic sense of Confessional. Before the Confessional will ascend to the next level, a mysterious voice asks Vincent a question and the player must choose between two answers; as an example, one is 'which is more "cheating"?', with the choices being 'An emotional tryst' and 'A physical fling'. Unlike other choices, however, this choice is framed more explicitly as one to the player, rather than Vincent – upon answering, the player is shown either how other players have answered, or the results of a survey on the question, broken down by gender. This framing complicates the concepts of choice and art-evil, by transgressing the line between player and player avatar. Further – though this point is integrated into the game but not made discernible to the player – it is the Confessionals that determine the game's final ending. As mentioned, in the game's ninth stage, the players are locked into a particular set of endings based on whether the gauge is at left, right or middle. At that point, the quality of ending depends on whether the answers to the final three confessional questions conform with the gauge position; for example, wishing for a peaceful life, refusing the excitement of chaos, and admitting you are ready to live in peace with the gauge pointing to the blue results in marriage with Katherine. In terms of the unit operation of choice, the final test of *Catherine* is less whether the player avatar is art-evil or not, but whether he or she is true to the choices that have been made.

Catherine and *Planescape: Torment* draw on gothic themes, to be sure, but in both games *choice* forms one of the primary unit operations, and in so doing, choice itself becomes a gothic device. Both games grant players a chance to navigate through a gothic system and come to their own conclusions, potentially adopting art-evil player avatars to explore alternate outcomes. In *Catherine*, that amounts to using Vincent in order to explore different models of desire, relationships and freedom, and staying committed to that choice – and at the same time, occasionally navigating your way around falling blocks. In *Planescape: Torment*, it means taking on the role of The Nameless One, and confronting the traumas of the past, by embracing monstrosity and ruling in hell, or seeking atonement. There are more video games than just these two that allow such gothic encounters, and more ways for video games to engage with the gothic than just choice-based unit operations. But these particular games make it clear that video games have more to offer the gothic beyond just 'figures on the screen and figures twitching in front of it'. Beyond repeating gothic storylines and devices, *Catherine* and *Planescape: Torment* expose the suppressed gothic underpinnings of video games per se. In complex ways, both games use choice to create a gothic game-play structure, and in so doing both use the notion of self-fashioning to undermine the very concept of Enlightenment individuality that such self-fashioning employs. In other words, *choice* itself becomes a gothic device in video games. These narratives are essentially Enlightenment *Bildungsroman*, in which one's own choices determine one's character; but, those choices are shown to be simultaneously within and beyond one's rational control. The Enlightenment model of a self that is predicated on reasoned action, which lies at the heart of such games, is shown to be inherently chaotic. The video game exposes the gothic self.

Conclusion: Redoubling the Digital

By way of a brief coda, I would like to return to Michael Fuchs's discussion of digital media and its simulacral doubling. If, as I argue above, video games turn the very act of choice into a gothic counterfeit, is this argument in turn reflected in other contemporary media? It could be that representations of video games and game play within other gothic-inflected media can invert this counterfeit, turning the recognition of limits of rational choice into a form of agential critique. Certainly one could think here of any number of American novels and films in which gamers are transformed into all powerful warriors precisely because of their skills at manipulating limits on choices. The resolution to the plots of such films as *War Games* (1983) or *The Matrix* (1999) depend upon the hero's ability to manipulate a digital environment without destroying it, even as *The Matrix* sequels critique this implicit Romantic narrative by highlighting the inescapable nature of this limited version of agency, as 'Neo', the 'new' transcendent figure becomes his own double, a software production designed to maintain the monster of the digital environment. Likewise, Orson Scott Card's novel *Ender's Game* (1985) and its sequel *Speaker for the Dead* (1986) critique – however inadvertently and Card's own politics aside – the ways in which simulated warfare can set the ideological and pedagogical frameworks for material acts of othering, terror and genocide, only to have those limits challenged by the military gamer. In such works, American violence, and a specifically male violence, is both perpetuated and challenged by its digital doubles.

But perhaps this play of media doubling and its relation to agency is best highlighted by Edgar Wright's *Shaun of the Dead* (2004), a British film parody and homage to the American zombie films of George Romero. *Shaun of the Dead* certainly echoes Romero's well-known critique of American consumerism and its neo-liberal commodification of 'human capital', with the zombies figuring the uncanny doubles of Shaun and his friends going about their daily lives. But in Wright's version, consumers can also 'haunt back', or perhaps 'eat back' – to adapt Teresa Goddu's phrase from a different context (Goddu 1997) – against the deadening effect of consumerism itself. If, in Botting's vision of gothic gaming, there 'is little difference ... between figures on the screen and figures twitching in front of it' (137), in *Shaun of the Dead* the active recognition of one's participation in, and enjoyment of, gaming transforms that twitching – the gothic non-choosing outlined above – into an act of *bricolage* that reclaims one's agency, if only in the moment. It is solely because of their gaming skills that Shaun and Ed are able to negotiate the neo-liberal zombie apocalypse. Ed may be (un)dead at the film's conclusion, but that's the life he chose. Gothic gaming may game the system, in the end.

Notes

1. Since PC also commonly stands for 'Personal Computer', avatar has been chosen as the less ambiguous term. The term avatar has many different definitions in the field of game studies and digital media studies in general, ranging from the very broad definition of 'a shorthand for experience of the networked subject, describing different practices of agency, identity and network capability' (Coleman 2011: 4) to the narrow case where avatar only refers to cases where the video game player has 'much creative control over the agent's appearance, skills and attributes' (Waggoner 2009: 9). For the purposes of this discussion, my conception of avatar hews closer to Waggoner, but without the stricter insistence on player creative control.
2. Jesper Juul explores the player's response to failure at great length in his book, *The Art of Failure: An Essay on the Pain of Playing Games* (2013).
3. Racing games in particular have embraced this sense of haunting, by including a translucent 'ghost car' that repeats the performance of the fastest time on a given track; the ghost car can be found in everything from Atari's 1988 *Hard Drivin'* to the *Super Mario Kart* franchise.
4. For a discussion of the role of the comic in the gothic, see Avril Horner and Sue Zlosnik's *Gothic and the Comic Turn* (2005).
5. Although to be fair to the game, Catherine's portrayal is generally much more sympathetic, as someone with mixed feelings about Mutton's ultimate goals.
6. For an overview of gender and sex as represented in video games, see Anita Sarkeesian's *Tropes vs. Women in Video Games* series (2013–) or Brenda Brathwaite's *Sex in Video Games* (2013). For a discussion on the relative shallowness of such depictions, see Tanya Krzywinska's 'The Strange Case of the Misappearance of Sex in Videogames' (2012).
7. The essential argument is over how video games are to be treated on a formal level, either as a traditionally defined game, in terms of being composed primarily of rules and play, as the group known as the ludologists would have had it, or as a representational narrative form, allowing the migration of existing methodology for film, drama and prose, as the narrativists would have it. The discussion was prominent in early twenty-first-century game studies – see, for example, the various arguments in play in Noah Wardrip-Fruin and Pat Harrigan's 2004 anthology, *First Person*. Though current discussion in game studies has largely moved to different subjects, the discussion's roots persist.

8. And in fact, as *Dungeons & Dragons* aficionados may be aware, *Planescape: Torment* borrows more than its rules from the series; the 'Planescape' in its title refers to the fact that the game is set within that Planescape subset of the *Dungeons & Dragons* multiverse.
9. For an example of how repetition and repression work into art-evil, a survey of players who play games multiple times showed that 63 per cent of them played as 'good' for their first playthrough, as opposed to only 9 per cent who played 'evil'; for these players, 'art-evil' was something to return to after the canonically 'good' playthrough (Lange 2014).
10. It is known that such checks are made because released design documents regarding the game allude to them (Avellone: 1; 44; 69). For a comparative example, in the *Mass Effect* series, the game measures choices based on two separate scales, Paragon and Renegade, which roughly corresponds to Order and Chaos. Any change to either scale is made immediately apparent to the player, and any time an option arises because of the current level of Paragon or Renegade, that option is marked through the game's colour-coding system, rendering those choices immediately discernible and overtly integrated.

References

Andriano, Joseph (1993), *Our Ladies of Darkness: Feminine Daemonology in Male Gothic Fiction*, University Park: Pennsylvania State University Press.
Avellone, Chris (2013), 'Ravel_Final', *RPGWatch*. Word document, n.d., web (last accessed 26 November 2013).
Bogost, Ian (2006), *Unit Operations: An Approach to Videogame Criticism*, Cambridge, MA: MIT Press.
Bogost, Ian (2010), *Persuasive Games: The Expressive Power of Videogames*, Cambridge, MA: MIT Press.
Botting, Fred (2008), *Limits of Horror: Technology, Bodies, Gothic*, Manchester: Manchester University Press.
Brathwaite, Brenda (2013), *Sex in Video Games*, Createspace.
Burn, Andrew and Gareth Schott (2004), 'Heavy Hero or Digital Dummy? Multimodal Player-Avatar Relations in Final Fantasy 7', *Visual Communication*, 3.2: 213–33.
Carr, Diane (2003), 'Genre and Affect in *Silent Hill* and *Planescape Torment*', *Game Studies: The International Journal of Computer Games*, 3.1: n.p.
Carroll, Noël (1990), *The Philosophy of Horror, or Paradoxes of the Heart*, New York: Routledge.
Catherine (2011), video game, produced by Katsura Hasino, Atlus.
Coleman, Beth (2011), *Hello Avatar: Rise of the Networked Generation*, Cambridge, MA: MIT Press.
Fuchs, Michael (2012), 'Hauntings: Uncanny Doubling in *Alan Wake* and *Supernatural*', *Textus* 3: 63–74
Gillen, Kieron (2007), 'Retrospective: Planescape: Torment', *Rock Paper Shotgun*, 25 September 2007, web (last accessed 26 November 2013).
Goddu, Teresa (1997), *Gothic America: Narrative, Nation, History*, New York: Columbia University Press.

Griliopoulous, Dan (2009), 'Retrospective: Planescape Torment', *Eurogamer.net*, 23 August 2009, web (last accessed 26 November 2013).
Horner, Avril and Sue Zlosnik (2005), *Gothic and the Comic Turn*, London: Palgrave McMillan.
Juul, Jesper (2005), *Half-Real: Video Games between Real Rules and Fictional Worlds*, Cambridge, MA: MIT Press.
Juul, Jesper (2013), *The Art of Failure: An Essay on the Pain of Playing Video Games*, Cambridge, MA: MIT Press.
Krzywinksa, Tanya (2012), 'The Strange Case of the Misappearance of Sex in Videogames', in *Computer Games and New Media Cultures: A Handbook of Digital Game Studies*, ed. Johannes Fromme and Alexander Unger, New York: Springer, 143–160.
Krzywinksa, Tanya (2013), 'Digital Games and the American Gothic: Investigating Gothic Grammar', in *A Companion to American Gothic*, ed. Charles L. Crow, Oxford: Wiley Blackwell, 505–16.
Lange, Amanda (2014), '"You're Just Gonna Be Nice": How Players Engage with Moral Choice Systems', *Journal of Games Criticism*, 1.1: n.p.
Mäyrä, Frans (2012), 'From the demonic tradition to art evil in digital games: Monstrous pleasures in *The Lord of the Rings Online*', in *Ringbearers:* The Lord of the Rings Online *as Intertextual Narrative*, ed. Tanya Krzywinska, et al., Manchester: Manchester University Press, 111–32.
Meteling, Arno (2010), '*Genus Loci*: Memory, Media, and the Neo-Gothic in Georg Klein and Elfriede Jelinkek', in *Popular Ghosts: The Haunted Spaces of Everyday Culture*, ed. María del Pilar Blanco and Esther Peeren, New York: Continuum, 187–99.
Miller, Kyle E (2010), 'Planescape: Torment', *RPGFan*, 27 June 2010, web (last accessed 26 November 2013).
Nelson, Victoria (2012), *Vampire Heroes, Human Gods, and the New Supernatural*, Cambridge, MA: Harvard University Press.
Planescape: Torment (1999), video game, designed by Chris Avellone et al., Black Isle Studios.
Salen, Katie and Eric Zimmerman (2003), *Rules of Play: Game Design Fundamentals*, Cambridge, MA: MIT Press.
Sarkeesian, Anita (2013-), *Tropes vs. Women in Video Games*, https://www.youtube.com/playlist?list=PLn4ob_5_ttEaA_vc8F3fjzE62esf9yP61, web (last accessed 29 July 2015).
Katie and Eric Zimmerman (2003), *Rules of Play: Game Design Fundamentals*, Cambridge, MA: MIT Press.
Sorens, Neil (2007), 'Rethinking the MMO', *Gamasutra.com*, 26 March 2007, web (last accessed 30 October 2014).
Wagonner, Zach (2009), *My Avatar, My Self: Identity in Video Role-Playing Games*, Jefferson: McFarland.
Wardrip-Fruin, Noah and Pat Harrigan (eds) (2004), *First Person: New Media as Story, Performance, and Game*, Cambridge, MA: MIT Press.
Webber, Andrew J. (1996), *The* Doppelgänger: *Double Visions in German Literature*, Oxford: Oxford University Press.

Part IV

American Creatures

Chapter 10

Screening the American Gothic: Celluloid Serial Killers in American Popular Culture
Sorcha Ní Fhlainn

'I'm setting the example.
And what I've done is going to be puzzled over
and studied and followed forever.'

John Doe, *Se7en*

This chapter situates the American gothic in post-1960 cinema by exploring the modern serial killer film and its distinctly American lineage, borne of the success of Alfred Hitchcock's *Psycho* (1960). Landmark critical films are used to chart the seismic shifts American cinema has undergone in the post-classical period – from *Psycho* to *The Texas Chainsaw Massacre* (1973), through to more recent invocations of serial killing in *The Silence of the Lambs* (1991), *American Psycho* (2000) and *Dexter* (2006–13). This chapter draws upon the popularity of the serial killer film, with careful consideration for the influence of significant real/reel American serial killers (such as Ed Gein and Ted Bundy), in order to argue that the figure of the serial killer is the embodiment of the counter-narrative American Dream: the consumerist and consumption-driven American nightmare. Frequently co-opted into horror cinema, this nightmare, at its heart, owes a significant debt to the aesthetics and fundamental roots of American gothic, which typically features monsters, old dark houses, psychological fragmentation, hauntings, hidden histories, serial murder, sexual repression and dark desires. The serial killer film has thus become an overtly modern American contribution to the gothic in popular culture. Primarily focused on the cinematic narratives beyond the fantastical ciphers of classical literary monsters, this chapter draws from a distinct set of moments where the serial killer becomes central to the understanding of, and continued fascination with, consumerist nightmares, destructive individualism and psychotic fractures so central to the American gothic narrative today. Evidenced by the continuation of such serial killer narratives as Hannibal Lecter (and other cross-pollinated serial killer texts which attempt to emulate its enduring success), the reel serial killer is an exemplary conduit of the American Nightmare. The chapter concludes with a focused study of Jonathan Demme's *The Silence of the Lambs* (1991), a landmark film that has garnered a prolific and celebrated afterlife across three decades of American gothic screen culture, through the continuation of Thomas Harris's series of 'Hannibal Lecter' novels, numerous film adaptations (1986–2007) and a television series, *Hannibal* (2013–15).

Serial Killers: The Real and the Reel History

Serial killing, contrary to popular belief, was not a product of the twentieth century. The figure of the serial killer in American culture has been noted as far back as the American Revolution, with the Harpe brothers of 1790s Tennessee possibly falling into the category. Such a lengthy genealogy, however, misses the fact that the serial killer, as a phenomenon, became popular in cinema, in films that explored killing in graphic and unique ways on-screen. But American gothic literature and other earlier forms do provide a necessary background for reading the serial killer as a particular instantiation of American gothic. The gothic writings of Edgar Allan Poe and Nathaniel Hawthorne, especially, prefigure this phenomenon by pointing to the darkness within protagonists who struggle with fractured psyches and personal damnations, leading them towards murder and the macabre. Unlike European gothic excess, where ruins and dark secrets lead to terrible acts of depravity and murder, often as a response to Catholicism and repression, American gothic turns inward: serial killers in fiction and film tend to be the product of deeply destructive psychological fractures: madness that masquerades just below the surface of everyday normalcy. Serial killers act out impulsive and buried desires that have been unleashed – recalling the split gothic self of Stevenson's *Jekyll and Hyde* (1886) or Edgar Allan Poe's unreliable murderous narrators in 'The Black Cat' (1843) and 'The Tell-Tale Heart' (1843) – filtered through a ferocious, destructive individualism, spawning countless screen and literary imitators. This rooting of the serial killer as a psychological product of 'cultural damage' or 'wound culture', as Mark Seltzer describes, is an important feature if we are to claim modern serial killer cinema as a product of American fascination with violence, excess and psychological trauma.

This psychological trauma also serves as a larger allegory for the nation. Through the history of cinema, we have witnessed the evolution of the serial killer, from folk tales to news coverage of real murderers, towards the contemporary valorization of the serial killer as a form of celebrity in the American popular imagination. Monsters have moved from the margins to the centre of our world, and it is through the collapse of these boundaries, previously separating them from us, that serial killers have become distorted mirrors of ourselves. Serial killers regularly feature as a form of the Other that lies just beneath the facade of the normal in our world. The terror of their aesthetic normalcy, of blending in, is central to understanding their invisibility. Yet serial killers on-screen, much like other filmic monsters such as the zombie and vampire, have evolved beyond their earlier perceived fixed states; unlike these monsters, serial killers have always worked from within society itself, and hide their chimeric faces amongst the crowd.

The fixation on the psychological is thus foundational to the modern, cinematic serial killer. The image of, and psychologized concept of, the modern American serial killer is largely shaped by the notorious figure of Ed Gein from Plainfield, Wisconsin. Gein's case, which came to light in 1957, included cannibalism, necrophilia, skinning his victims, grave robbing and decorating his home with body parts of the deceased; it is still figured as a shocking account of desecration and sexual perversion nestled within a small rural farming community. Gein's case featured in *Life* magazine (2 December 1957), complete with pictures of his filthy home, bringing the case to national attention, and it subsequently became inspirational for numerous screen depictions of serial killers. Gone was the suggestive European strangeness of Hans Beckert (Peter Lorre), from Fritz Lang's *M* (1931), and his ilk; American serial killers were now found and made in the homeland of Middle America. Though Gein was certainly not the first American serial killer since the inception of cinema – H. H. Holmes is believed to have committed at least thirty murders in his gothic 'Murder Castle', a labyrinthine hotel which housed unsuspecting visitors to Chicago's World's Fair in 1893 – Gein remains, without doubt, the most influential on contemporary film. He has become 'multiply interpretable' (Sullivan 2000: 45) and unfixed, repeatedly cited, re-imagined and revisited as the touchstone in serial killer narratives for its shocking and abject content.

While Gein was a partial inspiration for *The Texas Chainsaw Massacre* and *The Silence of the Lambs*, to which we will return, perhaps the most famous fictional adaptations inspired by his case are Robert Bloch's 1959 novel, *Psycho*, and its 1960 screen adaptation of the same name, directed by Alfred Hitchcock. Bloch's novel and Hitchcock's film both explore psychological trauma and murderous insanity through motel-manager and taxidermist Norman Bates (Anthony Perkins), an outwardly odd but passive man subject to the whims of his demanding, neurotic mother. That 'mother' and Norman are revealed to be one and the same ties *Psycho* very closely with contemporaneous thought on psychosexual dysfunction, expressed here as a violated and consumed psyche, and murderous impulses.

Beyond the psychological, *Psycho* is also the most infamous American film to align serial killing with a psychotic break from reality into a realm of fantasy and consumption, a pairing that finds its material echo in the proliferation of serial killer cinema. Alongside the post-*Psycho* rise of the slasher film of the 1970s and other representations of excess, serial killer cinema came to dominate in later years by sequelization, commodification and blatant imitation. As Brian Jarvis notes, there are numerous types of serial killer films, which cross-pollinate into other film genres, which ensure their endurance:

> Serial Killer cinema has many faces: there are serial killer crime dramas (*Manhunter* (1986), *Se7en* (1995) *Hannibal* (2001)), supernatural serial killers (*Halloween* (1978) *Friday the 13*th (1980), *Nightmare on Elm Street* (1984)), serial killer science fiction (*Virtuousity* (1995), *Jason X* (2001)), serial killer road movies (*Kalifornia* (1993), *Natural Born Killers* (1994)), . . . postmodern pastiche (*Scream* (1996), *I Know What You Did Last Summer* (1997)) and even serial killer comedies (*So I Married an Axe-Murderer* (1993), *Serial Mom* (1994), *Scary Movie* (2000)) . . . the serial killer has also become a staple ingredient in TV cop shows (like *CSI* and *Law and Order*) . . . (Jarvis 2007: 327–8)

Serial killers are now so ubiquitous as to be commonplace within multiple genres; indeed, they may even feel clichéd or tired as a metaphor for American malaise. Yet, there is something distinctly uncanny about their generic endurance and destructive individualism that is wholly bound to the foundations of the American imagination.

Thus, following *Psycho*, popular serial films of the mid to late twentieth century have linked psychological disturbances, murderous sexual desires and consumerism run amok; these connections give rise to at least a cursory understanding of the direct connection between what is represented as the serial killer's compulsive desire to kill again and again, and the larger culture that pours over the minutia of the killers' lives, their methodologies, and victims' wounds and corpses. Seltzer notes, 'Serial killing has its place in a culture in which addictive violence has become a collective spectacle, one of the crucial sites where private desire and public fantasy cross' (Seltzer 1998: 253). However, the source or drive of this compulsion has varied substantially on screen from 1960, from sexual deviance to expressions of psychosexual rage, social and economic exclusion, and political and cultural articulations on greed and consumption, through to representations of class, intellect and taste.

More recently, a near superhero status has been conferred onto twenty-first century serial killers through a highly problematic code of 'morality', which allows them to operate and thrive amongst the masses as near guardians of justice. That serial killers are hugely popular in film is unsurprising – those who cross moral boundaries are more interesting and appealing on-screen than those who strive to defend and delimit them. The fiction of presenting an embodiment of evil – one that looks like us – contains enormous narrative appeal, and acts as a framing device by which we encounter, experience and eventually contain the psychological or consumerist cultural threat (temporarily) through a filmic frame.

Contrary to the majority of film representations of serial killers in American cinema, real serial killers have been documented by reporters, psychologists and biographers as bland interfaces, rather than the monstrous figures we imagine. The banality of real-life serial killers in the face of such terrible deeds is in itself uncanny, as we desire the binary equivalence that they must be wholly different and separate from us, entirely other in some capacity, in order to act out in such extreme and violent ways. As Nicola Nixon notes:

> The real . . . Gacys, the real Bundys or Dahmers, unlike the charismatic gothic killers of, say, Thomas Harris's recent fiction, are deeply dull and blandly ordinary . . . it is precisely their ordinariness, their characteristic of 'sounding like accountants' and being employed in low-profile 'unexciting' jobs like construction/contracting, mail sorting, vat mixing at a chocolate factory that makes their crimes seem all the more shocking. (Nixon 1998: 223)

The conjunction between the real-life serial killers who dominated media in the 1970s and 1980s and film representations of charismatic figures and their shocking crimes all becomes blurred when an uninteresting, and distinctly un-cinematic, blank central figure is unmasked – the killer must be made visually interesting yet abject in order to match the gravity of his crimes and transgressions. Abhorring the narrative vacuum that reveals the true banality of evil, serial killers on-screen must present some depth and command attention if they are to contain, reflect or represent our collective cultural fears. Gothic monsters in fiction tend to mask their nightmarish selves by exuding charm, intellectualism and depth to lure unsuspecting victims. This is the fictive construct projected onto serial killers, which in turn contributes to their on-screen appeal, in that 'gothic paradigms allow for the creation of a compelling narrative and consequently the generation of character and plot out of "bland ordinariness" and incomprehensible randomness' (Nixon 1998: 226).

Serial Consumers

This need to place a false sense of order, rules and modes of recognition also fuels significant trends in serial killer representations within popular culture at large. The dynamic and charismatic villain comes into much sharper focus by the late 1970s and early 1980s as a figure who can ultimately be outsmarted and beaten (if only temporarily), provided generic rules and formulas are respected. By providing rules that override the terrible sense of random violence and unknown killers who hide in plain sight, serial killing was appropriated into popular horror cinema quite neatly via the slasher film. There is much to consider here in terms of cultural overlap: much like the serial killers' defined prerequisite of requiring a 'cool down' period between murders (differentiating them from the mass murderers who kill a group of victims in one prolonged act, such as the Columbine High School Massacre in 1999), screen slashers tend to become active around particular dates, events or rites of passage, when they re-emerge and re-enact wreaking havoc in order to exact vengeance on a community or group that either represent, or have enabled, a terrible past event. *Halloween* (1978), *Prom Night* (1980) and *Friday the 13*th (1980) underscore this narrative quite explicitly. For theorists like Carol J. Clover, slasher films are by their nature conservative, conformist, and possess a telling grammar whereby it becomes pleasurable in itself to detect the very rules which govern their formulaic diegeses (Clover 1992: 21–64). The films can also be read as 'morality tales', as John Kenneth Muir observes in Andrew Monument's 2009 documentary, *Nightmares in Red, White and Blue: The Evolution of the American Horror Film*, as warnings that such transgressive or immoral behaviour is aligned closely with an Old Testament vengeful God. Much like the masked slashers of the *Halloween* and *Friday the 13*th series, serial killers of the 1980s stand in as a blank embodiment of empty and rampant consumption and violence, behind a bland mask or distorted face – our greatest fear watching these blank faces is that they often do facilitate reading the killer as a horrific extension of our dark selves. Their 'facelessness' is crucial here, as the unknown serial killer also moves largely undetected while seeking out victims, only to become tabloid celebrities when caught, for our mass entertainment – they are 'nobodies' who become 'somebodies' due to a macabre popular fascination with their crimes.

Yet, on a cultural level, the act of achieving a visual catharsis out of watching such films also enables a fictional construct of containment, which cannot be applied to the real world. Victims on-screen represent us, but are not us, and so we can 'survive' the limit experience of such encounters without ever being in jeopardy. Slashers, like serial killers, are also highly repetitive in their actions – the seriality of their nature is that they continue their deeds unabated (until caught or killed), driven by the compulsion to re-enact and repeat their crimes again and again. As Seltzer notes, 'the real meaning of serial killing is a failed series of attempts to make the scene of the crime equivalent to the scene of the fantasy' (Seltzer 1998: 64), and the increased pursuit of the fantasy (and the failure to achieve it) promotes such repetition by attempting to merge the act with the *fantasy* of the act itself. The act of consumerist-driven fetishization and serial killing is galvanized by the same overriding compulsion – in order to achieve the fantasy, you must repeatedly consume and feed the addiction more and more in order to attain it.

During the economic dominance of the slasher film in the 1980s, increased hysteria and public outcries were also amplified by both the progression of sensationalist news coverage and talk show topics on *America's Most Wanted* (1988–2012) and *Geraldo* (1987–98), and the gradual move towards a twenty-four-hour news cycle and 'special investigative reporting'. Some of these shows overtly attempted to link the perceived rise in serial killer activity with moral slippage, or the erosion of conservative 'family values', in popular culture. Through this shift in media coverage and cultural hysteria, American gothic culture was both fascinated by, and seemed to be (re)producing, serial killers at an unprecedented rate. This process led to enormous public interest in series of extreme cases including The McMartin Pre-School Trial (1984–90), and the kidnapping and murder of six-year-old Adam Walsh in Florida in 1981, fuelling the frenzied perception that serial killers and satanic forces were active and recruiting followers. The increased popularity of the serial killer film is indebted to the 'low-brow' popularity of the 1970s and 1980s slasher film, which, through sequelization and box office profits ensured that the killer would rise and return to the multiplex, again and again, each year, for more gruesome thrills. But the commercial success of the slasher film also ties in very coherently to the consumer-led appetites that the serial killer and the Reaganomic culture of 'greed is good' had flaunted and encouraged in the 1980s. Slashers return for more victims to slay and to increase studio profits, capitalizing on this repetitive compulsion that more is better (body counts tend to multiply exponentially in sequels) and banking on the audience draw of more explicit and visceral material to encourage the spectacle further. As J. C. Oleson concludes, 'We have inverted our villains into strange heroes, commodifying their wickedness for legions of consumers' (Oleson 2005: 187).

In short, both the ongoing rise of graphic horror in the 1980s and the heightened terror that the serial killer embodied and exploited in 1980s culture were remarkably symbiotic, with the slasher sequel becoming both a lucrative annual staple film release and cathartic cultural experience. The seeds of discontent which marred the landscape from the late 1960s onwards – the political assassinations of Martin Luther King and Bobby Kennedy in 1968; race riots; the Manson Murders (1969); the failure of the countercultural movement; the oil crises of the 1970s; and the Watergate scandal (1972–4) – came to flourish in the 1980s, with a renewed emphasis on unbridled consumption to paper over the evident social and economic cracks. Slashers and serial killers transitioned from the depths of lowbrow culture of disavowed filth to the mass-marketed, studio-led sequel, making stars and media sensations of them by the decade's end; transgressors of law and order became the new iconic symbols of decadence in Reagan's America.

What became most apparent was the gothic lure of the killer as a charismatic anti-hero and the complete disposability of his or her victims: serial killer celebrity status demarcated the 1980s as *the* serial killer decade – bookended by Ted Bundy's conviction in 1979 to Jeffrey Dahmer's capture in 1992 – all the while their victims were lost amid the frenzy of interest, or were reduced to mere types or lurid details of the killer's modus operandi. Fans of slashers went to see *A Nightmare on Elm Street*, *Halloween* and *Friday the 13*th to witness anti-heroes Freddy Kruger, Michael Myers and Jason Voorhees dispose of their numerous victims in increasingly phantasmagorical ways, while body counts also served as a spectacle for more mordant wisecracks and visual excess. The enjoyment in later instalments of these franchises had less to do with any formalist study of the genre, or indeed a generic extension of Clover's concept of the 'Final Girl' (Clover 1992), and instead focuses its pleasures on the terrifying transgressive actions of the killer at the explicit expense of significant empathy with the victim. At their most depressing and nihilistic, late 1980s slasher films became increasingly disposable, interchangeable and narratively vacant, a lucrative commodity and bankable product bled dry by an over-saturated industry, having served a particular capitalist gory grist to the mill, which, coupled with their overfamiliar killer anti-heroes, had now lost their potency and frightening edge by their excessive visibility. When Freddy Kruger began appearing on children's pyjamas and Halloween masks, his gothic cachet was truly sacrificed at the altar of the almighty dollar.

Contemporary Killer Culture: Case Studies

Killer consumerism comes home, so to speak, in recent decades. According to Linnie Blake, serial killing and psychopathy have now become synonymous with extreme violent crime and with threats to the sanctity of the family and American idealism. Serial killer films thus appropriate and capitalize upon these societal fissures, making the serial killer 'a kind of conceptual shorthand for the degeneration of American dreams of cooperative endeavour into the atomised alienation of the present' (Blake 2008: 106). *Henry: Portrait of a Serial Killer* (1986) acts as a brutal reminder of the horrific actuality of serial killing, in direct opposition to 1980s slasher excesses, by repositioning serial killers Henry Lee Lucas (Michael Rooker) and Ottis Toole (Tom Towles) as mobilized murderers scouring for random victims along the highway, a vision of the American journey turned savage, with Lucas as its focused 'study of chilling blankness' (Murphy 2014: 62). The wisecracking anti-hero slashers have no place in this minimalist exploration of Lucas and his unending destruction – slashers are regulated by dates and rules, and fixated on past events, while Lucas is unbound by place or purpose. The film positions serial killing at its most visually confrontational and abject, stripping back the familiar layers of remove, phantasmagoria and gloss.

The blank exterior of serial killing, as documented by journalists and biographers, would also become the central focus of Bret Easton Ellis's controversial novel *American Psycho* (1991) and its later film adaptation released in 2000: Patrick Bateman (Christian Bale) is a self-proclaimed empty vessel of the 1980s yuppie consumerist nightmare, who is, like Lucas, also 'simply not there' (Easton Ellis 1991: 62). Leatherface and the Sawyer family in *The Texas Chainsaw Massacre* (1974) – also loosely inspired by Ed Gein – are mechanized out of the slaughterhouse business and turn to cannibalism as an apocalyptic end point under capitalist disenfranchisement; or perhaps, as Robin Wood asserts, cannibalism is *the* absolute logical progression of capitalism because it 'represents the ultimate in possessiveness, hence the logical end of human relations' (Wood 2004: 131). Patrick Bateman, however, wholly externalizes his psychopathology via consumption-led expressions of validation instead: his endless fashion labels, fetishized beauty-regimen products and murderous acts are all equally empty extensions of consumerist fantasies to compensate for his blank interior in late-stage capitalism. Whereas in *The Texas Chainsaw Massacre* at least a base need is being served, the devouring economic system in *American Psycho* feeds an acquired, unending appetite to accumulate and destroy purely for its own sake. Both the Sawyers and Bateman are positioned at opposite ends of this hyper-consumptive system, and both are equally unstable and faceless embodiments of its violence. Leatherface dons the skinned face of a previous victim and wears it as a mask, routing all visible identification back to his particular skillset, while Bateman is repeatedly misrecognized by his work colleagues, lacking an identity that emphasizes his insubstantiality. He is a postmodern void. That Bateman is an unstable, unreliable narrator is highly significant here, as the very system to which he is in thrall fundamentally destroys and anonymizes him (and cleverly destabilizes the foundations of Ellis's postmodern gothic novel). As Elizabeth Young notes, 'Patrick has been so fragmented and divided by his insane consumerism that he cannot "exist" as a person' (Young 1992: 104).

Sharing the same year of release with the publication of *American Psycho*, Jonathan Demme's *The Silence of the Lambs* (1991) ensures that both of its central serial killers are not only identifiable from the annals of serial killer and gothic literary history, but that they also originate from opposite ends of the capitalist spectrum. While Lecter's roots remained hidden until Harris's later novels *Hannibal* (1999) and *Hannibal Rising* (2006), it is clear from the outset that Lecter stems from the cultural elite, as his social standing and academic title is repeatedly emphasized throughout. Lecter's roots are traced back to European aristocracy in Harris's novels, adding an Old World flavour of bona fide gothic heritage; however, from the first mention of Lecter in Demme's *The Silence of the Lambs*, it is abundantly clear that Lecter is a cinematic gothic descendant of Stoker's *Dracula* (1897). As David Sexton observes (in a discussion of Harris's novel):

> Like Dracula, Lecter drains his victims. After meeting him for the first time, Clarice feels 'suddenly empty, as though she had given blood'. . . . Dracula's eyes are red, Jonathan Harker realises when he first meets him in the guise of a coachman . . . So too: 'Dr Lecter's eyes are maroon and they reflect the light in pinpoints of red. Sometimes the points of light seem to fly like sparks to his centre.' (Sexton 2001: 86)

Lecter's orality and dangerous touch, much like Dracula's magnetism and contaminating bite, is repeatedly emphasised in the film, from his mask which restricts his treacherous bite to his Plexiglas cell which categorically separates him from his cellmates on the prison block. Furthermore, when he shares a single moment of touch with Clarice Starling (Jodie Foster) through the bars of a makeshift cell (from which he will soon escape), it is a brief, almost intimate, yet dangerously charged, caress. Dr Lecter, like Dracula, is an icon of literary citation and excess – he is fundamentally forged from *fin de siècle* literature, combining Arthur Conan Doyle's Sherlock Holmes's deductive abilities with Professor James Moriarty's cunning, alongside Dracula's gothic physicality and lasting influence.

Buffalo Bill, aka Jame Gumb (Ted Levine), the oppositional serial killer to Lecter in *The Silence of the Lambs*, is a virtual composite of actual American serial killers. He is a carefully crafted assemblage of real and gothic horrors: he is both Victor Frankenstein and Frankenstein's Creature, creating his own monstrous other self in the form of a 'woman' flesh suit, stitched and grafted from the modus operandi of Ted Bundy, Gary Heidnik and Ed Gein. Gein's functional use of, and wearing, harvested skin as text(ile) is Buffalo Bill's most visible and chilling citation, but Heidnik's horrific basement hole and Bundy's disarming manipulations are equally evident. While Lecter's origins denote sophistication, Buffalo Bill's own roots are found in working-class Middle America – disenfranchised and dysfunctional like the Sawyer family in *The Texas Chainsaw Massacre*, and with an unhealthy obsession with his deceased prostitute mother (recalling his filmic 'brother', *Psycho*'s Norman Bates and so many other slasher killers with unhealthy mother fixations) (Clover 1992: 232), Bill's origins and acquired squalid squatters' house distinctly reference 'poor white trash', especially when compared with Lecter's gothic cell or indeed his intriguing mind *palace*. The film diminishes Bill's origins from its source novel, but his complexity and horrific capabilities are visually articulated through the rich *mise-en-scène* of his basement – the glowing moth hatchery; the skinning room with its mannequin displaying the patchwork 'woman' suit; the bathroom with its disintegrating corpse in the bathtub; and the prison-well with broken fingernails left from previous victims – Bill's traumas and horrific pursuits are carefully coded as a gothic descent into the mindscape of a dangerously split psyche. Like Lecter, he is also a ghastly triad of gothic reference, but significantly, the fundamental difference is that Bill is explicitly of American origin.

Clarice Starling, the trainee FBI agent, is at the helm of a huge paradigm shift in the serial killer film's plot structure at the beginning of the 1990s: the inclusion of the profiler/insightful investigator who must delve into the deranged mind of a psychopath in order to solve a heinous crime. This narrative device was popularized by Thomas Harris in his 1980 novel *Red Dragon* (and its film adaptation *Manhunter* (1986) directed by Michael Mann), but it was Starling's vulnerability and intellectual sparring with the terrifying Dr Lecter that shifted the American serial killer film paradigm to the extent that it became a virtual trope by the end of the 1990s. Their intense dialogues are extremely gothically inflected: the exchange of Starling's childhood traumas, the death of her father and the slaughtering of the lambs at the ranch, act as emotional currency (quid pro quo) through which Starling can elicit Lecter's psychological insights into Gumb's psychopathology. As Robert Cettl writes:

> The majority of serial killer films attempt in part to deal with the fantasies of the killer as something that the profiler must seek out. . . . In this sense, the profiler is structured as an inverse parallel of the killer. His task is to probe, analyse and understand aberrance – to look as long into the abyss as possible. . . . The serial killer is this emblematic of a malfunctioning order, and the profiler the agent of its cure and restoration. (Cettl 2008: 30–1)

The exchanges between Lecter and Starling unfold with ever-increasing urgency, emphasized through slow dolly shots resulting in claustrophobic extreme close-ups of both investigator/profiler and captive serial killer. Tak Fujimoto's cinematography reminds us of the psychological penetration Lecter can inflict (as does his supping on Starling's revelatory emotional pain) while building audience tension as Starling is racing to save Gumb's latest kidnap victim. Thus the film positions Starling as a questing heroine (in a typically masculine role) within a gothic fairy-tale structure, generically fusing detective fiction, horror motifs and a police procedural framing, with Lecter as its central source of wisdom as a vampiric dark oracle.

Harris's novels and their film adaptations are also meditations on the serial killer as destructive consumerist. At its most obvious level, this is revealed through their names: *Red Dragon*'s Francis Dolarhyde and Jame Gumb's Mr Hyde sewing business both explicitly recall money and the split psyche. Closer analysis reveals Dolarhyde's obsession with consumption as the ultimate act of transcendence when he devours William Blake's original painting 'The Great Red Dragon and the Woman clothed in sun' (1805–10), believing this will confer the dragon's power unto him. So too with Buffalo Bill, as he skins women to consume their hides as raw material which will confer a costumed transformation of gender. Both killers believe that consumerism will ultimately result in metamorphosis. Hannibal Lecter is also an avid consumer; not only do his cannibalism and gourmet interests place him at the top of the human food chain, his probing psychological torments are presented as consumptions of personal pain and suffering which nourishes his psychotic sadism. His knowledge of designer goods, brands and gourmet food indicate that even his incarceration hasn't stifled his investment in consumerism; his immediate cataloguing of Starling's perfume, skin cream, 'good handbag and cheap shoes' (*The Silence of the Lambs*,

1991) demonstrates his sharp grasp of consumerist conferrals of class, opportunity, biography and taste. After all, when we first encounter Dr Lecter in Harris's novel, he is reading the Italian edition of *Vogue* (Harris 2013: 17). Lecter's cultural elitism positions him as the good consumer of brands run amok into bad hyper-consumerism and cannibalism, whereas Dolarhyde and Gumb are lesser consumers of the wrong goods to begin with (and have always consumed people as goods for personal power and transformation), which irrevocably corrupts and marks them as truly irredeemable.

The critical and commercial success of *The Silence of the Lambs* has had a lasting influence. Later serial killer films in the 1990s acknowledge its influence in terms of structure by including a profiler or wise detective, or overtly attempt to modify and reuse the film's formula and confrontational style, as in the films including *Copycat* (1995), *Se7en* (1995), *The Bone Collector* (1999) or *The Cell* (2000). The explosion of serial killer titles since the 1990s cannot be underestimated, as filmmakers were keen to depict damaged profilers exploring terrifying mindscapes of serial killers as pioneered by Harris's novels and Demme's film in particular. As Brian Jarvis keenly observes, 'Since the early 1990s, the translation of serial killer shock value into surplus value has become an increasingly profitable venture. This market both reflects and produces an apparent insatiable desire for images and stories of serial killing in a gothic hall of mirrors' (Jarvis 2007: 328). The proliferation of serial killer narratives also bled across into long-form television series, such as *The X-Files* (1993–2002), *Twin Peaks* (1990–1) and *Millennium* (1996–9), culminating in the ultimate transformation of the serial killer as a fully fledged anti-hero in Showtime's TV series *Dexter*, loosely adapted from Jeff Lindsay's 2004 novel *Darkly Dreaming Dexter*.

Dexter dissolved the stark boundaries between serial killer and anti-hero; Dexter Morgan (Michael C. Hall) is a serial killer working within a strict moral code while also tracking and dispatching killers who have committed worse transgressions than himself. This positions Dexter as a marred, complex character with a deadly addiction to killing, while also eliciting empathy and narrative containment by explicitly directing his bloodlust on to murderers who have evaded justice. Serial killing in the series takes on a form of justified retribution while also encouraging audience investment and desire that Dexter remains undetected. While Harris merely hints at a behavioural code for Lecter, it is made explicit in *Dexter* via the Code of Harry (a moral code imparted to Dexter by his adoptive father Harry Morgan (James Remar)), thus taming the contemporary serial killer and actively encouraging audience sympathy. For Dexter must prove the guilt of his murder victims in order to legitimize killing them under Harry's moral code, transforming him into a vigilante serial killer, and gaining tacit approval verging on outright visual pleasure for his actions. Furthermore, Dexter occupies a unique space between the law enforcement profiler and the serial killer, all from within the Miami Metro Police Department, where he is a blood spatter analyst – not only does he detect murderers and solve cases, he also acts as a righteous judge, jury and executioner. As David Schmid notes, 'In a technique borrowed from Thomas Harris's *The Silence of the Lambs*, Dexter creates audience sympathy for the "good" serial killer by contrasting him with the "bad" serial killer' (Schmid 2010: 140), as each season Dexter is repeatedly pitted and polarized against horrific nemeses who cannot control their urges to kill, and also threaten to expose Dexter's own dark side. Borrowing this paradigm of competing representations of 'good' and 'bad' serial killing demonstrates not only how influential Thomas Harris's fiction and film adaptations have become on serial killer screen culture overall, but also that through shows like *Dexter* 'sympathetic serial killers have been embraced as part of the American mainstream' (Schmid 2010: 142).

To conclude, the recent return of Hannibal Lecter on NBC's TV series *Hannibal* (2013–15) continues the popular consumption of the serial killer narrative on-screen and returns to Harris's paradigm of profiler and killer by exploring the early years of Hannibal Lecter's (Mads Mikkelsen) and profiler Will Graham's (Hugh Dancy) alliance through various gothic cases set largely prior to Lecter's own capture. As with *Dexter*, *Hannibal* positions Lecter as the 'good' serial killer when contrasted against the horrific secondary serial killer (typically presented as 'killer of the week' alongside a chief antagonist for each season). Creating this narrative gap prior to *Red Dragon*'s timeline not only brings Harris's characters back for further exploration (and fan consumption) but it also visually presents gothic murders as beautiful and violent abject spectacles. The artistry of murder in the series, where corpses are violently rendered for extravagant exhibition, demonstrates that serial murder is here completely reconfigured and stylized into an inventive creative industry – victims' bodies are recast as raw materials to be transformed and commodified for our visual pleasure. What is most abject and most celebrated in *Hannibal* is not the duelling dance between Lecter and Graham, or its wry nods to Lecter's gourmet cooking, but rather its art direction, visual design and make up, all of which explicitly commodifies innocent flesh into abject works of art. Recall that this was also the prime pursuit of Ed Gein, who used skin as raw material to furnish his home, to display and wear his own horrific creativity. Whether it is through television, an Academy award-winning film, or studio-led excesses and consumerism since the 1960s, serial killer cinema within contemporary American gothic culture is never far from the long, all-consuming shadow cast by Ed Gein.

References

Blake, Linnie (2008), *The Wounds of Nations: Horror Cinema, Historical Trauma and National Identity*, Manchester: Manchester University Press.
Cettl, Robert (2008), *Serial Killer Cinema: An Analytical Filmography*, Jefferson, NC: McFarland.
Clover, Carol J. (1992), *Men, Women, and Chainsaws: Gender in the Modern Horror Film*, Princeton: Princeton University Press.
Easton Ellis, Bret (1991), *American Psycho*, London: Picador.
Harris, Thomas (1980), *Red Dragon*, New York: Putnam.
Harris, Thomas (1999), *Hannibal*, New York: Delacourte Press
Harris, Thomas [1988] (2013), *The Silence of the Lambs*, London: Arrow Books.
Jarvis, Brian (2007), 'Monsters Inc.: Serial Killers and Consumer Culture', *Crime, Media, Culture*, 3.3, 326–44.
Murphy, Bernice M. (2014), *The Highway Horror Film*, Basingstoke: Palgrave Macmillan.
Nixon, Nicola (1998), 'Making Monsters, or Serializing Killers', in *American Gothic: New Interventions in a National Narrative*, ed. Robert K. Martin and Eric Savoy, Iowa: University of Iowa Press, 217–36.
Oleson, J. C. (2005), 'King of Killers: The Criminological Theories of Hannibal Lecter, Part One', *Journal of Criminal Justice and Popular Culture*, 12.3, 186–210.
Schmid, David (2010), 'The Devil You Know: Dexter and the "Goodness" of American Serial Killing', in *Dexter: Investigating Cutting Edge Television*, ed. Douglas L. Howard, London: I. B. Tauris, 132–42.
Seltzer, Mark (1998), *Serial Killers: Death and Life in America's Wound Culture*, New York: Routledge.
Sexton, David (2001), *The Strange World of Thomas Harris: Inside the Mind of the Creator of Hannibal Lecter*, London: Short Books.
Sullivan, K. E. (2000), 'Ed Gein and the Figure of the Transgendered Serial Killer', *Jump Cut: A Review of Contemporary Media*, 43, July, 38–47.
Wood, Robin (2004), 'An Introduction to the American Horror Film', in *Planks of Reason: Essays on the Horror Film*, ed. Barry Keith Grant and Christopher Sharrett, Lanham, MD: Scarecrow Press, 107–41.
Young, Elizabeth (1992), 'The Beast in the Jungle, The Figure in the Carpet: Bret Easton Ellis' *American Psycho*', in *Shopping in Space: Essays on America's Blank Generation Fiction*, ed. Elizabeth Young and Graham Caveney, New York: Atlantic Monthly Press, 85–122.

Filmography

American Psycho, dir. Mary Harron, Lionsgate, 2000.
The Bone Collector, dir. Philip Noyce, Columbia Pictures, 1999.
The Cell, dir. Tarsem Singh, New Line Cinema, 2000.
Copycat, dir. Jon Amiel, Warner Brothers, 1995.
Dexter, Showtime, created by James Manos, Jr, 2006–13.
Friday the 13th, dir. Sean S. Cunningham, Paramount Pictures, 1980.
Halloween, dir. John Carpenter, Warner Brothers, 1978.
Hannibal, NBC, series developed by Bryan Fuller, 2013–15.
Henry: Portrait of a Serial Killer, dir. John McNaughton, Maljack Productions, 1986.
Manhunter, dir. Michael Mann, De Laurentiis Entertainment Group, 1986.
A Nightmare on Elm Street, dir. Wes Craven, New Line Cinema, 1984.
Nightmares in Red, White and Blue: The Evolution of the American Horror Film, dir. Andrew Monument, Lionsgate. 2009.
Prom Night, dir. Paul Lynch, Avco Embassy, 1980.
Psycho, dir. Alfred Hitchcock, Paramount Pictures, 1960.
Se7en, dir. David Fincher, New Line Cinema, 1995.
The Silence of the Lambs, dir. Jonathan Demme, Orion Pictures, 1991.
The Texas Chainsaw Massacre, dir. Tobe Hooper, Bryanstone, 1974.

Chapter 11

American Vampires
Jeffrey Andrew Weinstock

In 'Monster Culture (Seven Theses)', Jeffrey Jerome Cohen asserts that monsters of all varieties should be considered as 'cultural bodies' (Cohen 1996: 4) that embody specific cultural moments as they give shape to particular times, places and feelings. 'The monster's body', writes Cohen, 'quite literally incorporates fear, desire, anxiety, and fantasy . . . giving them life and an uncanny independence. The monstrous body is pure culture' (4). The vampire clearly serves this purpose, acting as a flexible metaphor condensing widely held yet culturally nuanced anxieties and desires. The vampire has found a congenial home in the United States where the 'pure culture' of its overdetermined body has materialized fears and fantasies related to preoccupations with racial, sexual and economic otherness – issues that have haunted the American psyche from the colonization of America by European powers to the present. In keeping with representations of other monsters, the American vampire has also undergone a metamorphosis over time, from something to fear into something to emulate.

This chapter will chart the development of the American vampire narrative in four sections. I will begin by outlining a 'prehistory' of the American vampire narrative. Although 'actual' vampires as supernatural blood drinkers are rare in pre-twentieth-century American literature, one can nevertheless identify 'proto vampires', particularly racialized cannibal blood drinkers and controlling women, which reflect nineteenth-century anxieties about race and gender. Furthermore, the appropriation of European vampire models becomes notable in the later part of the nineteenth century through adaptations for the American stage, providing a more familiar template for twentieth-century literary and cinematic representations. The second section will emphasize the legacy of Bram Stoker's 1897 *Dracula* in American literary and cinematic adaptations of the vampire narrative in the first part of the twentieth century, particularly the continued demonization of female sexuality in silent films of the 1910s and 1920s. Moving to the second half of the twentieth century, the third section will note the proliferation of vampire narratives via their emphasis on the increasing celebration of the vampire as a hero liberated from stultifying social convention and as an embodiment of post-Watergate scepticism of authority. My final section attends to twenty-first-century representations that extend the ironic humanization of the vampire, often in order to contest hegemonic structures of race, gender and sexuality. Lacking a reflection of its own, the vampire as pure culture nevertheless mirrors back culturally specific anxieties and desires.

The Pre-history of the American Vampire

Like Stoker's Renfield anticipating the arrival of Count Dracula, the cultural imaginary of nineteenth-century American literature was haunted by vampires prior to the actual emergence of the literary figure, and the vexed issue of American race relations is at the core of many of these 'proto-vampire' accounts. James Fenimore Cooper's *Last of the Mohicans* (1826) is a case in point. Cooper 'supernaturalizes' American Indians as spirits of the forest with almost magical abilities to appear, disappear and track their quarry. He then bifurcates this image into the Rousseauan 'noble savage', represented by the stoic Mohican Chingachgook and his courageous son Uncas, and the barbaric, conniving Huron Indian Magua. Borrowing elements of the Native American captivity narrative, such as *The Sovereignty and Goodness of God: Being a Narrative of the Captivity and Restoration of Mrs. Mary Rowlandson* (1682), in which Indians are presented as demonic 'ravenous beasts' and 'hell-hounds' (Rowlandson 2001: 308), the plot of *Mohicans* revolves around the kidnapping by Magua and attempted restoration of two white women, Cora and Alice. During a central scene, Indians massacre British soldiers peacefully vacating the surrendered Fort William Henry in the then-province of New York. In Cooper's words, 'as the natives became heated and maddened by the sight' of flowing blood that 'might be likened to the outbreaking of a torrent', 'many among them even kneeled to the earth, and drank freely, exultingly, hellishly, of the crimson tide' (Cooper 1982: 198).

Cooper's portrayal of the vampiric Indian also drew upon and influenced lurid anthologies of anti-Indian propaganda that proliferated across the nineteenth century. With titles such as *Horrid Indian cruelties!* (1799) and *Indian Atrocities! Affecting and Thrilling Anecdotes Respecting the Hardships and Sufferings of Our Brave and Venerable*

Forefathers, in Their Bloody and Heartrending Skirmishes and Contests with the Ferocious Savages (1846), these compendiums freely mixed fact with fantasy, often with avowedly genocidal intentions. As Kathryn Derounian-Stodola and James Arthur Levernier note, sensational accounts of murder and torture predominate in such works: 'Babies are thrown into cauldrons of boiling water, fried in skillets, eaten by dogs, or dashed against trees or rocks . . . The aged are dispatched with tomahawks and scalped. Women are sexually violated, and captives of all ages and both sexes are burnt at the stake, dismembered, and sometimes even devoured in orgiastic rituals said to be almost, but not quite, "too shocking a nature to be presented to the public"' (Derounian-Stodola and Levernier 1993: 33). Robert Montgomery Bird adopts this dim view of Indians in his popular *Nick of the Woods* (1837), written as a direct refutation of Cooper's romantic representation of noble Indians. Symbolically named protagonist Nathan Slaughter is an Indian hater intent on the destruction of his barbaric foes. The cannibalistic propensities of indigenous populations are also at the centre of Herman Melville's first novel, *Typee: A Peep at Polynesian Life* (1846), although Melville adopts a more tolerant perspective toward native characters. As in his more famous story 'Benito Cereno' (1855), which thematizes a shipboard slave revolt, *Typee* displaces antebellum American racial anxieties to the South Seas as the protagonist Tommo finds himself captive of the cannibalistic Typee tribe on the island of Nuku Hiva in the Marquesas Islands. Provoking the ire of conservative critics, Melville's novel seems to excuse the indigenous cannibalization of enemies slain in battle by comparing this horror in an otherwise pastoral society to Western white men consumed by greed, disease, anxiety and unfulfilled desire. The native's 'savage' practice pales in comparison to how modern existence debilitates and sucks dry 'civilized' men. To varying extents works by Cooper, Melville or Bird represent atavistic savagery as an intrinsic feature of indigenous populations whose racial otherness is then counterpoised against Anglo defenders of enlightened civilization enlisted to combat the hellish creatures of night and forest. While not immortal or literally able to transform, Indians are nevertheless both more and less than human, possessing almost supernatural powers of stealth and observation. They are savage, demonic creatures able to appear and disappear at will, to move silently, to sense and control nature, and to track their quarry across forbidding terrain.

Unlike James Malcolm Rymer's serialized account of Varney in his Victorian 'penny dreadful' *Varney the Vampire; or, The Feast of Blood* (1845–7), which influenced Bram Stoker's *Dracula* (1897), there is no known nineteenth-century American literary equivalent of an 'actual' vampire. While nineteenth-century American fiction restricts blood drinking as a literal or conscious act to non-white races, it is nonetheless rife with psychic vampires who possess seemingly supernatural powers to drain the vitality of others. Like the fears of racial difference in the above accounts of dark-skinned cannibals, these narratives reflect American anxieties about exploitative power relations and often pivot around issues of sexual difference and control embodied by a vampiric female figure. Not surprisingly, such demonic entities figure in the dark romantic writings of Edgar Allan Poe and Nathanial Hawthorne, as well as the gothic fictions of Mary E. Wilkins-Freeman and Ambrose Bierce. In both Poe's 'Ligeia' (1838) and 'Morella' (1835), for instance, mysterious and powerful females captivate their male companions and appear to defy death. After the demise of the eponymous Ligeia, the melancholic narrator remarries and, depending upon how one interprets the ambiguous conclusion, observes Ligeia's spirit taking possession of his dying second bride. The titular character of 'Morella' similarly refuses to succumb to death, despite her apparent dissolution during childbirth. American literary critic Allen Tate has compared the surviving daughter – also named Morella and a doppelgänger of her namesake – to a vampire returning 'to wreak upon her "lover" the vengeance due him' for his lack of passion (Tate 1963: 385). Tate also considers Lady Madeline of Poe's 'The Fall of the House of Usher', 'back from the tomb, neither dead nor alive', as someone who suffocates her brother in the vampire's 'sexual embrace' (387).

A more obvious case of psychic vampirism is featured in Poe's 'The Oval Portrait' – originally titled 'Life in Death', an allusion to the vampiric figure in Samuel Taylor Coleridge's *Rime of the Ancient Mariner* (1798) – in which an injured traveller seeking refuge in an abandoned chateau discovers an eerie account of a captivatingly realistic portrait. Providing a template for Oscar Wilde's later *The Picture of Dorian Gray* (1891), the narrative explains how the portrait's eccentric creator grew so obsessed with the artistic process that he neglected his model: his young bride. Upon completing the portrait, he exclaims, 'This is indeed Life itself!', followed immediately by his discovery of the death of his bride, her vitality drained and transferred to the portrait. One of many Poe tales about the death of a beautiful woman, 'The Oval Portrait' also allegorizes the artistic process as a vampiric one that entails the 'murder' of the thing represented. A gothic painting connected to life and blood similarly takes centre stage in Hawthorne's *The House of the Seven Gables* (1851). The stern portrait of Colonel Pyncheon, scion of the Pyncheon family upon whom the curse 'God will give him blood to drink' was laid following the unjust appropriation of the land of accused witch Matthew Maule, casts its long shadow over the Pyncheon line. The colonel was indeed served up blood to drink, fittingly choking to death on his own before the events of the novel. Thus his blood drinking is figured as either supernatural payback or poetic justice for having spilt the blood of a disempowered other. In a more metaphoric sense, both Hawthorne's Roger Chillingworth, the cuckolded husband in *The Scarlet Letter* (1850) who drains the life out of the guilt-ridden Reverend Dimmesdale, and (with interesting parallels to Poe's 'The Oval Portrait') the alchemist Aylmer in Hawthorne's 'The Birth-Mark' (1843), who 'perfects' his wife only at the cost of her life, feed vampirically on those over whom they exert control.

Two more explicitly supernatural early vampire tales – both of which thematize the grasp of controlling women – are Mary E. Wilkins-Freeman's 'Luella Miller' (1902) and Ambrose Bierce's 'The Death of Halpin Frayser' (1891). The former presents the account of the delicate eponymous character whose suitors and servants waste away and die. Seemingly incapable of caring for herself, Luella too sickens and dies when the townspeople will no longer approach her. In Bierce's strange tale, a distraught mother returns from the grave, like Poe's Lady Madeline, to wreak vengeance upon the son, Halpin Frayser, who left her. In one surreal scene, Frayser lies down in the woods and dreams of blood 'about him everywhere', only to find himself 'staring into the sharply drawn face and blank, dead eyes of his own mother, standing white and silent in the garments of the grave!' Frayser then 'dreamed he was dead' (Bierce 2013: 222), which may or may not be the case. Anticipating contemporary queer vampire stories, both tales associate vampirism with excessive or 'unnatural' affective attachment. Luella feeds upon the energy of those drawn to her, while the relationship between Frayser and his mother, who 'were not infrequently mistaken for lovers' (Bierce 2013: 220), transforms into blood-soaked violence and revenge from beyond the grave. Indeed, Bierce's scenario, in which a revenant plagues its immediate family, is much truer to the folkloric roots of the vampire than most literary accounts.

Blood drinkers also emigrated from Europe and England to the nineteenth-century American stage, which 'produced a steady stream of plays about vampires, originating in France and quickly "cannibalized" by the English and Americans' (Stuart 1994: 3). For example, Dion Boucicault's *The Vampire, A Phantasm in Three Dramas*, an adaptation of Alexander Dumas's 1851 *Le Vampire* (itself inspired by Charles Nodier's 1820 play, also titled *Le Vampire*, itself an adaptation of John Polidori's 1819 'The Vampyre'), was first presented in Philadelphia using the title *The Phantom* in 1856. Both as *The Phantom* and in at least one pirated version (*The Grand Legendary Drama, Vampire! or, The Spectre of Mount Snowden!*), the play had successful American runs in the late 1850s and early 1860s (see Stuart 1994: 145–55).

The First Half of the Twentieth Century

The above cultural crossings set the stage for a key moment in the evolution of the American vampire tale at the turn of the twentieth century: the 1897 publication of Bram Stoker's *Dracula*, which crystallized the vampire archetype in the popular imagination. Although not explicitly indebted to Stoker, F. Marion Crawford's 'For the Blood is the Life' (1905), continuing the American tradition of correlating vampirism with enervating female sexuality, displays the influence of both *Dracula* and Joseph Sheridan Le Fanu's 1872 novella *Carmilla* (Carter 2007: 625). At the heart of this story within a story is the tragic tale of a murdered gypsy girl who rises from the grave first to prey upon the young man indifferent to her love and subsequently upon any man who accidentally crosses her path. Unlike stories by Poe, Wilkins-Freeman and Bierce, in which physical violence is either entirely absent or off-stage (but very much in keeping with Stoker), Crawford's story renders vampirism explicitly as the red-lipped revenant Cristina, who lays kisses upon her paramour Angelo's throat and drains his blood.

Yet with this notable exception or the popular 1927 Broadway adaptation of Hamilton Deane's 1924 British staging of *Dracula*, the early twentieth-century American vampire narrative was primarily a cinematic affair. In keeping with Poe, Wilkins-Freeman, Bierce and Crawford, the first film vampires were not charismatic male seducers but rather 'vamps', predatory women who contravened the 'laws of nature'. Early vamps such as Helen Gardner, Louise Glaum, Valeska Suratt, and particularly Theda Bara, established a pattern of supernaturalizing feminine sexuality. They neither had fangs, drank blood, nor were undead, but still seduced their male victims and drained their vitality. Frank Powell's *A Fool There Was* (1915), for instance, inspired by and quoting Rudyard Kipling's poem 'The Vampire' (1897), chronicles the downfall of a man seduced by Theda Bara, named only 'The Vampire', who mesmerizes men, drives them to drink, and leaves them forlorn and debilitated as she moves on to her next victim.

The vamp films of the 1910s and 1920s suggest a conservative retrenchment in the face of the late-Victorian New Woman's defiance of traditional gender expectations. Even as they titillated the movie-going public, representations of the vamp as a chaotic force of social disruption demonized her less inhibited female sexuality. Adaptations of Stoker's novel, which retain the plot of brave men fighting with Dracula over control of women, suggest similar anxieties about women stepping outside of their prescribed roles. Such films reassert women's dependence on men and emphasize the pernicious consequences of giving in to 'sinful' desires. In the 1927 Broadway stage adaptation of *Dracula*, Lucy Westenra and Mina Murray were fused into a single character, the chaste and innocent Lucy Seward, daughter of Dr. John Seward, who must be protected from the aristocratic vampire Dracula – famously played by Bela Lugosi – by the commanding Van Helsing (played by Edward Van Sloan). Mina's agency in the novel, her role in combating Dracula, was wholly absent from this stage adaptation – one that then served as the impetus for the 1931 film version. Various early films, most notably F. W. Murnau's 1922 *Nosferatu, eine Symphonie des Grauens* (1922), remain somewhat faithful to Stoker's novel. Dracula did not arrive on the American silver screen, however, until the famous 1931 Universal Pictures film directed by Tod Browning. With its central contest between Dracula and Van Helsing and its greatly truncated conclusion culminating in the offstage staking of Dracula in Carfax Abbey, the film capitalized upon the success of the 1927 play as much as it does Stoker's novel by reprising Lugosi's charismatic stage performance. Lugosi's iconic film Dracula cements the contemporary vampire archetype as a foreign aristocrat in evening wear who preys upon attractive women. This cinematic Dracula gave American audiences both an escape from and a reflection of inchoate anxieties about the Great Depression. The classic 1930s monster films – Universal's *Frankenstein* (1932), *The Mummy* (1932), and *Werewolf of London* (1935), and RKO's *King Kong* (1933) – depicted 'average' people afflicted by supernatural threats that, like Dracula, arrive suddenly, but also showed misunderstood monsters cursed by forces beyond their control. These films offered film viewers momentary relief from their concerns but also empathic identification with citizens and monsters victimized by problems not of their own making.

Insofar as American vampire narratives of the nineteenth and early twentieth centuries gave shape to underlying gender and sexual anxieties and desires, they suggest how vampires are inevitably 'queer', highlighting as they do the social construction of normative sexuality precisely through their transgressions of social expectations (see Weinstock 2012: 7–9). One can see this queerness at play, for example, in the incestuous desire underpinning 'Morella', 'The Fall of the House of Usher', and 'The Death of Halpin Frayser'; in the hyperbolic feminine helplessness of 'Luella Miller'; and in the transgression of conventional gender expectations in

A Fool There Was. Of particular note to film critics interested in queer theory and recovering the traces of homosexual history embedded in film has been Lambert Hillyer's *Dracula's Daughter* (1936), in which the title character, Countess Marya Zaleska (Gloria Holden), enters into psychotherapy with Dr Jeffrey Garth (Otto Kruger) in order to cure her blood-drinking 'obsession'. When therapy fails, the Countess, resigned to her vampirism, determines to make Dr Garth her vampire companion, luring him to her Transylvania castle by kidnapping his assistant/love interest Janet (Marguerite Churchill) only to be shot through the heart by her jilted assistant Sandor (Irving Pichel) whom she had promised to make into a vampire. According to Harry Benshoff in his groundbreaking *Monsters in the Closet* (1997), Zaleska, who preys upon men but relishes young women, and who seeks assistance to combat her deviant desire, is 'the most obviously "lesbian" monster movie of the classical period' (Benshoff 1997: 77). Zaleska is, of course, punished in the end for her transgressions as order is restored and the monstrous potential for alternate sexualities is seemingly foreclosed – but not before cracks have appeared in the edifice of hegemonic heterosexuality as the vampire has lead us to contemplate tabooed sexual desire even as the film works to diminish and demonize those same alternative sexual possibilities.

The 1930 implementation of the US Motion Picture Production Code (or Hays Code), whose censorship guidelines were in effect until 1968, ensured that post-1930 representations of sexuality and violence were relatively tame by comparison with films of the preceding two decades. Compensating for this cinematic restraint were American pulp magazines such as *Weird Tales*, *Strange Tales of Mystery and Terror*, *Horror Stories* and *Terror Tales*, which offered a steady stream of lurid, gruesome vampire narratives from authors including Conan-creator Robert E. Howard, Seabury Quinn, Clark Ashton Smith, Frank Belknap Long, August Derleth and *Psycho* creator Robert Bloch. Among the most interesting are two 1937 stories from *Weird Tales*, H. P. Lovecraft's 'The Shunned House' (originally written in 1924) and science fiction great Henry Kuttner's 'I, the Vampire'. Lovecraft claimed to eschew gothic clichés, but occasionally introduced supernatural creatures. 'The Shunned House' recasts the vampire tale as a quasi-scientific story of horrific discovery in which an unnamed protagonist and his uncle investigate a house haunted with a century-long history of sickness and death. The house's monstrous vitality-sapping resident is ultimately defeated not with holy water and communion wafers but with sulphuric acid. Kuttner's story adopts the playful premise that the actor to appear in a horror film titled *Red Thirst* is himself a vampire. Anticipating Francis Ford Coppola's romantic 1992 cinematic adaptation of Stoker's novel,

Kuttner's vampire believes the film's leading lady to be the reincarnation of his lost love, which leads to a rather maudlin conclusion in which the vampire sacrifices himself.

Both stories demonstrate an early twentieth-century metatextual vampire consciousness by re-scripting and extending the vampire's literary and cinematic history. Showcasing the vampire as an embodiment of culturally specific anxieties and desires, Lovecraft's narrative, on the one hand, substitutes a rationalist framework for interpreting the vampire for the conventional supernatural one but, on the other, introduces his characteristic 'cosmic fear': the sense that the universe is governed by monstrous forces that render humans insignificant. In Lovecraft's story science displaces religion as a bulwark against the forces of darkness, but ultimately reveals the precariousness of human existence. Kuttner's less innovative updating nevertheless shifts attention from religion to science and technology through its playful emphasis on the movie camera. Anticipating E. Elias Merhige's excellent film *Shadow of the Vampire* (2000), Kuttner's story intimates how film creates legions of the living dead as the camera transfers life from the physical actor to his screen avatar. In this way, Kuttner supernaturalizes technology, suggesting in turn how modern cinema projects an uncanny semblance of life onto the silver screen in the absence of living actors.

The Second Half of the Twentieth Century

In the later twentieth century a staggering proliferation of American vampire narratives in literature, film and, later, television emphasizes the vampire as a protean metaphor for shifting social anxieties and desires. Richard Matheson's novel *I Am Legend* (1954) functions as a kind of vampiric pivot point by not only rethinking sedimented conventions of the genre, but in a remarkably prescient way foregrounding political and environmental themes that will become central to late twentieth-century culture. Protagonist Robert Neville is apparently the lone survivor of an apocalyptic pandemic that has transformed the world's population into vampires. Seeking answers to what has happened, he conducts research and traces the root of the disease to a strain of bacteria that infects both living and dead hosts. Along the way he draws conclusions as to why various vampire prophylactics are effective and develops increasingly efficient ways to kill his undead antagonists. In the novel's famous conclusion (spoiler warning!), Neville is stunned to discover that the vampires he has been indiscriminately killing during their daytime dormancy have in fact established a society of their own that fears him as the monster that comes while they sleep. In a world of vampires, the human being is the monster.

Matheson's novel constitutes a prophetic amalgamation of contemporary themes. As a story about the aftermath of a global pandemic, it anticipates the current preoccupation with viruses and zombie apocalypses. By seeking a rational explanation for seemingly supernatural affliction, it speaks to the modern faith in science to unlock the secrets of the universe, but also to science as a double-edged sword by connecting the pandemic to rampant militarism and biological warfare among nations. Most notably, the novel's surprising conclusion undoes the knee-jerk equation of difference with monstrosity through a relativist view of culture exemplified particularly in later films for children, such as *Shrek* (2001) and *Monsters, Inc.* (2001). Matheson's novel thus anticipates a later scepticism toward authority and celebration of the vampire as hero liberated from stultifying social convention.

That monsters should be construed as 'cultural bodies', as Cohen puts it, giving shape to particular times, feeling and places, is particularly evident in Stephen King's punningly titled post-Watergate 1975 novel, *'Salem's Lot*. The Nosferatu-styled vampire, Kurt Barlow, is an imperial force of evil who, like Dracula, travels across the ocean to invade fresh territory in the rural Maine town of Jerusalem's Lot, an apparently pastoral refuge from modern life that slowly reveals the banal evils of covetousness, bigotry, lust and selfishness. The loss of faith in authority, religion and the clichéd wholesomeness of small-town life is embodied by the alcoholic priest Father Callahan who falls prey to the vampire, who in turn materializes the evil already lurking in the poisoned heart of the town whose inhabitants are gradually transformed into a legion of the walking dead. In King's novel, the traditionally villainous antagonist reflects a postmodern scepticism about authoritative frameworks and metanarratives (Lyotard 1984) and thus a heightened sense of cultural relativism. This post-1970s re-evaluation of monstrousness transforms the vampire from threatening antagonist to sympathetic protagonist beset by conservative culture intent upon demonizing sexual and racial difference.

Following Fred Saberhagen's sympathetic first-hand retelling of Stoker's novel from the vampire's perspective in *The Dracula Tape* (1975), Anne Rice's *Vampire Chronicles* series (now including ten novels) exemplifies this shift in the vampire's moral status through its non-judgmental representations of affectively intense same-sex relationships. The series' first three novels in particular – *Interview with the Vampire* (1976), *The Vampire Lestat* (1985) and *Queen of the Damned* (1988) – reinvent vampire culture and mythology by presenting vampires as superheroes (and literally in *Lestat* as rock stars) endowed with immortality, supernatural strength and speed, and even the ability to fly. No longer subject to God's curse, vampires in Rice's saga are freed from their conventional antagonism to social mores, their fluid sexuality reflecting the natural expression rather than transgression of a more evolved vampiric consciousness. In an ironic reflection of the 1970s gay rights movement, Louis and Lestat even 'adopt' a daughter in the form of the child vampire Claudia. Unlike *Dracula's Daughter*, which excises the queer vampire with an arrow through Zaleska's heart, Rice celebrates queer as the new normal whose progressive attitude toward erotic relationships disregards conventional gender expectations.

Although not told from a first-person perspective, Jewelle Gomez's lesbian feminist vampire novel *The Gilda Stories* (1991) completes the inversion of monstrosity initiated by Rice and others. The eight sections of this episodic work chronicle the life of the eponymous protagonist, from her experience as a young runaway slave rescued in 1850 and introduced into a vampire family of sorts in Louisiana, to a dystopian future 200 years later in which vampires reveal their presence to the world. As Amy Harlib notes, Gomez constructs a form of 'benevolent vampirism' that 'involves the non-fatal sharing of blood that happens alongside the sharing of dreams and life force to the mutual benefit of both individuals involved in the encounter' (Harlib 2014). *The Gilda Stories* reimagines vampirism as a form of symbiosis benefitting both parties, a model appropriated by Octavia Butler in *Fledgling* (2005), discussed below, while associating true vampirism with the oppressive regimes of slavery and white hetero-patriarchy.

Similarly, the *Blade* (1998, 2002, 2004) and *Underworld* (2003–) film franchises harken back to American proto-vampire narratives, but with an updated message: those who would assert a racialized social hierarchy based on 'purity' of blood are mired in the past and the source of social strife. Emphasizing the 'half-breed' as hero, both series reject an earlier paranoia over contamination of blood by proposing miscegenation as the answer to racism in Western culture. In the *Blade* series' thinly veiled allegory of American race relations, vampires, defined by wealth and power, stand in for whites and humans for minorities. Loosely based on a Marvel Comics character, the films centre on the black vampire Blade (Wesley Snipes), who has special abilities because he was born soon after his mother was bitten by a vampire. As a result, he is a 'daywalker', a human/vampire hybrid whose powers outstrip those of both races. As a 'hybrid', he also possesses the moral compass and empathy for 'mortals' that the vampires in the series, believing themselves to be superior to humans, lack. In this racial allegory, rather than one blood type overwhelming the other, the mixing of blood produces a superior race – one that shares the white/vampire thirst for domination but recognizes it as evil and controls it. The fantasy of miscegenation as the solution to contemporary racial anxieties embedded in the *Blade* films is shared and rendered even more explicitly in the *Underworld* films. The fundamental premise informing this series is that aristocratic vampires are at war with their former slaves, lycans (short for lycanthropes). The potential to resolve racial tension resides in the relationship between two 'hybrids' – Michael (Scott Speedman) and Selene (Kate Beckinsale) – whose powers ultimately exceed those of either vampires or werewolves alone. Like the *Blade* series, the *Underworld* films feature vampire elders who fight to preserve the status quo and refuse to acknowledge their shared relation with those they consider beneath them. Both series show that this type of thinking is obsolete in the modern world and that racial mixing invigorates rather than enervates bloodlines.

By emphasizing class as well as race, George Romero's *Martin* (1977) is perhaps 'the most thoroughgoing, sophisticated re-examination of the vampire figure yet attempted' (Newman 1988: 130). Eschewing the conventional vampire formula, Martin (John Amplas) is not sexy, aristocratic or commanding; he does not speak with a Transylvanian accent or garb himself in evening wear – indeed, there is nothing to confirm Tata Cuda's (Lincoln Maazel) accusations that Martin is an 84-year-old vampire with European origins or Martin's own assertions to a radio talk-show host (Michael Gornick) about his vampirism. Instead, *Martin* re-scripts the vampire as a white working-class twenty-something going through the motions in an economically depressed post-industrial town, associating dread and desire with the vampire's class location. *Martin* is thus the exception proving the rule that vampire cinema is undergirded by a racialized discourse about social class in which foreign aristocrats prey upon domestic citizens. As with Browning's *Dracula* or King's *'Salem's Lot*, Romero's *Martin* suggests that the vampire's foreign otherness distracts attention from the fact that vampires are the product of domestic forces such as hopelessness, boredom and financial stress.

In the same way *Martin* revises entrenched class positions of the vampire cinematic tradition, Joss Whedon's TV series *Buffy the Vampire Slayer* (1997–2003), taking its cue from the 1992 film written by Whedon and directed by Fran Rubel Kuzui, inverts – and thereby reveals the sedimented nature of – the vampire narrative's established gender conventions A female-empowerment narrative, *Buffy* turns the history of vampire cinema on its head through its central character, Buffy (Sarah Michelle Gellar), a perky blonde teenage girl who protects the fictional town of Sunnydale, California – and the rest of the world – from the forces of darkness, including vampires.

While more conventional than other narratives discussed in this section, Francis Ford Coppola's lush big-budget *Bram Stoker's Dracula* (1992) nevertheless participates in the twentieth-century undoing of the correlation between vampirism and villainy by superimposing a romantic backstory that transforms Dracula into a melancholic lover. To Stoker's tale Coppola adds a prelude in which Vlad Dracula (Gary Oldman) returns from war against the Turks to discover that his wife, Elisabeta (Winona Ryder), has committed suicide after receiving a false report of her husband's death. The enraged Dracula renounces God, which seemingly gives rise to his vampiric state. When Dracula later emigrates to London, he becomes convinced that Mina Harker (Winona Ryder) is in fact the reincarnation of his lost bride. Sympathetically played by Gary Oldman, Dracula is more tragic than horrific. Coppola's film elicits a contemporary desire to rethink monstrosity by understanding the monster's motivations. Indeed, what Stoker carefully refuses the reader in *Dracula* (apart from a speech to Jonathan Harker about his proud martial lineage) is any real elaboration on Dracula's motives that might allow readers to sympathize with him. What Coppola significantly adds to his *Bram Stoker's Dracula* that is in fact nowhere present in Bram Stoker's *Dracula* is a romantic backstory that promotes the sympathy for the vampire that Stoker precisely rejects. Coppola's Dracula in this way is humanized and softened. His motivations are comprehensible and his actions, if not excusable, are at least understandable. Reflecting a contemporary distrust of authority and emphasis on the free expression of individuality, those who hunt Dracula, in contrast, are presented as increasingly priggish and narrow-minded.

The Twenty-First-Century American Vampire Narrative

The vampire narrative is among the most self-referential of literary and cinematic traditions. Later texts insistently allude to, directly reference and innovate on earlier narratives, especially Stoker's novel as ur-text, in the process assuming audience familiarity with the tradition and its transformations. Matheson's *I Am Legend* both references and rejects Stoker's ideas about vampires, for example, as protagonist Robert Neville seeks to understand and combat his antagonists. In King's *'Salem's Lot* the vampire hunters prepare by reading up on the entire vampire tradition, including *Varney* and *Dracula*, and the reader discovers, together with King's unfortunate character Father Callahan, that, contra Stoker, religious icons possess no inherent power to ward off the vampire; rather, their power is an extension of the religious faith of their wielder. Anne Rice's vampires, seeking to understand their own nature, introduce and reject Stoker as well, discovering for themselves an ancient tradition and culture.

While an in-depth analysis of the reasons for this vampiric variant of Harold Bloom's 'anxiety of influence' (Bloom 1973) is beyond this chapter's scope, it is clear that twenty-first century American vampire texts continue to demonstrate a pronounced metatextual element as they play with the conventions of vampire narratives in very conscious ways. A dramatic case in point is E. Elias Merhinge's delightful *The Shadow of the Vampire* (2000), a fictional narrative about the making of another fictional narrative, Murnau's *Nosferatu*, which in the process provocatively asserts the vampiric nature of film itself. Count Orlok, played by Willem Dafoe, is a real vampire masquerading as the human actor Max Schreck. Contemplating a 'real' actor playing a vampire playing a human playing a vampire, the film's viewer is interpolated into *Shadow*'s playful structure of meaning – its interrogation of the genre's theatricality and cinema's role in producing the vampires it endlessly pursues and destroys. Throughout the film, Murnau (John Malkovich), the director, is paralleled with Count Orlok, the vampire. Murnau 'consumes' his actors, uses them as tools in the production of his art and drains them of life and vitality, just as readily as Orlok drinks their blood. The film then culminates with an inspired effect: when exposed to sunlight, both Count Orlok and the film go up in smoke. At the end of *Nosferatu*, the vampire grabs his chest, raises his arm, and dissipates in a rather disappointing puff of smoke. In *Shadow*, the light obliterates all as the film stock itself seems to melt and burn up. As projections of one another, both vampire and film are uncanny creations of shadow and light that can only survive in the dark.

The twenty-first century American vampire is an increasingly humanized, even deified figure. In the novels and film adaptations of Stephenie Meyer's *Twilight* series (2005–8), vampires and werewolves are presented as powerful and beautiful. At the series' centre is human protagonist Bella (Kristen Stewart in the films) who falls in love with Edward Cullen (Robert Pattinson), who turns out to be a vampire – albeit a 'vegetarian' who resists drinking human blood. Although 'traditionally' a monster, Edward is more angel than demon: powerful, immortal (barring certain forms of physical violation), handsome, caring, faithful and, except in the case of Bella, capable of reading everyone's mind. He is, in sum, the apotheosis of the modern sensitive man rather than a repellent monster and he offers to Bella love, excitement, protection and escape from the mundane. HBO's *True Blood* (2008–14), based on *The Southern Vampire Mysteries* series of novels by Charlaine

Harris (2001–13), similarly presents vampires as powerful and alluring. In keeping with modern inversions of monstrosity that demonize restrictive social norms and celebrate the outsider's individuality, *True Blood* directly parallels the situation of vampires and homosexuals in Western culture. Following the invention of a synthetic blood substitute that liberates vampires from the necessity of consuming human blood, they have 'come out of the coffin' and revealed their existence to humankind. In a parody of conservative Christian homophobia, religious zealots such as the anti-vampire Church of the Sun greet this revelation with dismay. Indeed, each show's opening credits feature a church sign on which the hate slogan 'God hates fags' has been altered to read 'God hates fangs'.

The joke at the centre of Tim Burton's 2012 film of the American TV soap opera *Dark Shadows* (1966–71) is that the vampire, Barnabas Collins (Johnny Depp), is more normal than the hyperbolic and absurd 1970s culture into which he awakens, complete with lava lamps, hippie pot circles, and Alice Cooper. Viewed from the perspective of the monster and Burton's audience, particularly those conversant with the history of cinematic horror, this strange and fantastic 'real world' serves as the backdrop for the more comprehensible world of witchcraft and vampirism. More darkly, in *Let Me In* (2010), the American remake of Thomas Alfredson's 2008 *Let the Right One In* (*Låt den Rätte Komma In*), the real world is an abusive place. Owen (Kodi Smit-McPhee) is a lonely twelve-year-old boy neglected by his divorcing parents and bullied at school. When a young girl named Abby (Chloë Grace Moretz) and her 'father' (Richard Jenkins) move in next door, Owen develops an unusual friendship with Abby – a vampire who has been twelve for a very long time. At the film's climax Abby becomes a superhero who rescues Owen, who then in turn decides to abandon the life he has known to serve as caretaker for Abby. *Let Me In* insists that the world is a harsh place full of 'vampires' who prey upon the weak and different, but who, by understanding what it means to be an outsider, also exemplify the compassion humans lack.

Ostensibly leaving the human world almost entirely behind is Butler's novel *Fledgling*, which introduces vampires as a separate race called the Ina who are nocturnal, extremely long-lived and physically and mentally superior to the humans from whom they derive nourishment. With parallels to Gomez's *Gilda Stories*, the vampires in *Fledgling* form symbiotic relationships with humans, who not only experience intense pleasure from the vampire's bite, but derive enhanced immune systems and extended longevity from the bond. With a connection to the *Blade* and *Underworld* film franchises, the protagonist of *Fledgling*, Shori, is dark-skinned, the result of genetic experimentation by the Ina to produce resistance to daylight (and as with Abby in *Let Me In*, Shori appears quite young, despite being much older). As a consequence of her colour, Shori is victimized by racist Ina, a predicament that drives much of the novel's plot. Here again, the outsider vampire becomes the central figure in a morality tale pitting the forces of racist exclusionism against those of openness and tolerance.

Ironically, even a contemporary film in which vampires are unambiguously evil still manages to convey tolerance. The conceit at the heart of Timur Bekmambetov's campy *Abraham Lincoln: Vampire Hunter* (2012) is that Lincoln (Benjamin Walker) has sworn vengeance against vampires after the death of his mother at the hands of vampire slave owner Jack Barts (Marton Csokas). Through the film's rather unsubtle parallel between vampirism and slavery (the Confederate troops are vampires), Lincoln thus effects a dual emancipation: liberating African Americans from slavery and the human race from the tyranny of vampires.

Countering the impression that all contemporary American vampire narratives utilize the vampire sympathetically as a thinly veiled metaphor for otherness is Guillermo del Toro and Chuck Hogan's *The Strain Trilogy* (2009–11). Fusing the vampire narrative with contemporary anxieties relating to the prospect of global pandemics and nuclear annihilation, the series borrows freely from sources ranging from Stoker, Rice and King to Matheson, *Blade* and even the graphic novel *30 Days of Night* by Steve Niles (adapted for film in 2007 by David Slade). In the first instalment, *The Strain* (2009), the human protagonists confront a vampire 'virus' with New York City as the epicentre. In the sequel, *The Fall* (2010), human civilization is taken over by a vampire faction lead by a renegade vampire 'Ancient one'. In the trilogy's post-apocalyptic conclusion, *The Night Eternal* (2011), the remnants of human resistance make use of nuclear weapons to liberate themselves from vampiric servitude.

While the vampire conventionally possesses the power to morph into a bat, wolf or mist, its true power of transformation inheres in its ability to give shape to shifting cultural anxieties and desires. Prior to the emergence in American narrative of the vampire as the familiar supernatural blood-drinking character, vampirism already infiltrated American culture through racist characterizations of indigenous populations as bloodthirsty cannibals or misogynistic anxieties concerning the debilitating powers of female sexuality. The vampire paradoxically was already here, anticipating its own arrival. With the importation of European stage plays featuring vampires and then Stoker's *Dracula* at the end of the nineteenth century, vampiric anxieties and discourse were concretized and amplified in the form of the familiar supernatural creature, the vampire as 'undead' monster, whose unrestrained sexuality threatens even as it titillates. Twentieth-century American adaptations then took the constellation of themes already associated with the vampire – its racialization, its queerness, its embodiment of exploitative power relations foremost among them – and, with a self-referential eye toward the conventions of the vampire tradition already established, repeatedly redeployed and updated these themes to reflect shifting cultural emphases, notably recasting the vampire not as villain but as hero resisting the stultifying expectation of social conformity. The outsiderdom of the vampire, its queer sexuality, its refusal to respect authority all become causes of celebration rather than castigation – and, in an increasingly secular society, the vampire's association with satanic forces waned, while leaving its longevity and superpowers intact.

From a scourge to be eradicated to a symbol for unjust ostracism, and from a metaphor for threatening female sexuality to an embodiment of post-human promise, the metamorphic power of the vampire showcases the monster as an embodiment of 'pure culture'. Twenty-first-century American iterations of the vampire in the texts addressed above – as well as even more recent texts, such as the television drama *The Vampire Diaries* (2009–) and Jim Jarmusch's film *Only Lovers Left Alive* (2014) – continue to demonstrate the interest the vampire commands, the trend of its humanization and the ways in which vampire narratives are invariably, on some level, precisely *about* vampire narratives, as new re-scriptings anticipate audience awareness of the tradition being utilized and updated. Lacking a reflection of its own, the vampire continues to reflect back to the reader or viewer the anxieties and desires of its cultural moment.

References

Benshoff, Harry (1997), *Monsters in the Closet: Homosexuality and the Horror Film*, Manchester: Manchester University Press.
Bierce, Ambrose [1891] (2013), 'The Death of Halpin Frayser', in *American Gothic: From Salem Witchcraft to H. P. Lovecraft. An Anthology*, 2nd edn, ed. C. Crow, Malden, MA: Blackwell, 217–26.
Bird, Robert Montgomery [1837] (1967), *Nick of the Woods. Or, The Jibbenainosay: A Tale of Kentucky*, ed. C. Dahl, Lanham, MD: Rowman & Littlefield.
Bloom, Harold (1973), *The Anxiety of Influence: A Theory of Poetry*, Oxford: Oxford University Press.
Butler, Octavia (2005), *Fledgling*, New York: Grand Central Publishing.

Carter, Margaret L. (2007), 'The Vampire', in *Icons of Horror and the Supernatural: An Encyclopaedia of our Worst Nightmares*, ed. S. T. Joshi, Westport, CT: Greenwood Press, 619–52.

Cohen, Jeffrey Jerome (1996), 'Monster Culture (Seven Theses)', in *Monster Theory: Reading Culture*, ed. J. Cohen, Minneapolis: University of Minnesota Press, 3–25.

Cooper, James Fenimore [1826] (1982), *The Last of the Mohicans*, New York: Bantam.

Crawford, F. Marion [1905] (1911), 'For the Blood is the Life', in *Wandering Ghosts*, New York: The Macmillan Company, 165–94.

Del Toro, Guillermo and Chuck Hogan (2009), *The Strain*, New York: Harper.

Del Toro, Guillermo and Chuck Hogan (2010), *The Fall*, New York: Harper.

Del Toro, Guillermo and Chuck Hogan (2011), *The Night Eternal*, New York: Harper.

Derounian-Stodola, Kathryn and James Arthur Levernier (1993), *The Indian Captivity Narrative, 1550–1900*, New York: Twayne Publishers.

Gomez, Jewelle (1991), *The Gilda Stories*, Ann Arbor: Firebrand Books.

Harlib, Amy (2014), rev. of *The Gilda Stories*, Online, http://www.queerculturalcenter.org/Pages/Gomez/GomezGida.html (last accessed 21 February 2014).

Hawthorne, Nathaniel [1851] (2006), *The House of the Seven Gables*, ed. R. Levine, New York: Norton.

Hawthorne, Nathaniel [1843] (2007), 'The Birth-Mark', in *The Norton Anthology of American Literature*, 7th edn, ed. N. Baym, New York: Norton, 1320–31.

Hawthorne, Nathaniel [1850] (2009), *The Scarlet Letter*, ed. Brian Harding, Oxford: Oxford University Press.

King, Stephen (1999), *'Salem's Lot*, New York: Pocket Books.

Kuttner, Henry (1992), 'I, the Vampire', in *Weird Vampire Tales: 30 Blood-Chilling Stories from the Weird Fiction Pulps*, ed. R. Weinberg, S. Dziemianowicz and M. Greenberg, New York: Gramercy Books, 207–22.

Lovecraft, H. P. (2004), 'The Shunned House' in *The Dreams in the Witch House and Other Weird Stories*, ed. S. T. Joshi, New York: Penguin Books, 90–115.

Lyotard, Jean-François (1984), *The Postmodern Condition: A Report on Knowledge*, trans. G. Bennington and B. Massumi, Manchester: Manchester University Press.

Matheson, Richard [1954] (2007), *I Am Legend*, New York: Tor Books.

Melville, Herman [1846] (1996), *Typee: A Peep at Polynesian Life*, New York: Penguin Books.

Newman, Kim (1988), *Nightmare Movies: A Critical Guide to Contemporary Horror Films*, New York: Harmony Books.

Poe, Edgar Allan, 'Morella' [1835] (1996a), in *Poe: Poetry, Tales, & Selected Essays*, ed. P. Quinn and G. R. Thompson, New York: Library of America, 234–9.

Poe, Edgar Allan [1838] (1996b), 'Ligeia', in *Poe: Poetry, Tales, & Selected Essays*, ed. P. Quinn and G. R. Thompson, New York: Library of America, 262–77.

Poe, Edgar Allan, 'The Oval Portrait' [1891] (1996c), in *Poe: Poetry, Tales, &*

Selected Essays, ed. P. Quinn and G. R. Thompson, New York: Library of America, 481–4.
Rice, Anne (1976), *Interview with the Vampire*, New York: Alfred A. Knopf.
Rice, Anne (1985), *The Vampire Lestat*, New York: Alfred A. Knopf.
Rice, Anne (1988), *Queen of the Damned*, New York: Alfred A. Knopf.
Rowlandson, Mary [1682] (2001), *The Sovereignty and Goodness of God: Being a Narrative of the Captivity and Restoration of Mrs. Mary Rowlandson*, in *Early American Writings*, ed. C. Mulford, A. Vietto, and A. Winans, New York: Oxford University Press, 307–27.
Saberhagen, Fred (1975), *The Dracula Tape*, New York: Warner.
Stuart, Roxana (1994), *Stage Blood: Vampires of the 19th-Century Stage*, Bowling Green, OH: The Popular Press.
Tate, Allen (1963), 'Our Cousin, Mr. Poe', in *Modern Criticism: Theory and Practice*, ed. W. Sutton and R. Foster, New York: Western Publishing Company, Inc., 383–90.
Weinstock, Jeffrey Andrew (2012), *The Vampire Film: Undead Cinema*, New York: Columbia University Press.
Wilkins-Freeman, Mary E. [1902] (2013), 'Luella Miller', in *American Gothic: From Salem Witchcraft to H. P. Lovecraft. An Anthology*, 2nd edn, ed. C. Crow, Malden, MA: Blackwell, 344–52.

Filmography

A Fool There Was, dir. Frank Powell, Box Office Attractions, 1915.
Abraham Lincoln: Vampire Hunter, dir. Timur Bekmambetov, 20th Century Fox 2012.
Bram Stoker's Dracula, dir. Francis Ford Coppola, Columbia Pictures, 1992.
Dark Shadows, dir. Tim Burton, Warner Brothers Pictures, 2012.
Dracula, dir. Tod Browning, Universal Pictures, 1931.
Dracula's Daughter, dir. Lambert Hillyer, Universal Pictures, 1936.
Let Me In, dir. Matt Reeves, Overture Films, 2010.
Martin, dir. George A. Romero, Libra Films International, 1977.
The Shadow of the Vampire, dir. E. Elias Merhinge, Lions Gate Films, 2000.

Chapter 12

Consumed out of the Good Land: The American Zombie, Geopolitics and the Post-War World

Linnie Blake

Since 1845, when Edgar Allan Poe brought the American zombie into being in the brief tale 'The Facts in the Case of M. Valdemar', this simultaneously dead and yet perversely living figure has proffered a highly gothic challenge to the primacy of instrumental rationality on which the post-Enlightenment discourse of national identity rests. For the dead should stay dead. They should not reanimate or communicate. They should certainly not affect in any way the lives, or selfhood, of the living. And yet they do. What is more, zombie narratives allow for a revisitation of a number of themes familiar from the American gothic canon. For the zombie-apocalypse narrative estranges us from the erstwhile familiarity of its setting, now uncannily populated by a range of American selves that have been transformed into agents of chaos by an external entity. With alarming rapidity, these will destroy those markers of cultural identity Americans hold most dear: the proactive individual, the home, the family, civil society and democratic individualism itself. In gothic terms, this thematic of assault on the national endeavour stretches back to Cotton Mather's warnings of satanic intervention in American life that Hawthorne would develop in his depiction of the civil body corrupted. Here is a sense of the fundamental manipulability of American subjects, the essential instability of their cultural institutions and the duplicitous complicity of their chosen mode of government with those very forces that are inimical to the interests of the people. All are familiar paradigms, characterizing the New England gothic tradition from Brockden Brown to Poe and H. P. Lovecraft. The zombie narrative, with its additional investment in discourses of bodily corruption, has brought this matrix of concerns into the present moment echoing, in the process, Southern Gothic's concern with degenerative deliquescence whilst drawing on science fiction's contagion dynamics and body horror's allegorization of the corporeal. The zombie is, then, an exceptionally gothic creature and, for all its Caribbean origins, a very American one too.[1]

This chapter will argue that the zombie narrative of the post-war period has drawn on the conceptual resources of the gothic mode to undertake a new and terrifying interrogation of national selfhood in the light of the traumatic dislocations of post-war geopolitics. These range from the 1950s fear of Communist infiltration and full-scale nuclear war to the neo-colonialist catastrophe of Vietnam, from the consumer fetishism and economic collapse of the 1970s to the contemporary economic dominance of global neo-liberalism. For in the present age of governmental disinvestment from the public sector, corporate governance of domestic and foreign policy and large-scale infrastructural collapse, the howling monsters of the gothic tradition have come to overrun all aspects of contemporary culture. And of all the myriad monsters that populate our screens, our pages and our streets it is the zombie who holds sway over the vampires and werewolves, ghosts and demons, mad scientists and serial killers. This is witnessed in the enormous profitability of the US zombie economy which comprises 'novels, comic books, magazines, television programming, videogames, the digital world, conventions, events and walks as well as the more traditional Halloween costumes' and is currently valued at more than '$5.74 billion', and even that figure is 'grossly undercalculated' (Ogg 2011: 1). In the zombie horde's total disregard for national borders and its capacity to reduce survivors to traumatized subhumans huddled in the wreckage of civil society we can see, then, a highly gothic interrogation of the economic problems of the current age, specifically the enormous transformative impact of global neo-liberalism. For like the free market, the zombie horde sweeps away traditional agents of identity formation such as 'community groups, libraries, public schools, neighbourhood organizations, cooperatives, public meeting places, voluntary associations and trade unions' (McChesney 1999: 11). What replaces it is a world in ruins, where the weakest are the first to die and zombie and survivor alike become beings that are 'only body, without empathy, without respect for life: very like the marketplace, in fact' (Webb and Byrnard 2008: 91).

It is possible to trace the emergence of the modern zombie not to the New England cannibals of Romero's *Night of the Living Dead* (1968), as is commonly claimed, but to the zombie-vampire hybrids of Richard Matheson's novel, *I am Legend* (1954). Set within the American suburbs, to which the new middle class had fled in the years following World War II, the novel articulates the period's twin horrors of infection and depersonalization, the red menace being allegorized as an infectious agent carried by dust storms that destroy all animal life. Thus, the social divisions of the 1950s are made both noticeable and strange: the affluent selfhood of the protagonist Richard Neville being counterpoised to the increasingly tattered remnants of his neighbours who stalk the streets outside his highly fortified home.[2] Our inherently conservative protagonist thus sets about protecting his property from the onslaught of infected alterity in a manner highly evocative of those Cold War narratives of individualistic patriotism that were insistently counterpoised to the homogenizing imperialism of foreign communism.[3] Certainly, Matheson's monsters possess distinctively vampiric characteristics. They sleep by day and feed on blood. They are repelled by garlic and, if Christian in life, the cross. They are effectively dispatched by a stake through the heart. But these are not the aristocratic vampires of the *Dracula* (1897) tradition, being stinking horde-creatures who 'walked and walked about on restless feet, circling each other like wolves, never looking at each other once, having hungry eyes only for the house and their prey inside the house' (Matheson 2006: 55). They fall upon that prey in a now familiar frenzy of feeding – their victims being unceremoniously 'torn to pieces' (Matheson 2006: 120). For this is the only form of sociality demonstrated by these creatures, who infest the increasingly shabby streets and lawns they inhabited when alive, leaving our morally ambiguous hero barricaded in his family home; the last survivor of his family, community and ultimately species. As is the case in many zombie narratives, moreover, the origin of these creatures is material and man-made – an infectious agent born of war infecting a compliant population that sickens and dies; scientific diagnosis of their more vampiric symptoms being provided as Neville seeks a rational explanation for his plight. As would become the case in numerous subsequent zombie narratives too, Neville's survival is won at the cost of his humanity – his ability to torture and kill the infected turning him into 'a scourge even worse than the disease' (Matheson 2006: 160) that ended the world. For this is a world in which '[e]verything was gone, everything' (Matheson 2006: 37). Those who survive the onslaught as mutants witness this eradication of the old order and memorialize that witnessing in the mythologization of Neville himself. He becomes the legendary scourge of their people, embodiment of all that was wrong with the old world: home and family, state and nation, class-based gender roles and consumer capitalism.

But for all Matheson's pioneering work, it was indeed the film director George A. Romero who first capitalized on the zombie's potential to address the disjunction between the foundational dream of a perfectible nation and the contemporary realities of American life. Spanning the period from the Vietnam War to the presidency of George W. Bush, the first three films of Romero's *Living Dead* series respectively chart the ignominy of the United States' defeat in neo-colonialist war, the crash of consumer capitalism in the 1970s and the rise of neo-liberal economic models in the 1980s, models that brought our own world into being and positioned the zombie as avatar of the modern condition.

Thus, *Night of the Living Dead* (1968) established the flesh-eating proclivities of the 'silent majority' as they converge on a remote Pennsylvania farmhouse in which the American family eats itself, the heterosexual couple burns and the proactive protagonist, who is also black, is destroyed by militiamen unable to recognize his humanity. *Dawn of the Dead* (1978) deploys the motif to undertake a sustained critique of the media (that feeds the populace on a diet of 'moral bullshit' and false information), the state (that undertakes an inept forced relocation that leads many to their deaths but fails entirely to protect the population) and the ordinary American citizen, whose will to survive has been fatally compromised by self-interest and cupidity encapsulated in the shopping mall to which our hapless band of survivors flees. Drawing extensive parallels between the survivors and the zombies – both of which are driven to consume by factors beyond their will – the film thus undertakes, as I have argued elsewhere (Blake 2008), a sustained evocation of the stagflationary economics of the American 1970s. The subsequent film, *Day of the Dead* (1985) would, in turn, target the disaster capitalism complex generated by Reaganite economics, a network of power that had 'much farther-reaching tentacles than the military-industrial complex that in the 1950s Dwight Eisenhower warned against' (Klein 2007: 12). Thus the belligerently sexist Captain Rose embodies the US military's ongoing will to conquer the alterity of the Communist threat whilst the mad scientist Dr Logan's experiments on zombies echo the techniques of torture, first codified in the *Kubark Counterintelligence Interrogation* manual of 1963 that would be exported under Reagan to Central and South America as a ready means of exterminating opposition to corporate globalization (McSweeney 2010: 111).

And if *Day of the Dead* provided an updated narrative of national degeneration for the bellicose 1980s, then *Land of the Dead* (2005) set 'Some Time' after the zombie apocalypse, illustrates how the society that rises from the ashes of the old world is every bit as corrupt, exploitative and segregated as that it replaced. The film thus focuses on the sharp economic polarization of survivors. The power-crazed Kaufman, a thinly veiled impersonation of Donald Rumsfeld, is CEO of Fiddler's Green, a luxury apartment complex that Romero affirms unequivocally in the DVD commentary '*is* the Bush administration' (*Land of the Dead*, 2005). For whilst the denizens of Fiddler's Green operate exclusively in their own interests, an ethnically mixed population of survivors huddle in the Green Zone that lies at its feet – hemmed in by the zombies outside and ruthlessly exploited by their economic masters within. Kaufman is played, moreover, by Dennis Hopper – a countercultural icon since the 1960s, who here enacts the cataclysmic impact of his generation's chosen economic model on participatory democracy. For as the film makes clear, contemporary Americans are every bit as trapped as the 99 per cent of survivors, inhabiting the uneasy space between government policies that dismantle public services whilst exempting both corporations and the rich from fair taxation and a media-generated insistence that neo-liberalism not only serves democracy but is the *only* viable economic model. In *Land of the Dead*, 'If you can drink it, shoot it up, fuck it or gamble on it' it belongs to Kaufman. In our own world, the top 1 per cent of Americans own 40 per cent of the nation's wealth, a proportion that is growing year on year (Stiglitz 2011).

In a manner directly evocative of the Suburban Gothic of *I am Legend*, it is actually a Canadian film, *Fido* (2006), that builds most creatively on Romero's linkage of the zombie and the self under neo-liberal capitalism. The film is set in a highly colour-saturated 1950s-encoded smalltown America that simultaneously evokes both the Sirkian melodrama and the nostalgic fetishization of the decade by the conservative mass culture of the Reaganite 1980s.[4] This is Willard and it is named for the town around which *Night of the Living Dead* is set. Willard has made a good economic recovery from the horrors of the zombie wars some years previously. Consumer capitalism is unquestioningly accepted as the only viable system of economic exchange and the propagandistic militarism that underscores everyday life is utterly normalized. The citizens of Willard fear external dissent and external threat in equal measure, echoing the ways in which Red Scare Americans remained vigilant in the face of a putative Communist threat, first-generation neo-liberals quashed all ideological opposition at home and abroad and more recent 'warriors against terror' have looked suspiciously on anyone of a vaguely Middle Eastern persuasion. Children are trained in the use of weapons and shown *Duck and Cover* (1951) style films that equip them to survive another zombie outbreak. The newly deceased are decapitated – separate interment of the head being so desirable as to have generated, in classic neo-liberal mode, a new market for appropriate prepayment plans. Like the American small town of 1950s mass culture, which bore no relation to the actualities of the urban ghetto at home or neo-colonialist war in Korea, Willard is an ideologically driven and historically unanchored fantasy. It self-consciously differentiates itself from the zombie-infested hinterland to which all nonconformists are banished and promotes itself as a peaceful and affluent community of aspirational nuclear families.

Most notable here are the new social structures, institutions and organizations that have taken over control of society in the wake of the shock of war, most specifically the enterprising Zomcom Corporation, which has invented a remote-control collar that suppresses the zombies' flesh-eating appetites, enabling them to be enslaved in menial service-sector jobs including sex work. In this thoroughly corporatized society the family is the primary unit of consumer culture – possession of a zombie house-servant being a significant status symbol. The less-than-human, less-than-American zombie thus echoes not only the historic plight of enslaved African Americans but also the contemporary economic enslavement of foreign workers at the hands of US corporations, which perpetrate gross human rights violations whilst outlawing both collective bargaining and strikes. It also evokes the contemporary plight of domestic workers whose 'freedom of association is under sustained attack in the United States', the government frequently 'failing its responsibility under international human rights standards to deter such attacks and protect workers' rights' (Human Rights Watch: n.d.). So, whilst the film ostensibly tells the story of Timmy Robinson's friendship with the zombie he names Fido, his parents' loveless marriage and the possibility of human-zombie romance, what is of real interest here is the Zomcom Corporation. This is a company town with Zomcom as sole employer and self-proclaimed guarantor of outsourced civil liberties. But it operates by enslaving the undead and propagandizing the living through its control of the news media. In this too, the world of *Fido* echoes that of the global news media. As is the case with the 2009 film *Zombieland,* which opens with a distorted version of Hendrix's 'Star Spangled Banner' playing over a 90 degree tilted shot of a burning White House, the zombie pandemic has the capacity to render the supposedly 'normal' sufficiently strange as to enable us to see beyond the ideological obfuscations of the present. In the transmutation of people into zombies we can see the ways in which dominant ideologies render us less than human. In the inept response of central government to the horde we can see the duplicitous fallibility of our elected representatives. 'Welcome', says the narrator 'to the United States of Zombieland.'

Such interrogations of national selfhood are not confined to the world of film and television, however – Max Brooks's 2006 novel *World War Z: an Oral History of the Zombie Wars* draws insistent parallels between the zombie apocalypse and the multinational globalism of the neo-liberal free market. In this, I would argue, Brooks remains true to the historic deployment of the American zombie for the purposes of national self-examination. For in his act of memorialization, the narrator consistently addresses the ironic disjunction between the cultural isolationism of the United States and its overweening control of global economies, critiques the role of the military and exposes the corrupt complicity of small government and big business in our own contemporary world. Originally commissioned by the United Nation's Postwar Commission to write an impact study of the recent global conflict, the narrator's preliminary report was rejected, he tells us, for containing '[t]oo many opinions, too many feelings' (Brooks 2006: 1) to meet his given brief. The present work is a response to that rejection, setting out to capture 'the human factor' (Brooks 2006: 2) as a means of understanding the past and imagining a future beyond the present. For following the zombie onslaught, the survivors now find themselves inhabiting a world that is, itself, the logical conclusion of contemporary geopolitics. Here 'global life expectancy is a mere shadow of its former pre-war figure' due to 'malnutrition, pollution [and] the rise of previously eradicated ailments'. Here 'the physical and psychological casualties' (Brooks 2006: 2) of the war find their treatment entirely under-resourced.

The zombie apocalypse in this novel has not ended the world, then, but has radically transformed it, the internationally focused, multi-chapter, witness-testimony format providing perspectives from every continent and allowing for a comparison of the ways in which differing ideological systems responded to the global threat as it manifested itself within its sovereign territory. The totalitarian regime of North Korea, which has historically trapped its people within its borders and within punitive labour camps in which any whisper of opposition to the regime is ruthlessly silenced, opts for isolation. Its entire population disappears underground so totally that even years after the war nobody knows if 'those caverns are teeming with twenty-three million zombies, emaciated automatons howling in the darkness and just waiting to be unleashed' (Brooks 2006: 203). Israel builds a wall, keeping the zombies out and an improbably mixed population of Israelis and Palestinians in, positing perhaps a future that is considerably more hopeful than is currently the case. Meanwhile, the rest of the world attempts to control the spread of the virus through extermination of its agent: the living dead. Some countries are more centralized than others in their approach, sacrificing strategically placed populations for the greater good in a triumph of orchestrated national effort. South Africa has the Redeker Plan that revisits the taxonomies of apartheid to decide who will survive, scoring citizens on a scale that 'included income, IQ, fertility and an entire checklist of "desirable qualities", including the subject's location to the potential crisis zone' (Brooks 2006: 107). Germany had the Prochnow

Plan that pulled all troops into the North, leaving the Southern populations to their fate. Both ensured the survival of large swathes of the population and both relied on a 'jihad against emotions' (Brooks 2006: 110) that further traumatized those who survived.

It is notable that in the United States no such plans exist, for unlike those countries that mobilise the resources of the state for the benefit of the majority of the population, the US acts only in the interests of the markets. Thus, the President, who like George W. Bush presides over 'one of the most business-friendly administrations in American history' (Brooks 2006: 55), opts not for centrally planned and funded civil defence measures, but the investment of public monies in pharmacology he knows to be ineffective. It is the President himself who railroads the antiviral Phalanx through the FDA whilst proclaiming 'people don't need big government, they need big protection, and they need it big time!' (Brooks 2006: 56). In a frightened society that has itself internalized the values of the free market, this is a popular move in the short term, not least because '[e]verybody got to be heroes, everyone got to make money' (Brooks 2006: 57). In the medium term, of course, incidences of zombie infection increase exponentially. But it is not the recovery of the people that interests the government; it is the recovery of the markets. As Breckenridge 'Breck' Scott, the CEO of the company that produced Phalanx boasts: 'Because of Phalanx, the biomed sector started to recover, which, in turn, jump-started the stock market, which then gave the impression of a recovery, which then restored consumer confidence to stimulate an actual recovery! Phalanx hands down ended the recession' (Brooks 2006: 58). Holed up in his Antarctic fortress some years after the cessation of the Wars, Scott eschews all responsibility for millions of deaths and blames, instead, his victims. They were 'sheep'. They made the choice to use his product. He is not to blame. 'I never hurt anybody', he says 'and if anybody was too stupid to get themselves hurt, boo-fuckin-hoo' (Brooks 2006: 58).

In turning its attention to global biotechnologies, the contemporary zombie narrative therefore illustrates the potentially lethal short-termism of corporations that wield massive control over the future health of the planet whilst being motivated solely by short-term financial considerations.[5] Those profits are safeguarded, of course, by neo-liberal governments that decry the state when it comes to welfare provision but happily plunder its resources to the tune of 700 billion dollars to bankroll failing banks (Herbst 2013). In such a world, corporate executives come to play a powerful role in domestic and foreign policy – Defence Secretary Donald Rumsfeld, for example, being long-standing CEO of a company that not only owns the patents on four AIDS treatments but as Melanie

Klein has illustrated, 'spends a great deal of energy trying to block the distribution of cheaper generic versions of its lifesaving drugs in the developing world' (Klein 2007: 290). Three years after the publication of *World War Z*, of course, the Bush administration would stockpile one and a half billion dollars' worth of Tamiflu as ostensible protection against the 2009 swine flu pandemic, itself a strain of the H1N1 virus responsible for the decimation of world populations in the years following World War I. As was the case with Phalanx, the government simply ignored the fact that the drug's manufacturers had sponsored all trials into its efficacy and had suppressed the evidence that it was entirely ineffective in reducing the spread or severity of the illness (Krumholz 2013).

The utter absurdity of placing the public health in the hands of companies driven by financial considerations is further developed in *World War Z*'s delineation of the international organ trade. For whilst economically advantaged individuals may, the novel affirms, believe themselves to be free to consume what they choose, that freedom can only be exercised within a closed system of economic exchange in which the consumers are themselves subject to the vicissitudes of the markets whilst producers are effectively enslaved. It is a situation we have seen before in *Land of the Dead*. The metaphor of infection thus encapsulates the un-freedom of consumer and producer alike – the transnational organ trade enabling the virus to spread rapidly from person to person and state to state. In this world, we are told:

> China used to be the largest exporter of human organs on the world market. Who knows how many infected corneas, infected pituitary glands . . . Mother of God, who knows how many infected kidneys they pumped into the global market. And that's just the organs! You want to talk about the 'donated' eggs from political prisoners, the sperm, the blood? You think immigration was the only way the infection swept the planet? (Brooks 2006: 27)

Of course, nobody asks where the organs are coming from, 'be it a slum kid from the City of God or some unlucky student in a Chinese political prison. You didn't know. You didn't care. You just signed your travellers checks, went under the knife then went back home to Miami or New York or wherever' (Brooks 2006: 28). For all the protests of neo-liberal ideologues, the deregulated market symbolized by corporatized biotechnologies is once more shown to be entirely un-free, and utterly inimical to the rights and freedoms of the individual. And it is the zombie who conveys the message.

In *World War Z*, the motif of infection that is so central to the zombie genre comes therefore to echo the strategies of neo-liberalism itself. For as the precepts of the free market have infected both public institutions and governmental policy, available models of subjectivity have themselves mutated, creating the neo-liberal subject – realized in zombie narratives by the infected and uninfected alike. As Jodi Dean has argued, those 'symbolically anchored identities (structured according to conventions of gender, race, work, and national citizenship)' of the past have given way to neo-liberalism's 'imaginary injunctions to develop our creative potential and cultivate our individuality, injunctions supported by capitalism's provision of the ever new experiences and accessories we use to perform this self-fashioning' (Dean 2008: 62). Under the onslaught of neo-liberalism's bellicose consumerism, people may believe themselves to be both free and unique. But as the cultural ubiquity of the zombie attests, we have been made monstrous by neo-liberal conceptions of the self, becoming highly infectious transnational organisms locked within a static subjectivity that entirely lacks self-reflexivity and affirms, at every turn, the inescapability of the status quo. Thus, the situation in *Fido*'s Willard is poignantly echoed in Season Three of *The Walking Dead* (2010–), the Governor's town of Woodbury offering the traumatized survivors of the zombie plague a putative stability in the form of a barricaded small town run by an empire-building megalomaniac masquerading as a benevolent humanitarian. Woodbury thus encapsulates the defence of neo-liberalism propounded by its defenders, existing social systems having failed and the Governor's rule appearing to be the only feasible course of action to take; neo-liberalism being 'the only economic system possible' (McChesney 1999: 8). Such 'end of history' discourse is entirely suited to the mindset of the Governor, a man whose world came to an end with the sequential infection, death, resurrection and termination of his daughter. And it echoes Henry Giroux's sense that neo-liberalism has consumed the future (Giroux 2011). It culminates in the Governor massacring his subjects, losing everything and ultimately dying himself. History, needless to say, stumbles on without him.

But lest we accept too unquestioningly a sense that purgation of the corrupt present guarantees the redemption of those who survive, *World War Z* is keen to warn that a careless repetition of the mistakes of the past will lead us again to perdition. Citizens of the post-war society of survivors, cleansed of their consumer-fetishism by the harsh realities of total war, must now acknowledge personal responsibility for the role they played in ending the world. A woman formerly 'worried about [her] car payments and Tim's business loan . . . worried about that widening crack in the pool and the new non-chlorinated filter that still left an algae film . . . worried about [her] portfolio' (Brooks 2006: 64) thus comes to acknowledge personal responsibility for her role in the crisis, affirming '"I'm the American system . . . we all gotta take the rap"'

(Brooks 2006: 334). In condemning 'the baby boomers, the "me" generation' that 'fucked it all up' (Brooks 2006: 334), Brooks foregrounds, therefore, the necessity of ethical engagement and individual action. The survivors of the Zombie Wars may have 'stopped the zombie menace' but they have also become aware that 'we were the ones that let it become a menace in the first place' (Brooks 2006: 334).

In order to tackle the 'starvation, disease [and] homelessness' of a world in which 'industry was in shambles [and] transportation and trade had evaporated' (Brooks 2006: 136), the post-war United States returns, therefore, to a form of New Deal Keynesianism. This is diametrically opposed to the neo-liberalism of our present, relying as it does on state control of the markets, an affirmation of governmental responsibility for the welfare of the population and a concomitant investment in education and healthcare. Central is the creation of a viable manufacturing economy. In order to bring forth a new and better world, Brooks affirms, it is necessary 'to break from our comfortable, disposable consumer lifestyle' and institute a programme of state-run collective action designed to reject the class-privilege of old and transform a nation of 'sedentary, overeducated, desk-bound, cubicle mice' (Brooks 2006: 139) into something more socially useful and existentially whole. Such a model clearly flies in the face of contemporary ideology of the free market, which is conceptually equated with the zombie onslaught throughout the novel. Most notably, the post-war administration eschews the 'hands off' fiscal policies of neo-liberalism, the 'money cop' Arthur Sinclair working to move the county away from a barter economy and to instil 'trust in the American dollar again' (Brooks 2006: 337). To do this, of course, it is necessary to catch and punish 'not just the penny-ante looters but the big fish as well, the sleazebags who're trying to buy up homes before survivors can reclaim them, or lobbying to deregulate food and other essential survival commodities' (Brooks 2006: 337). Even Breckenridge Scott, the CEO responsible for the Phalanx debacle, faces extradition to the US to be held accountable for his actions. Nonetheless, the Saratoga Conference, at which the US convinces the world to 'go permanently on the offensive, marching forward every day until . . . every trace was sponged and purged and, if need be, blasted from the surface of the earth' (Brooks 2006: 265), offers pause for thought. For whilst the US attack plan evokes the old doctrine of Manifest Destiny to convince the world to 'take the long, hard road back to humanity' (Brooks 2006: 267), it also predicates economic security on military investment and retrenches the superpower status of the United States in the post-apocalyptic world. The imagined history of the Zombie Wars closes with a warning but is characterized by a sense of hope for the future that in the world of the novel's readers is almost entirely lacking in all but the 1 per cent.

In recent years, as the housing bubble has collapsed and ten years of war in Iraq and Afghanistan have transformed the United States 'into the world's biggest debtor and stripped millions of their jobs, pensions, and dreams of home ownership' (McCormick 2012: 3), the zombie apocalypse has become a particularly potent metaphor, the monster encapsulating the terrors of our age of infrastructural collapse, societal degeneration, mismanaged pandemic scenarios and governmental indifference and corruption. Such circumstances, I have argued, have made the zombie our generation's monster of choice, the Season Four premier of AMC's *The Walking Dead* (2010–), broadcast in October 2013, becoming the most popular programme on American television by attracting an audience of over twenty million people (Bibel 2013). For the zombie is a highly adaptable monster crossing generic boundaries as easily as it breeches national borders. Thus zombie films have been transformed into television programmes (*Zombieland* (2013)), graphic novels have been adapted for TV (*The Walking Dead*; *Rachel Rising* (2012)) and both games (the *Resident Evil* franchise (2002–12)) and the 2012 novel by Isaac Marion (*Warm Bodies*) have been made into films. These narratives display a variety of approaches to their subject matter that range from low–budget comedy (*Midget Zombie Takeover* (2013)) to politically engaged explorations of the contemporary workplace (*Dead Man Working* (2013)). Some deploy the zombie for the purposes of humorous historical revisionism (*Abraham Lincoln vs Zombies* (2012)) whilst others reference, parody and pastiche a range of archetypally American genres. These include the ghetto movie (*Gangs of the Dead* (2006)), the road movie (*Deadheads* (2011)) and the western (*Gallowwalkers* (2013)). Some are overt in their engagement with the United States' mission into the Middle East and Afghanistan, *The Revenant*'s (2009) undead Iraq War veteran going on a crime spree at home whilst *Ozombie* (2012) has Osama Bin Laden rise from his watery grave to expropriate the chemicals with which the US sought to counter 'insurgency' in the region and use them to create an army of jihadist zombies. In each of these scenarios, it is for contemporary zombie narrative to expose and challenge the socio-economic certitudes of the present, enabling us to attain knowledge of our own condition whilst working through the existential dislocations it has engendered. For as this chapter has argued, the role of the zombie narrative has always been to offer a sustained interrogation of the degeneration of the body politic and an exploration of both the nature and the value of human life. For every generation since World War II, it seems, John Winthrop's warning from the 1630s has come to pass. Americans have indeed sought to 'prosecute [their] carnal intentions, seeking great things for [themselves] and [their] posterity'. And in turn they have been 'consumed out of the good land' (Winthrop 1996: 9–10) by monsters of their own making.

Notes

1. As echoed in the earliest cinematic rendering of the monster: *White Zombie* (1932) and consolidated by *I Walked With a Zombie* (1943).
2. This being an era in which despite the primacy of consumer culture, one in five Americans continued to live in poverty, The National Poverty Centre at the University of Michigan affirming that 'In the late 1950s, the poverty rate for all Americans was 22.4 per cent, or 39.5 million individuals' (National Poverty Centre).
3. I am thinking of films such as the independently produced *Invaders from Mars* (1953) and *Killers from Space* (1954) and the rather better known *Invasion of the Bodysnatchers* (1956).
4. A tendency encapsulated by films such as *Back to the Future* (1985, 1989, 1990), *Dirty Dancing* (1987) and *Peggy Sue Got Married* (1986) amongst numerous others and memorably parodied by David Lynch in *Blue Velvet* (1986).
5. The global biotechnology is made utterly monstrous in the *Resident Evil* franchise (2002–12). In these films, the Umbrella Corporation is itself responsible for the zombie apocalypse, having unleashed a virus upon the world. It is a plot that echoes the ways in which the 'terminator seeds' of the Monsanto Corporation threaten to spread famine and ecological cataclysm across the world by replacing indigenous strains and altering the RNA of non-modified plants through cross pollination.

References

Bibel, Sara (2013), '*The Walking Dead* Season 4 Premiere is Highest Rated Episode Ever With 16.1 Million Viewers & 10.4 Million Adults 18–49', *Zap2it*, http://tvbythenumbers.zap2it.com/2013/10/14/the-walking-dead-season-4-premiere-is-highest-rated-episode-ever-with-16-1-million-viewers-10-4-million-adults-18-49/208857/ (last accessed 31 July 2015).

Blake, Linnie (2008), *The Wounds of Nations: Horror Cinema, Historical Trauma and National Identity*, Manchester: Manchester University Press.

Brockden Brown, Charles (1998), *Three Gothic Novels: Wieland, Arthur Mervyn, Edgar Huntly*, ed. Sydney J. Krause, New York: Library of America.

Brooks, Max (2006), *World War Z: An Oral History of the Zombie Wars*, London: Duckworth.

Dean, Jodi (2008), 'Enjoying Neoliberalism', *Cultural Politics*, 4.1, 47–72.

Giroux, Henry A. (2011), *Zombie Politics and Culture in the Age of Casino Capitalism*, London: Peter Lang.

Hawthorne, Nathaniel (1937), *Complete Novels and Selected Tales*, ed. Norman

Holmes Pearson, New York: Modern Library.
Herbst, Moira (2013), 'The bank bailout cost US taxpayers nothing? Think again', *Guardian,* 28 May 2013, http://www.theguardian.com/commentisfree/2013/may/28/bank-bailout-cost-taxpayers (last accessed 31 July 2015).
Human Rights Watch (2000), 'Unfair Advantage: Workers' Freedom of Association in the United States under International Human Rights Standards', http://www.hrw.org/reports/2000/uslabor/ (last accessed 31 July 2015).
Klein, Naomi (2007), *The Shock Doctrine,* London: Penguin.
Krumholz, Harlan (2013), 'The Myth of Tamiflu: 5 Things You Should Know', *Forbes,*http://www.forbes.com/sites/harlankrumholz/2013/01/08/the-myth-of-tamiflu-5-things-you-should-know/ (last accessed 31 July 2015).
Lovecraft, H. P. (2005), *Tales,* ed. Peter Straub, New York: Library of America.
Marion, Isaac (2010), *Warm Bodies,* New York: Random House.
Mather, Cotton (2005), *Wonders of the Invisible World,* 1692, repr. as *On Witchcraft,* Mineola, NY: Dover.
Matheson, Richard [1954] (2006), *I am Legend,* repr. London: Gollantz.
McChesney, Robert (1999), 'Introduction' to Noam Chomsky, *Profit Over People: Neoliberalism and Global Order,* New York: Seven Stories, 7–16.
McCormick, Patrick (2012), 'Zombie Economics: The Harrowing and Hungry Living Dead Serve as Stand-Ins for the Unspoken Fears of an Uncertain Generation', *U.S. Catholic,* 77.7, 1–3.
McSweeney, Terence (2010), '*The Land of the Dead* and the Home of the Brave: Romero's Vision of a Post-9/11 America', in *Reframing 9/11: Film, Popular Culture and the War on Terror,* ed. Jeff Birkenstein, Anna Froula and Karen Randell, New York: Continuum, 107–16.
National Poverty Center (n.d.), 'Poverty Facts', http://www.npc.umich.edu/poverty/ (last accessed 31 July 2015).
Ogg, Jon C. (2011) 'Zombies Worth Over $5 Billion to Economy' *24/7 Wall St,* 3 pages, http://247wallst.com/investing/2011/10/25/zombies-worth-over-5-billion-to-economy (last accessed 31 July 2015).
Poe, Edgar Allan (1984), *Poetry and Tales,* ed. Patrick F. Quinn, New York: Library of America, 1984.
Stiglitz, Joseph E. (2011), 'Of the 1%, By the 1%, For the 1%', *Vanity Fair,* May 2011, http://www.vanityfair.com/society/features/2011/05/top-one-percent-201105 (last accessed 31 July 2015).
Webb, Jennand Sam Byrnand (2008), 'Some Kind of Virus: The Zombie as Body and as Trope', *Body & Society,* 14.83, 83–98.
Winthrop, John (1996), 'A Model of Christian Charity', in *The Journal of John Winthrop, 1630–1649,* abr. edn, ed. Richard S. Dunn and Laetitia Yeandle, Cambridge, MA: Harvard University Press, 1–11.

Filmography

Abraham Lincoln vs Zombies, dir. Robert Schenkman, Four Score Films, 2012.
Back to the Future I, II, and *III,* dir. Robert Zemeckis, Universal Pictures, 1985, 1989, 1990.
Blue Velvet, dir. David Lynch, De Laurentiis Entertainment Group, 1986.
Dawn of the Dead, dir. George A. Romero, United Film Distribution, 1978.

Day of the Dead, dir. George A. Romero, United Film Distribution, 1985.
Deadheads, dir. Brett Pierce and Drew T. Pierce, Fro Bro Films, 2011.
Dead Man Working, dir. L. E. Salas, L5 Multimedia, 2013.
Dirty Dancing, dir. Emile Ardolino, Great American Films, 1987.
Duck and Cover, dir. Anthony Rizzo, Archer Productions, 1951.
Fido, dir. Andrew Currie, Anagram Pictures / British Columbia Film Commission / Telefilm Canada, 2006.
Gallowwalkers, dir. Andrew Goth, Sheer Films, 2013.
Gangs of the Dead, dir. Duanne Sinnett, Outside Productions, 2006.
Invaders from Mars, dir. William Cameron Menzies, National Pictures, 1953.
Invasion of the Bodysnatchers, dir. Don Siegel, Allied Artists, 1956.
I Walked With a Zombie, dir. Jacques Touneur, RKO Pictures, 1943.
Killers from Space, dir. W. Lee Rider, RKO Pictures, 1954.
Land of the Dead, dir. George A. Romero, Universal Pictures, 2005.
Midget Zombie Takeover, dir. Glenn Berggoetz, Continuum Motion Pictures, 2013.
Night of the Living Dead, dir. George A. Romero, The Walter Reade Organization, 1968.
Ozombie, dir. John Lyde, Arrowstorm Entertainment, Mainstay Productions, 2012.
Peggy Sue Got Married, dir. Francis Ford Coppola, Tristar Pictures, 1986.
Resident Evil (film series), various directors, written by Paul W. S. Anderson, Constantin Film, 2002–12.
The Revenant, dir. D. Kerry Prior, Putrefactory Limited, 2009
The Walking Dead, created by Frank Darabont, AMC, 2010– .
Warm Bodies, dir. Jonathan Levine, Mandeville Films, 2012.
White Zombie, dir. Victor Halperin, United Artists, 1932.
Zombieland, dir. Rubin Fleischer, Columbia Pictures, 2009.
Zombieland, dir. Eli Craig, Sony Pictures Television, 2013.

Contributors

Linnie Blake is Principal Lecturer in the Department of English at Manchester Metropolitan University and Director of the Manchester Centre for Gothic Studies. She has published widely on topics as diverse as zombie apocalypticism, Edgar Allan Poe and the Situationist International and the queer nationalism of *Torchwood*. She is author of *The Wounds of Nation: Horror Cinema, Historical Trauma and National Identity* (2008) and co-editor of two forthcoming collections: *Digital Horror: Haunted Technologies, Network Panic and the Found Footage Phenomenon* (for I. B. Tauris) and *International Gothic in the Neoliberal Age* (for Manchester University Press). She is currently working on a monograph on gothic television for the University of Wales Press.

Joel Faflak is Professor in the Department of English and Writing Studies at Western University, where he is Director of the School for Advanced Studies in the Arts and Humanities. He is author of *Romantic Psychoanalysis* (2008), co-author of *Revelation and Knowledge* (2011), editor of De Quincey's *Confessions* (2009), and editor or co-editor of eight volumes, including *The Handbook to Romanticism Studies* (2012), *The Public Intellectual and the Culture of Hope* (2013), and *Romanticism and the Emotions* (2014). He is currently working on two books: 'Romantic Psychiatry: The Psychopathology of Happiness' and 'Get Happy! Utopianism and the American Film Musical'.

Sorcha Ní Fhlainn is a Lecturer in Film Studies and American Literature at Manchester Metropolitan University, UK. Ní Fhlainn has published extensively on Gothic and Horror Studies, and on the representation of monstrosity and subjectivity on-screen. She is the author and editor of numerous publications on popular Hollywood Cinema, American popular culture and Vampire Studies. Publications include

The Worlds of Back to the Future: Critical Essays on the Films (2010), *Our Monstrous (S)kin: Blurring the Boundaries between Monsters and Humanity* (2010), and forthcoming publications on Clive Barker, Christopher Nolan and Postmodern Vampires.

Christoph Grunenberg is Director of the Kunsthalle, Bremen and Honorary Professor at the Hochschule für Künste, Bremen. Grunenberg did his MA and PhD at the Courtauld Institute of Art. He has been Director of the Tate Liverpool, and has held professional positions at the National Gallery of Art in Washington, DC, the Kunsthalle in Basel, the Institute of Contemporary Art in Boston, and the Tate Gallery in London. Among many publications, he is author of *Gothic: Transmutations of Horror in Late Twentieth-Century Art* (1999), *Elsworth Kelly* (2008), *Magritte: A to Z* (2012), *Summer of Love: Art of the Psychedelic Era* (2005); and co-author of *Picasso and the Model: Sylvette, Sylvette, Sylvette* (2014), *Picasso: Peace and Freedom* (2010), *The Summer of Love: Psychedelic Art, Social Crisis and Counterculture in the 1960s* (2005), and *Mike Kelley: The Uncanny* (2004).

Michael Hancock is a PhD candidate in the Department of English Language and Literature at the University of Waterloo, and book review editor for the online publication *First Person Scholar*. His primary interest is digital media studies, with a focus on textual representation in video games. Other areas of interest include representations of nature in fantasy literature and popular culture studies.

Jason Haslam is Associate Professor in the Department of English at Dalhousie University, where he teaches American literature, science fiction and popular culture. He is the author or editor of several books, including, most recently, the monograph *Gender, Race, and American Science Fiction: Reflections on Fantastic Identities* (2015), the essay collection *The Public Intellectual and the Culture of Hope* (2013; with Joel Faflak), the textbook, *Thinking Popular Culture* (2015), and a scholarly edition of Edgar Rice Burroughs' *Tarzan of the Apes* (2010). He has published on science fiction, the gothic and non-realist modes more generally in other collections, and in such journals as *College Literature*, *ESC*, *Gothic Studies*, and *Modern Language Studies*.

Christopher Lloyd is a fractional lecturer at Goldsmiths, University of London and an associate tutor at the University of East Anglia and London South Bank University, where he teaches modules on American culture and cultural memory. He gained his PhD from Goldsmiths in the

Department of English and Comparative Literature. Lloyd's first book is *Rooting Memory, Rooting Place: Regionalism in the Twenty-First-Century American South* (Palgrave Macmillan 2015). It examines texts such as Cormac McCarthy's *The Road*, Spike Lee's *When the Levees Broke* and the photographs of Sally Mann. He also has an essay published on Dave Eggers' *Zeitoun* in the collection *Ten Years After Katrina* (Lexington Books), and an introduction on American Exceptionalism in a special issue of the *European Journal of American Culture*, which he co-edited. His current research project examines race and corporeality in contemporary culture from the American South.

Andrew Loman, Associate Professor of English Language and Literature at Memorial University of Newfoundland, is the author of *'Somewhat on the Community-System': Fourierism in the Works of Nathaniel Hawthorne* (Routledge, 2005). He has published articles in *PMLA*, *ESQ*, *Journal of American Studies*, and *Children's Literature*, and has contributed a chapter on Art Spiegelman's *Maus* to *The Rise of the American Comics Artist: Creators and Contexts* (2010). His thought piece on fictions of empire and the late nineteenth-century trade in wild rubber will appear in the forthcoming study *Fueling Cultures*, edited by Imre Szeman, Jennifer Wenzel and Patricia Yaeger. He is currently writing two books: one on Nathaniel Hawthorne's city fiction, the other on Alan Moore and Dave Gibbons's graphic novel *Watchmen*.

Arthur Redding is Professor of English at York University in Toronto. He is the author of *Raids on Human Consciousness: Writing, Anarchism, and Violence* (1998), *Turncoats, Traitors, and Fellow Travellers: Culture and Politics of the Early Cold War* (2008), and *'Haints': American Ghosts, Millennial Passions, and Contemporary Gothic Fiction* (2011).

Sherry R. Truffin is Associate Professor of English at Campbell University in Buies Creek, North Carolina, where she teaches courses in Rhetoric, Writing and American Literature. In addition to her monograph, *Schoolhouse Gothic* (2008), she has published essays on the fiction of James Baldwin, Edgar Allan Poe, Donna Tartt, Stephen King, Bret Easton Ellis, Chuck Palahniuk and Joyce Carol Oates, as well as a piece on the sci-fi television show *The X-Files*. In addition, she has delivered papers at regional and national conferences on works by Lydia Davis, Flannery O'Connor, Walker Percy, Toni Morrison and Alice Walker. She is currently working on an essay on New Orleans literature for an upcoming collection titled *A Handbook of Southern Gothic*.

Jeffrey Andrew Weinstock is Professor of English at Central Michigan University and the author or editor of sixteen books including *The Ashgate Encyclopedia of Literary and Cinematic Monsters* (2014), *The Works of Tim Burton: Margins to Mainstream* (Palgrave 2013), *The Vampire Film: Undead Cinema* (Columbia University Press 2012), and *Charles Brockden Brown* (University of Wales Press 2011).

Julia M. Wright is Professor of English at Dalhousie University. She is a former Canada Research Chair (2002–12), and the author or editor of fourteen volumes, including *Irish Literature, 1750–1900: An Anthology* (2008), and over forty articles and chapters. Her recent publications include *Representing the National Landscape in Irish Romanticism* (2014), an edition of Lady Morgan's *The O'Briens and the O'Flahertys* (2013), and the co-edited *Handbook of Romanticism Studies* (2012). Her next book is on masculinity and gothic television.

Christine Yao is a PhD candidate in English Literature at Cornell University. She works on intersections of race, gender and sexuality in the American long nineteenth century. Her dissertation is entitled *Feeling Subjects: Science and Law in Nineteenth Century America*.

The editors would also like to acknowledge John Sears's contribution to the developmental stage of this volume.

Index

9/11, 63, 72, 162

A Fool There Was (Powell), 208
abject, abjection, 16, 29, 30, 98, 145, 152, 154–7, 189, 191, 195, 200
abolition, 12, 44, 47
Abraham Lincoln: Vampire Hunter, 217–18
Abstract Expressionism, 149, 151
Abu-Jaber, Diana, 63
Addams Family, The, 130, 132, 133, 136
African Americans, 12, 47, 50, 55, 57n5, 86, 88, 89, 98, 132, 218, 227; *see also* race; slavery
Agamben, Giorgio, 41n4
Albright, Ivan Lorraine, 156
Alexie, Sherman, 41n5
  Indian Killer, 61
Allen, Paula Gunn, 69
Allston, Washington, 148–9
  Lectures on Art and Poems, 149
  Tragic Figure in Chains (painting), 148
Alter, Robert, 102
Althusser, Louis, 110
Altmejd, David, 160
American Dream, 1, 3, 5, 10, 19, 187
American Gothic, 2, 6, 7, 8, 15–19, 20, 25, 26, 29, 30, 31, 32, 33, 36, 40, 40n1, 44–57, 60–5, 80, 94, 97, 175, 222
  art, 3, 145–63, 163n1
  criticism, 9–15
  film, 187–201
  painting, 149–50
  series, 137, 145, 149, 154, 187
  television, 129–42
  urban, 14, 18, 92–108

American Gothic, Washington D.C. (Parks) (photograph), 150
American Horror Story, 136, 137, 138, 141
American Indian Renaissance, 67
American Psycho, 187, 195, 196
American wilderness (the frontier) 7, 10–11, 17, 25, 27–8, 30, 32, 37, 38–9, 41n2, 60, 147, 148
America's Most Wanted, 193
Andriano, Joseph, 173
animality, 29, 30; *see also* bestial, bestiality
antebellum, 18, 47, 92, 93, 94, 100; *see also* Civil War
avatar, 19, 166, 167–9, 171, 172, 175, 176, 177, 178, 179, 180, 182n1, 211, 225; *see also* chimera; cyborg; doppelgänger; the uncanny; video games

Baer, Richard, 132
Baldick, Chris, 112
Ball, Alan *see True Blood*
Barthes, Roland, 52
Baudrillard, Jean, 1, 2, 16, 131, 167
Bearheart (Vizenor), 61
Beat art/artists, 152, 153
Beguiled, The (Cullinan), 79
Bell, Book, and Candle, 130
Bell, Michael Davitt, 92
Bergson, Henry, 123n9
bestial, bestiality, 25–41
Bewitched, 130, 132, 136
Bierce, Ambrose, 206, 207, 208
  'Death of Halpin Frayser, The', 207
Bierstadt, Albert, 148

Bildungsroman, 19, 66, 180
Birth of a Nation (Griffith), 47
Black Snake Moan (Brewer) (film), 79, 81, 87–9
Blade (films), 213–14, 217, 218
Blake, William, 6, 148, 198
  America, 6
Bless Me, Ultima (Anaya), 67–9
Bloch, Robert, 189, 210
Bloom, Harold, 215
Bogost, Ian, 175–6
Bone (Ng), 71
Botting, Fred, 3, 161, 166, 167, 181
Boucicault, Dion
  Poor of New York, The, 92
  Vampire, A Phantasm in Three Dramas, The, 207
Boyd, Collen E., 26
Bram Stoker's Dracula (Coppola), 214–15
Brite, Poppy, 12
British gothic, 46, 49
Brogan, Kathleen, 64–5, 69, 70
  Cultural Haunting, 64
Brown, Charles Brockden, 7, 8, 9, 17, 25–40, 40–1n1, 92, 96, 101, 222
  Address to the Government of the United States on the Cession of Louisiana, An, 36
  Arthur Mervyn, 92, 96, 101, 102
  Edgar Huntly, 7, 8, 17, 25–40, 96
  Wieland, 96
Bruhm, Steven, 131
Buffy, the Vampire Slayer (Whedon), 130, 131, 136, 137, 138, 214
Bundy, Ted, 187, 191, 194, 197
Burke, Edmund, 5, 53, 130, 135, 162; see also sublime: Burkean
Burn, Andrew, 176
Burnham, Michelle, 61
Burns, Allan, 132
Burns, Sarah, 147, 148, 149, 159, 163n2
Burton, Tim, 217
Bush, George W., 72, 224, 225, 229, 230
Butler, Judith, 6, 52
Butler, Octavia, 12, 17, 40, 51, 54, 213, 217
  Fledgling, 213, 217
  Kindred, 12, 50, 54, 56

Caesar's Column (Donnelly), 99, 101
Cajete, Gregory, 29

Candygothic, 161
cannibals, cannibalism, 17, 19, 25, 26, 27, 28, 29, 30–1, 33, 34, 35, 41n3, 41n5, 103, 189, 195, 198, 199, 203, 205, 206, 207, 218, 223
capitalism, 1, 6, 9, 44, 50, 111, 153, 195, 226, 231
  consumer, 224, 225, 226
  disaster, 225
  Gothic, 154
Capote, Truman, 82
Card, Orson Scott
  Ender's Game, 181
  Speaker for the Dead, 181
Carr, Diane, 173
Castle, Terry, 3
censorship, 131, 140, 142, 154
  Comics Code, 132, 142
  Hays Code, 210
Césaire, Aimé, 34
Cettl, Robert, 198
Cherry, Brigid, 84–5
Cheyfitz, Eric, 29, 31, 40
Child, Lydia Maria, 93–4
  Letters from New York, 102–3, 107
Chiles, Katy, 32
chimera, chimerical, 7, 17, 25, 26, 32, 33, 34, 35, 36, 39, 40, 41n6, 189; see also avatar; cyborg; doppelgänger; the uncanny; video games
Cholera Fiend, The (Averill), 99, 102
Christophersen, Bill, 34, 37
city-mysteries, 92, 94–5, 97; see also American gothic: urban
Civil War (American), 3, 10, 18, 79; see also antebellum
civilization, civilized, 10, 11, 13, 26, 27, 28, 29, 30, 31, 32, 35, 41n3, 55, 61, 95, 101, 110, 153, 205, 218
Clansman, The (Dixon), 47
Clark, T. J., 152
class, 11, 13, 18, 45, 49, 62, 82, 84, 92, 94, 99, 103, 106, 110, 115, 119, 120, 132, 133, 157, 190, 199, 214, 224, 232
  middle, 20, 96, 99, 101, 102, 132, 136, 157, 223
  working, 99, 100, 103, 106, 163n6, 197, 214
Clover, Carol J., 192, 194, 197
Cohen, Jeffrey Jerome, 25, 26, 203, 212
Cole, Teju, 63
  Open City, 72–3

Cole, Thomas, 149
Coleridge, Samuel Taylor, 133–4, 136, 206
  Rime of the Ancient Mariner, 206
Collins, Wilkie, 61
colonial, colonialism, 7, 11, 12, 25–36, 38, 223, 225, 226
Columbus, Christopher, 17, 27–8
Connelly, Joe, 132
Conner, Bruce, 152
Cooper, James Fenimore, 7, 8, 9, 204, 205
Crewdson, Gregory, 155, 156, 158
Cronon, William, 95
Crownshaw, Richard, 81
cyborg, 155, 158
  Cyborg Manifesto, A (Haraway), 41n6
  see also avatar; chimera; doppelgänger; the uncanny; video games

Dahmer, Jeffrey, 191, 194
Dark Knight Rises, The (film), 92
Dark Shadows, 133, 136, 137, 138, 217
Darkly Dreaming Dexter (Lindsay) (novel), 199
Dean, Jodi, 231
del Toro, Guillermo, 218
  Devil's Backbone, The, 62
  Pan's Labyrinth, 62
  see also Strain Trilogy, The
Delbanco, Andrew, 162
Deleuze, Gilles, 4, 156
Demme, Jonathan see Silence of the Lambs
Derounian-Stodola, Kathryn, 205
Derrida, Jacques, 29–30, 41n4, 72
Dexter (television show), 19, 187, 199–200
Diable amoureux, Le (Cazotte), 173
Dickinson, Emily, 9
Die Geheimnisse von New Orleans (Reizenstein), 94
disease, 96, 100, 101, 155, 156, 205, 211, 224, 232
Disney, Walt, 1, 5, 8, 16, 20
Disneyland, 1, 2, 16, 17
Django Unchained (Tarantino), 54
doppelgänger, 158, 167, 168, 174, 176, 206; see also avatar; chimera; cyborg; the uncanny; video games
doubling, 19, 51, 166, 167, 170, 174, 177, 181; see also performance; repetition; unit operation; video games
Douglass, Frederick, 12, 17, 48, 50
  Narrative of the Life of Frederick Douglass, The, 48
Dracula, 19, 130, 155, 204, 208, 209, 212, 214, 215, 224; see also *Bram Stoker's Dracula*; *Dracula's Daughter*; *Dracula Tape, The*; Stoker, Bram
Dracula Tape, The, 212
Dracula's Daughter, 210, 213
DuBois, W. E. B., 57n8
  Souls of Black Folk, 53
Dumas, Alexandre, 207
Dungeons and Dragons (game), 178–9, 183n8; see also video games

Eagleton, Terry, 155, 158, 163n6
Eakins, Thomas, 148
Edmundson, Mark, 153–4
Ellison, Ralph, 13, 44, 56
  Invisible Man, 13, 56
Emerson, Ralph Waldo, 148
Enlightenment, 2, 13, 18, 19, 96, 110, 111, 119, 121, 122, 146, 166, 171, 177, 180, 222
Erickson, Gregory, 85
Eye-Killers (Carr), 62

Faulkner, William, 8, 11, 18, 44, 79–80, 82, 97, 111, 112, 113, 114, 115, 116, 123n6, 123n9, 157
  Absalom, Absalom!, 111, 113–14
  As I Lay Dying, 113
  Hamlet, The, 113
  Sanctuary, 80, 114
  Sound and the Fury, The, 18, 111, 113–15
Felman, Shoshana, 15
femininity, feminism, feminist, 12, 69, 87, 103, 132, 133, 156, 208, 209, 213
Fido, 226–7, 231
Fiedler, Leslie, 8, 9–10, 37, 40, 40–1n1, 44, 46, 53, 60, 80, 81, 85, 159
  Love and Death in the American Novel, 40n1, 80
Flight from Nevèrÿon (Delany), 45
Fludernik, Monika, 57n2
'For the Blood of Life' (Crawford), 208
Foucault, Michel, 11, 110
  Discipline and Punish, 114

Frankenstein (films), 16, 209; *see also* Shelley, Mary
Frankenstein (monster), 197; *see also* Shelley, Mary
freedom, 13, 17, 45, 52, 53, 54, 55, 56, 57, 72, 138, 154, 171, 177, 180, 227, 230
Freud, Sigmund / Freudian, 3, 8, 14, 15, 26, 64, 73, 96, 97, 158, 167
 'Mourning and Melancholia', 73
Friday the 13th, 190, 192, 194
Fuchs, Michael, 167, 181
Fuseli, Henry, 148

García, Cristina, 73
 Dreaming in Cuban, 62, 70–1
Gardner, Jared, 31, 32
Gein, Ed, 11, 187, 189, 195, 197, 200, 201
gender, gendered, 11, 12, 14, 18, 45, 81, 84, 86, 89, 93, 110, 120, 133, 157, 174, 180, 182n6, 198, 203, 204, 208, 209, 213, 214, 224, 231
Ghost and Mrs. Muir, The, 132, 133
Ghost Singer (Walters), 61
Gilda Stories, The (Gomez), 213, 217
Giles, Paul, 73
Ginsberg, Lesley, 47
Giroux, Henry, 110, 231
Glance at New York, A (Baker), 93
Gleeson-White, Sarah, 82, 85
Gober, Robert, 155, 157–8, 159, 162
 Untitled (Closet) (artwork), 157
Goddu, Teresa, 12, 18, 45, 46, 48, 49, 51–2, 54, 55, 57n3, 60, 64, 80, 82, 85, 97, 181
Good Scent from a Strange Mountain, A (Butler), 64
Gordon, Avery, 81
Goya, Francisco, 3, 18
Great Gatsby, The (Fitzgerald), 6, 15
Greenberg, Clement, 151–2
Grotesque, the, grotesqueness, 44, 47, 99, 102–3, 145, 146, 147, 154–6
 Southern grotesque (or Gothic), 19, 82–4
 Techno-grotesque, 159
Guattari, Félix, 156

Halloween, 190, 192, 194
Hamlet (Shakespeare), 111, 123n1, 123n7, 134
Hannibal, Hannibal Lecter *see* Harris, Thomas

Haralovich, Mary Beth, 132
Haraway, Donna *see* cyborg
Harlib, Amy, 213
Harris, Charlaine, 84, 216; *see also True Blood*
Harris, Thomas
 Hannibal, Hannibal Lecter, *Hannibal Rising*, 187, 188, 190, 196, 198, 200
 Red Dragon, 197, 198, 200
 Silence of the Lambs, The, 11, 187, 188, 189, 196–9, 200
 see also Manhunter
Hartman, Geoffrey H., 51
Hawthorne, Nathaniel, 8, 9, 12, 46, 93, 97, 102, 188, 206–7, 222
 'Birth-Mark, The', 207
 Blithedale Romance, The, 11
 House of the Seven Gables, The, 206
 'Lady Eleanore's Mantle', 102
 'My Kinsman, Major Molineux', 95, 99
 Scarlet Letter, The, 11, 207
Heidnik, Gary, 197
Hemenway, Robert, 46
Henry: Portrait of a Serial Killer, 195
Hitchcock, Alfred, 189
 Afred Hitchcock Presents, 130–1
 Psycho, 11, 187, 189–90, 210
Hogan, Chuck, 218; *see also Strain Trilogy, The*
Hogle, Jerrold E., 6, 9, 14, 15, 53, 57, 169
Hollering Creek (Cisneros), 64
Holmes, H. H., 189
Homer, Winslow, 148
homosexual, homosexuality, 15, 86–7, 209, 216
Hopper, Edward, 19, 149
Howe, Daniel Walker, 93
Huckleberry Finn (Twain), 53
Hungry Ghosts, The (Selvadurai), 63

Indians *see* Indigenous, Indigenous peoples
Indigenous, Indigenous peoples, 4, 6, 7, 10, 11, 26–7, 29, 39, 41n3, 62, 63, 66, 68, 151, 153, 205, 218
 American Indian, Indian, 7, 9, 25–40, 40n1, 60, 66, 68, 80, 204–5
 Native Americans, 17, 25–40, 41n2, 41n5, 60, 61, 67, 80, 204
infection, 20, 101, 211, 223, 224, 229, 230–1

Inge, M. Thomas, 88, 89
Ironweed (Kennedy), 64
Irving, Washington, 8, 98
Island of Dr. Moreau (Wells), 135

Jacobs, Harriet, 12, 17, 49, 50, 54, 55
  Incidents in the Life of a Slave Girl, 45, 48, 54
James, Ed, 132
James, Henry, 8, 9, 11, 15
  'Beast in the Jungle, The', 15
  'Jolly Corner, The', 98
Jameson, Frederick, 14
Jamestown (colony), 30, 31
Jarvis, Brian, 190, 199
Jekyll and Hyde (Stevenson), 188
Jim Crow, 81, 85, 98
Jørgensen, Bo Hakon, 122
Juhl, Marianne, 122
Juul, Jesper, 175
  Art of Failure, The: An Essay on the Pain of Playing Games, 182n2

Kafter, Peter, 36
Kakutani, Michiko, 162
Kalifornia Gothic, 152–3
Kant, Kantian, 2, 5, 52, 57n7, 116, 117
Kawash, Samira, 137–8
Kelley, Mike, 155–6, 158
Kelting, George, 131
Key Into the Language of America, The (Williams), 28–9
Kienholz, Ed, 152
Kilgour, Maggie, 14, 31, 96
King, Martin Luther, 194
King, Stephen, 8, 32, 79–80, 84, 85, 175, 218
  Carrie, 12, 110
  Danse Macabre, 79
  Salem's Lot, 212, 214, 215
  'Suffer the Little Children', 110
Kiss of the Fur Queen (Highway), 62
Klein, Naomi, 225, 229–30
Klein, Richard, 154
Krause, Sydney J., 36
Kristeva, Julia, 156, 163n2
Krzywinska, Tanya, 175, 182
Kucich, John J., 55

La Ferla, Ruth, 160
Lacan, Jacques, 15, 54
  Lacanian Real, 6, 7, 15, 52, 53, 188
Lavender-Smith, Jordan, 134, 142

Lawrence, D. H., 60
Ledwon, Lenora, 129
Lee, Joanna, 132
Lenni-Lenape (Indigenous people), 26, 32, 33, 35, 36, 37, 38, 39
Leslie, Phil, 132
Let Me In, 217
Let the Dead Bury their Dead (Kenan), 62
Levernier, James Arthur, 205
Lhamon, W. T., 98, 108n1
Lights Out (radio series), 130, 131
Lindsay, Jeff *see Darkly Dreaming Dexter*; *Dexter*
London, Jack, 118, 121
Lord of the Flies (Golding), 135
Los Angeles gothic, 152
Lost (Abrams), 134–6
Lovecraft, H. P., 210, 211, 222
  'Horror at Red Hook, The', 92
Lucas, Henry Lee, 195

M (Lang), 189
Madsen, Deborah, 11, 16
Malchow, H. L., 46
Man-Eating Myth, The (Arens), 41n3
Manhunter, 190, 197
Manifest Destiny, 4, 10, 15, 232
Marxism, Marxist approaches, 10, 14, 15, 97, 163n6
Mather, Cotton, 11, 16, 20, 222
Matheson, Richard, 132, 218
  I Am Legend (film), 92, 132, 211–12, 215, 223–4, 226
Mäyrä, Frans, 177
McCabe, James Dabney, 103
  Secrets of the Great City, The, 103–7
McCarthy, Paul, 156
McCay, Winsor, 5, 16
  Gertie the Dinosaur, 5
McChesney, Robert, 223, 231
McCullers, Carson, 82
McPherson, Tara, 86, 87
Melmoth the Wanderer (Maturin), 139
Melrose Place, 154
Melville, Herman, 9, 14, 205
  'Benito Cereno', 205
  Typee: A Peep at Polynesian Life, 205
Meteling, Arno, 168
Miles, Robert, 4, 45
Millennium (Carter), 137–41, 142, 154, 199
Miller, John, 156

miscegenation, 8, 14, 17, 19, 60, 82, 86, 88, 89, 213; *see also* infection; race; racism
Moi, Toril, 139–40
Monk, The (Lewis), 139
Monkey Beach (Robinson), 62
Monsters in the Closet (Benshoff), 210
monsters, monstrosity, monstrous, 2, 3, 19, 20, 25–41, 82, 83, 89, 92, 99, 103, 110, 111, 118, 134, 135, 136, 147, 155–9, 169, 170, 171, 172–5, 177, 180, 181, 187, 189, 191, 197, 203, 209–19, 223, 224, 231–4, 234n5
Montaigne, Michel de, 31
Montrose, Louise, 48
Morgan, Darin, 138, 139, 140
Morgan, Edwin S., 30
Morris, David B., 129, 130, 131
Morrison, Toni, 8, 11, 12, 13, 14, 15, 17, 53, 54, 60, 62, 92, 97
  Beloved, 12, 49, 62, 70, 110
  Playing in the Dark, 46
Mourt's Relation, 28
Muir, John Kenneth, 192
Munsters, The, 130, 132, 136, 142
Mystères de Paris, Les (Sue), 94, 95, 107
Mysteries and Miseries of New York (Buntline), 93, 94
Mysteries of London, The (Reynolds), 96
Mysteries of Udolpho, The (Radcliffe), 93, 95

Native Americans *see* Indigenous, Indigenous peoples
Nelson, Victoria, 172
Neo-liberalism, 20, 167, 169, 171, 177, 181, 182, 223, 225, 226, 227, 229, 230, 231, 232
New Historicism, 14, 48
Newman, Kim, 214
Newman, Robert D., 34
Ng, Andrew Hock Soon, 71
Nick of the Woods (Bird), 205
Nightmare on Elm Street, A (Craven), 157, 190, 192
Nightmares in Red, White, and Blue: The Evolution of the American Horror Film (Monument), 192
Nixon, Nicola, 191
Nora, Pierre, 65
Norwalk, Pennsylvania, 33, 36, 37, 38, 39

Nosferatu, eine Symphonie des Grauens, 209
Novak, Barbara, 148–9

Oates, Joyce Carol, 110–24, 239
  Accursed, The, 18, 110–22, 123n4, 123n8, 123n10
  Beasts, 110, 111
  Bellefleur, 113
  Zombie, 110
O'Connor, Flannery, 8, 11, 82, 83, 84, 97
  Violent Bear It Away, The, 110
  Wise Blood, 83, 88
Of Plymouth Plantation (Bradford), 28
Oleanna (Mamet), 110
Oleson, J. C., 193
Oliver Twist (Dickens), 96
Only Lovers Left Alive (Jarmusch), 219
Otherness, 6, 19, 31, 44, 51, 60, 85, 86, 97, 98, 156, 203, 205, 214, 218
Others, The (Amenábar), 72
Owens, Louis, 60, 61, 66
  Sharpest Sight, 61

Passion for Consumption, A: The Gothic Novel in America (Sonser), 113
performance, 98, 168, 176, 182n3, 209; *see also* doubling; repetition; unit operation; video games
Picture of Dorian Gray (Wilde), 206
Plymouth Colony, 17, 28
Poe, Edgar Allan, 8, 12, 14, 17, 32, 46, 47, 97, 107, 110, 111, 130, 149, 151, 154, 188, 207, 208, 222
  Black Cat, The, 12, 47, 188
  'Fall of the House of Usher', 132, 206, 209
  'Ligeia', 206
  'Man of the Crowd, The', 98, 102
  'Morella', 206, 209
  'Murders in the Rue Morgue, The', 99, 102
  Narrative of Arthur Gordon Pym, The, 25, 92, 120
  'Oval Portrait, The', 206, 207
  'Purloined Letter, The', 15
  'Tell-Tale Heart, The', 188
Pollock, Jackson, 149, 151
  Gothic (painting), 151
  Seascape (painting), 149
postmodern, postmodernism, 8, 51, 141, 145, 190, 196, 212

gothic, Gothick, 154–7, 196
  theory, 9, 167
Praisesong for the Widow (Marshall), 64
Psycho see Hitchcock, Alfred
psychoanalysis, 6, 14, 50, 51, 52, 64, 96
Punter, David, 4, 155
Puritanism, Puritans, 3, 10, 11–12, 28, 29, 30, 146, 154, 157

Quaker City, The (Lippard), 99, 106
queer *see* sexuality

race, 10, 11, 12, 13, 14, 18, 31, 32, 36, 46, 53, 84, 85, 86, 87, 89, 97, 99, 110, 123n3, 124n11, 132, 140, 147, 157, 160, 194, 203, 204, 213–14, 217, 231
racism, racist, 12, 13, 18, 34, 45, 46–7, 57, 61, 67, 82, 101, 150, 159, 213, 217, 218
Reagan, Reaganomics, 153, 193, 194, 225, 226
Real, the *see* Lacan, Jacques: Lacanian Real
realism, 16, 18, 84, 89, 122, 129, 130–3, 134, 136, 138, 139, 140, 141, 142, 148, 149, 150, 158
  magical, 62, 63
  televisual, 137
Red Dragon see Harris, Thomas
repetition, 4, 19, 45, 51, 52, 53–4, 55, 161, 166, 167, 168–9, 171, 172, 176, 177, 183n9, 193; *see also* doubling; performance; unit operation; video games
Resident Evil, 233, 234n5
Reynolds, David S., 93, 99
Rice, Anne, 8, 130, 212–13, 215, 218
  Interview with the Vampire, 12, 212
  Queen of the Damned, 212
  Vampire Chronicles, The, 212
  Vampire Lestat, The, 212, 213
Ringe, Donald A., 7
Romantic, Romanticism, 2, 8, 10, 56, 146, 148, 181
  Dark Romanticism, 148
Romero, George, 157, 224, 225, 226
  Day of the Dead, 225, 230
  Land of the Dead, 225–6
  Martin, 214
  Night of the Living Dead, 157, 223, 224, 225, 226
Romine, Scott, 86

Rowe, John Carlos, 35
Ruddell, Caroline, 84–5
Rumsfeld, Donald, 225, 229
Ruskin, John, 146–7
Russ, Joanna, 12
Ryden, Mark, 161
Ryder, Albert Pinkham, 149
  Flying Dutchman, The (painting), 149

Salt Eaters, The (Bambara), 62
Samuels, Shirley, 40
Sankofa (Gerima), 57n6
Savoy, Eric, 6, 9, 15, 31, 40, 51, 52, 60, 64, 81
Schoolhouse Gothic, 18, 110–24
Schott, Gareth, 176
science fiction, 9, 50, 56, 190, 210, 222
Sedgwick, Eve Kosofsky, 11, 15
Seltzer, Mark, 188, 190, 193
serial killers, 2, 4, 11, 19, 139, 141, 153, 157, 223
  and film, 187–201
Sexton, David, 196
sexual abuse, sexual violence, 8, 50, 55, 87; *see also* violence
sexuality, 11, 13, 14, 81, 82, 84, 85, 86, 87, 88, 89, 131, 163n6, 171, 210, 212–13
  female, 204, 208–9, 218–19
  queer, 19, 219
  sexual otherness, 19
  see also sexual abuse, sexual violence; violence
Shadow of the Vampire, The (Merhinge), 211, 216
Shaun of the Dead (Wright), 181, 182
Shelley, Mary, 130
  Frankenstein (book), 56, 130, 155, 159
Sherman, Cindy, 156
Silence of the Lambs, The (film), 11, 187, 188, 189, 196–9, 200; *see also* Harris, Thomas
Silko, Leslie Marmon, 41n5, 61, 67, 69
  Ceremony, 67, 69
  Gardens in the Dunes, 61
Simmons, Gary, 160–1
  Ghost Ship (painting), 160
  Light House (painting), 160
simulacra, simulation, 1, 167, 169, 181
Sinclair, Upton, 118, 121, 122
  The Jungle, 118
Sixth Sense, The (Shyamalan), 72

slavery, slaves, 6, 8, 10, 12–13, 17–18, 36, 44–57, 57n1, 57n5, 57n6, 60, 62, 80, 82, 86, 88, 89, 112, 147, 159, 160, 178, 213, 214, 218, 227, 230
Slotkin, Richard, 34, 41n2
Smith, Adam, 2–3, 50
Smith, Allan Lloyd, 7, 10–14, 71–2
Smith, Christopher, 87
Smith, Jon, 88
Smith, Kiki, 156
So Far from God (Castillo), 62
Southern Gothic, 8, 11, 14, 19, 79–89, 154, 159, 222
Spann, Edward K., 94
   New Metropolis: New York City, The, 107–8
Spaulding, A. Timothy, 51
Stallybrass, Peter, 97, 100
   Politics and Poetics of Transgression, The, 97
Stoker, Bram, 130, 196, 203, 204, 205, 208, 209, 210, 212, 214, 215, 218
   Dracula (novel), 196–7, 203, 204, 205, 208–9, 214–15, 224
Stowe, Harriet Beecher, 49, 55
   Uncle Tom's Cabin, 12, 47
Strain Trilogy, The, 218
sublime, 3, 55, 134, 145, 148, 149, 160, 162
   Burkean, 5, 130, 162
   Kant, 5, 57n7
succubus, 148, 169, 171, 172, 173, 174
Supernatural, 130, 136, 137, 141, 142, 143n3, 167
Surrealism, 149, 151, 156
Surrounded, The (McNickle), 66
Suspense (radio series), 130

Tartt, Donna, 239
   Secret History, The, 110, 111
Tate, Allen, 206
Tchelichew, Pavel, 156
Television Ghost, The, 131
television, 2, 18, 129–43, 160, 167, 199, 200, 211, 223, 233
   gothic, 16, 18
   see also individual television shows
Texas Chainsaw Massacre (film), 25, 187, 189, 195, 197
That Girl!, 132
Thompson, Gary Richard, 148

Thompson, George, 103, 106
   City Crimes, 95, 97–8, 99, 100–1, 102
Thoreau, Henry David, 148
Thrush, Coll, 26
Toole, Ottis, 195
'Tooth, The' (Jackson), 12
Town, Charles H., 94
Tracks (Erdrich), 64
Trash Humpers (Korine), 79, 81, 83–4, 87, 88
trauma, 6, 14, 17, 18, 20, 31, 38, 50–1, 52, 53, 55, 56, 64, 65, 67, 72, 73, 79, 80, 81, 83, 85, 86–7, 89, 135, 153, 156, 159, 180, 188, 189, 197, 198, 223, 229, 231
   of history, 8, 19, 25, 40, 54, 56, 62, 81, 146
   of slavery, 45–51, 52, 53, 55
   see also repetition
Trivia: or, The Art of Walking the Streets of London (Gay), 96
True Blood (Ball) (television show), 79, 81, 84–7, 88, 89, 131, 216
Turner, Nat, 47, 55
Twilight (Meyer), 172, 216
Twilight Zone, The, 131, 132, 134
Twin Peaks, 129, 137, 199

uncanny, the, 1, 2, 3, 4, 5, 17, 19, 26, 83, 85, 92, 129, 138, 145, 155, 157, 158, 159, 167, 172, 173, 181, 190, 191, 203, 211, 216
   'Indian uncanny', 26, 40, 45
   Uncanny, The (exhibition), 158, 238
   see also doppelgänger
Unclaimed Experience (Caruth), 54
Underworld (films), 213–14, 217
unit operation, 169, 175–6, 177, 180; *see also* doubling; performance; repetition, video games

Vampire Diaries, The, 219
vampires, 4, 19–20, 84–7, 112, 130, 131, 132, 148, 172, 189, 203–19, 223, 224; *see also Buffy, The Vampire Slayer*; *Dracula*; individual 'vampire' entries; Matheson, Richard; Stoker, Bram
Varney the Vampire; or, The Feast of Blood (Rymer), 205, 215
video games, 2, 5, 8, 16, 18, 19, 166–82, 182n1, 182n6, 182n7
   Alan Wake, 167, 175

Catherine, 169, 170–1, 173–5, 176, 177, 178, 179–80, 182n5
DOOM, 166
Final Fantasy VII, 176
Papers, Please!, 176
Planescape: Torment, 169–70, 171, 172–3, 175, 176, 177, 178–9, 180, 183n8
Secret World, The, 175
Silent Hill, 166
see also doubling; performance; repetition; unit operation
violence, 1, 3, 7, 10, 18, 25, 27, 28, 29, 40, 41n2, 44, 45, 47, 49, 62, 68, 73, 79, 81, 82, 83, 85, 87, 88, 89, 99, 101, 106, 113, 120, 131, 136, 138, 140, 142, 147, 159, 181, 188, 190, 192, 196, 207, 208, 210; *see also* sexual abuse
Violette, Banks, 160, 162
Vocabulum; or, The Rogue's Lexicon (Matsell), 99

Walker, Kara, 19, 159
Subtlety, A, 92
Walking Dead, The, 231, 233
Walpole, Horace, 5, 14, 18, 20, 96, 133, 134, 136
Castle of Otranto, The, 5, 16, 95, 96, 129, 133
Webber, Andrew, 167–8, 174
Welty, Eudora, 82
Wesley, Marilyn C., 55
West, Paul, 132
Westworld (Crichton), 16–17
What Is Told (Melnyczuk), 64
Wheatley, Helen, 130, 137, 142
Whisper in the Dark (Bruchac), 61

White, Allon, 100
Politics and Poetics of Transgression, The, 97
Wilkins-Freeman, Mary E., 206, 207, 208
'Luella Miller', 207
Williams, Anne, 14, 96, 97
Williams, Tennessee, 8
Winkler, Harry, 132
Winter in the Blood (Welch), 67
Winthrop, John, 1, 16, 20, 28, 38, 232–3
witches (witchcraft), 67, 68, 69, 130, 148, 207, 217
Woman Warrior, The (Kingston), 61, 66
Wood, Grant, 3, 19, 149–50
American Gothic (painting), 150
Wood, Robin, 195
World War Z: an Oral History of the Zombie Wars (Brooks), 227–32
World's End (Boyle), 64

X-Files, 137, 140, 154, 199

Yaeger, Patricia, 82
'Yellow Wallpaper, The' (Gilman), 12
Young, Elizabeth, 196

Zamora, Lois Parkinson, 68
Žižek, Slavoj, 5
Zombieland, 227
zombies, 4, 100, 110, 169, 172, 189, 222–34
apocalypse, 20, 182, 212, 222, 225, 228, 233, 234n5
films, 181
Zone One (Whitehead), 92

EU representative:
Easy Access System Europe
Mustamäe tee 50, 10621 Tallinn, Estonia
Gpsr.requests@easproject.com